VOLUME 5

TODD MCFARLANE

JAVI FERNANDEZ

KEVIN KEANE

VOLUME 5

TODD McFARLANE
SCRIPT / PLOT

JAVI FERNANDEZ
ISSUES 25-30
KEVIN KEANE
ISSUE 27: PAGES 11-20
ARTISTS

THOMAS HEALY — EDITOR-IN-CHIEF
YVETTE ARTEAGA — PUBLISHING COORDINATOR
RYAN KEIZER — PRODUCTION ARTIST
ZABRIEL KENNEDY — PRODUCTION ARTIST
IMANI DAVIS — INTERN
ERIC STEPHENSON — PUBLISHER FOR IMAGE COMICS

SPAWN CREATED BY TODD MCFARLANE

IVAN NUNES
COLOR

ANDWORLD DESIGN
LETTERING

MARCIAL TOLEDANO
COLLECTED EDITION COVER

FEDE MELE
MIKE DEODATO JR.
DAN PANOSIAN
ZÉ CARLOS
FEDERICO SABBATINI
FRANCESCO TOMASELLI
JAVI FERNANDEZ
KAEL NGU
DON AGUILLO
MARCIAL TOLEDANO
FRANCESCO MATTINA
COVER ARTISTS

September 2024. First Printing. Published by Image Comics, Inc. Office of publication: PO BOX 14457, Portland, OR 97293 USA. Originally issue format as King Spawn issues #25-30. Spawn, its logo and its symbol are registered trademarks © 2024 Todd McFarlane Productions, Inc. acters are TM and © 2024 Todd McFarlane Productions, Inc. All rights reserved. The characters, events and stories in this publication are entirely the Image Comics logos are registered trademarks of Image Comics, Inc. No part of this publication may be reproduced or transmitted, in any (except for short excerpts for journalistic or review purposes), without the express written permission of Todd McFarlane Productions, Inc., or INTED IN CANADA. ISBN: 978-1-5343-2750-4

image
TODD McFARLANE
PRODUCTIONS
McFARLANE.COM

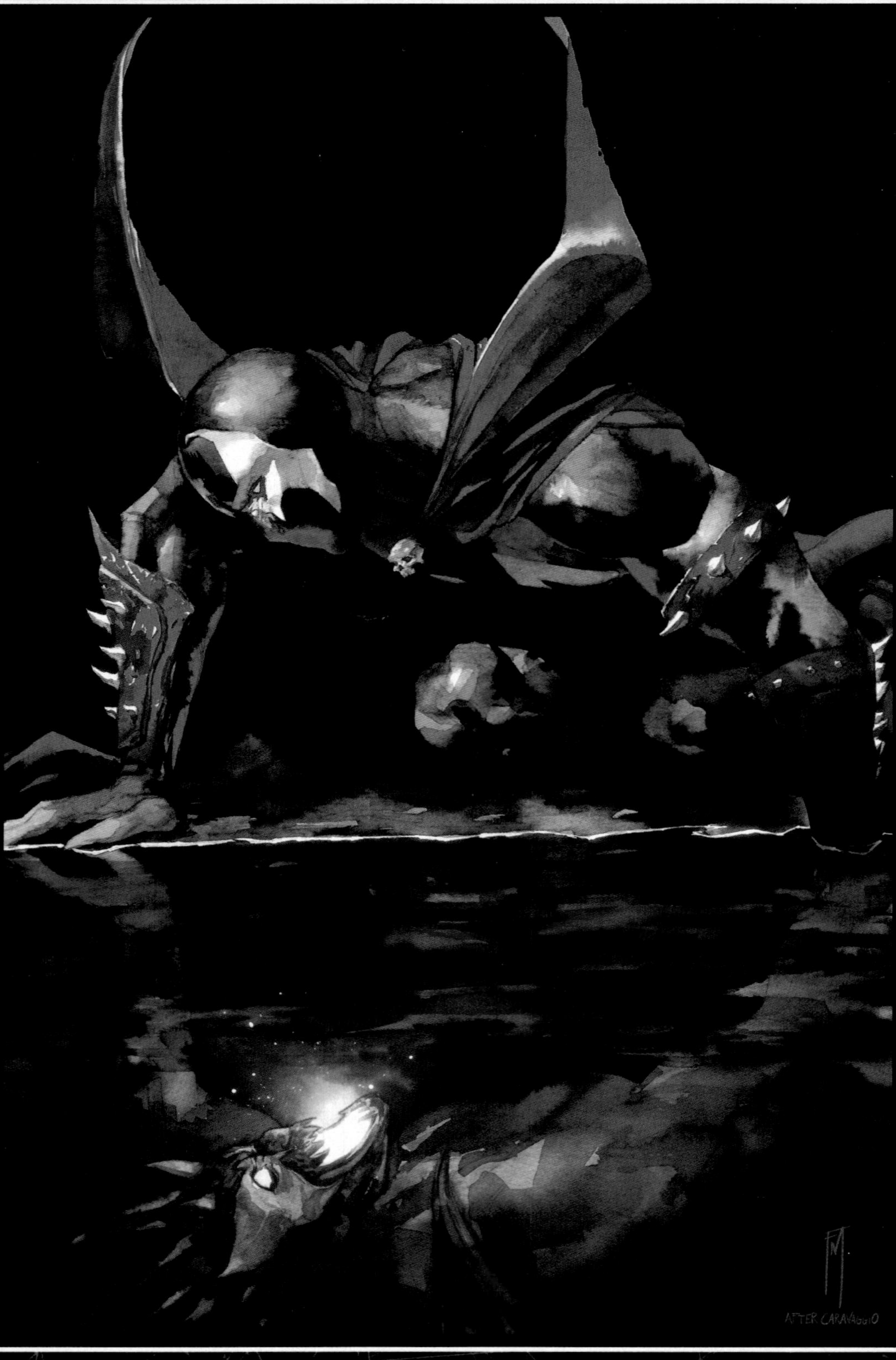
AFTER CARAVAGGIO

King Spawn #25 Cover by Fede Mel

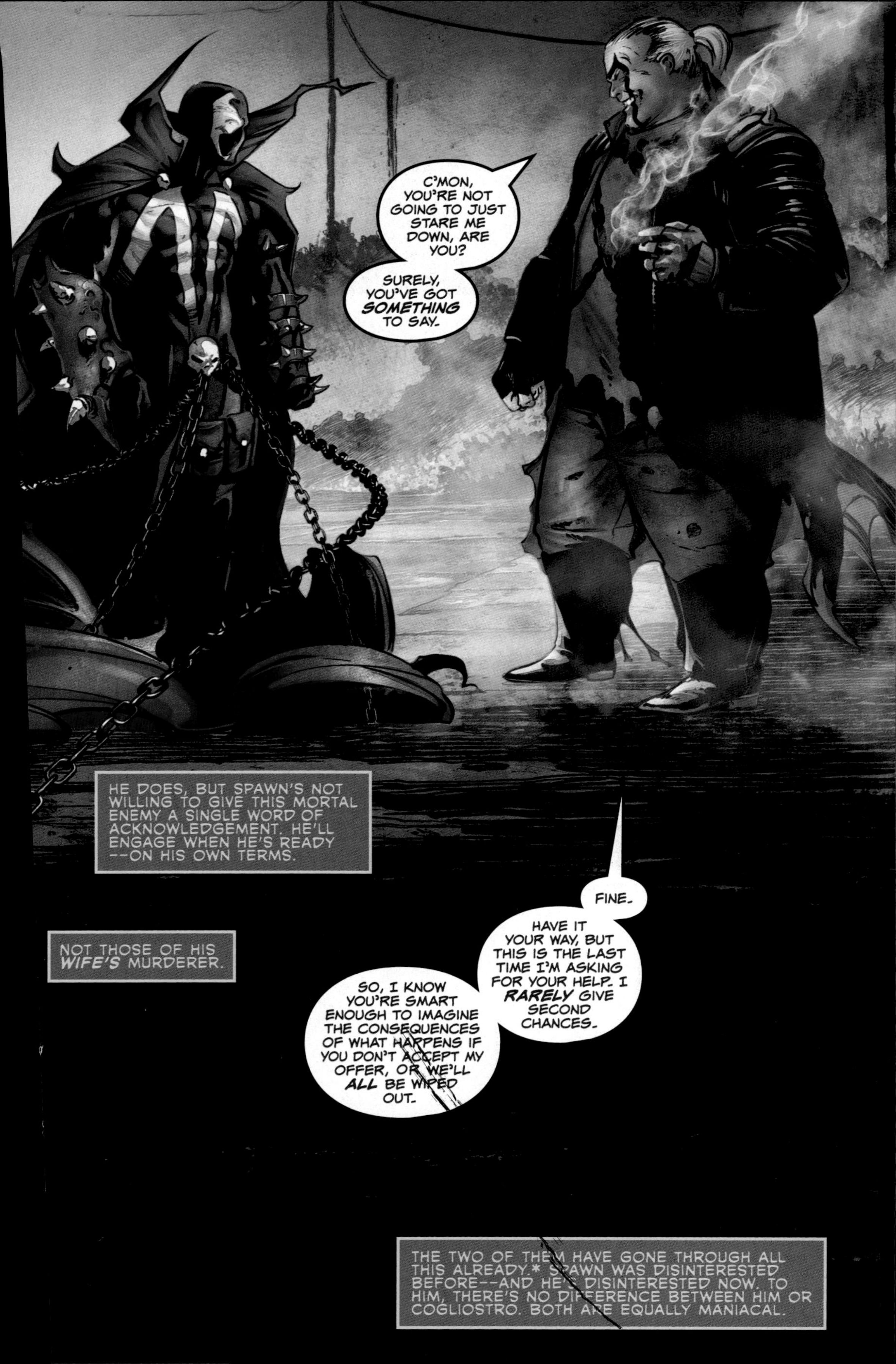
C'MON, YOU'RE NOT GOING TO JUST STARE ME DOWN, ARE YOU?
SURELY, YOU'VE GOT SOMETHING TO SAY.
HE DOES, BUT SPAWN'S NOT WILLING TO GIVE THIS MORTAL ENEMY A SINGLE WORD OF ACKNOWLEDGEMENT. HE'LL ENGAGE WHEN HE'S READY --ON HIS OWN TERMS.
NOT THOSE OF HIS WIFE'S MURDERER.
FINE.
HAVE IT YOUR WAY, BUT THIS IS THE LAST TIME I'M ASKING FOR YOUR HELP. I RARELY GIVE SECOND CHANCES.
SO, I KNOW YOU'RE SMART ENOUGH TO IMAGINE THE CONSEQUENCES OF WHAT HAPPENS IF YOU DON'T ACCEPT MY OFFER, OR WE'LL ALL BE WIPED OUT.
THE TWO OF THEM HAVE GONE THROUGH ALL THIS ALREADY.* SPAWN WAS DISINTERESTED BEFORE--AND HE'S DISINTERESTED NOW. TO HIM, THERE'S NO DIFFERENCE BETWEEN HIM OR COGLIOSTRO. BOTH ARE EQUALLY MANIACAL.

*N ISSUE 343 - THOMAS

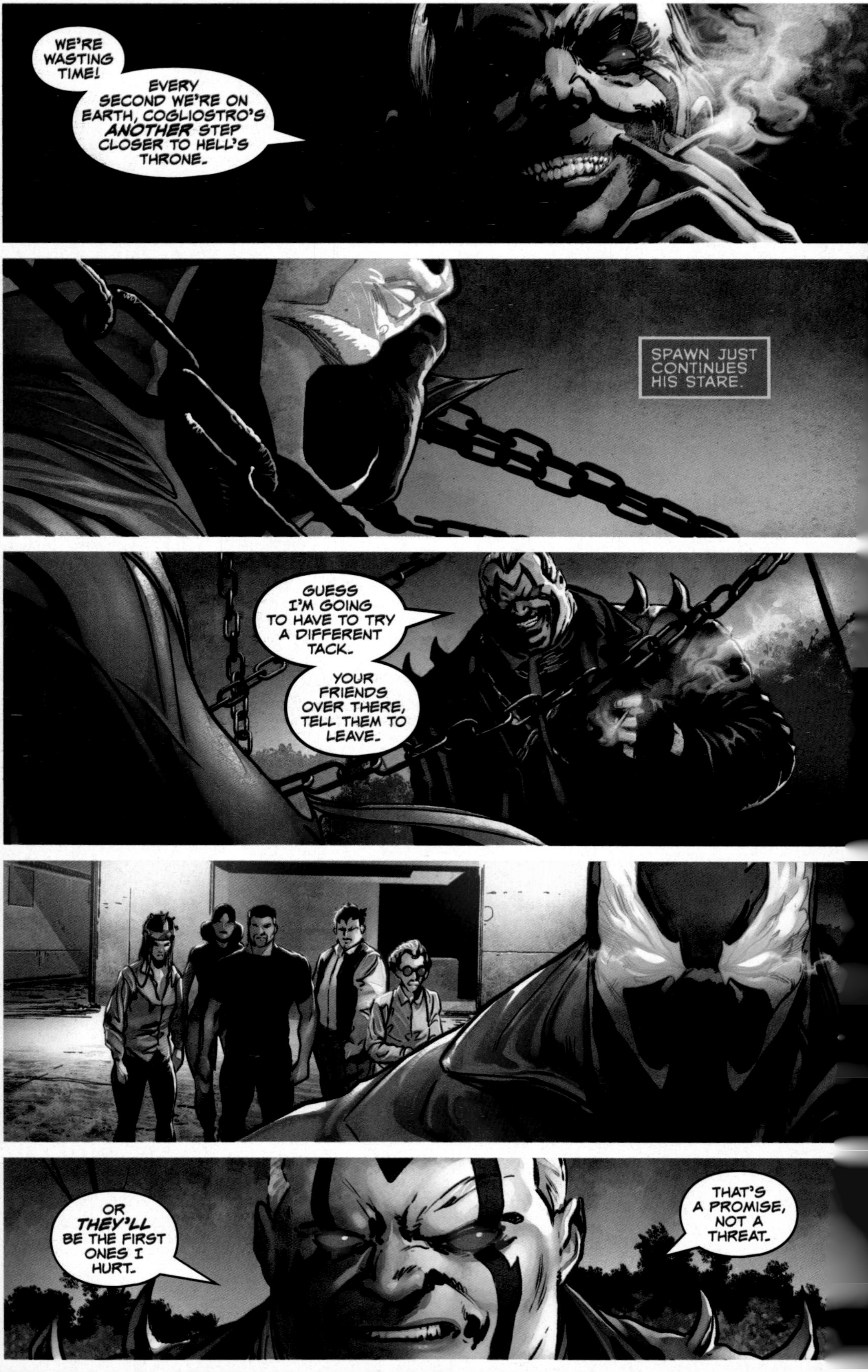

WE'RE WASTING TIME!
EVERY SECOND WE'RE ON EARTH, COGLIOSTRO'S ***ANOTHER*** STEP CLOSER TO HELL'S THRONE.
SPAWN JUST CONTINUES HIS STARE.
GUESS I'M GOING TO HAVE TO TRY A DIFFERENT TACK.
YOUR FRIENDS OVER THERE, TELL THEM TO LEAVE.
OR ***THEY'LL*** BE THE FIRST ONES I HURT.
THAT'S A PROMISE, NOT A THREAT.

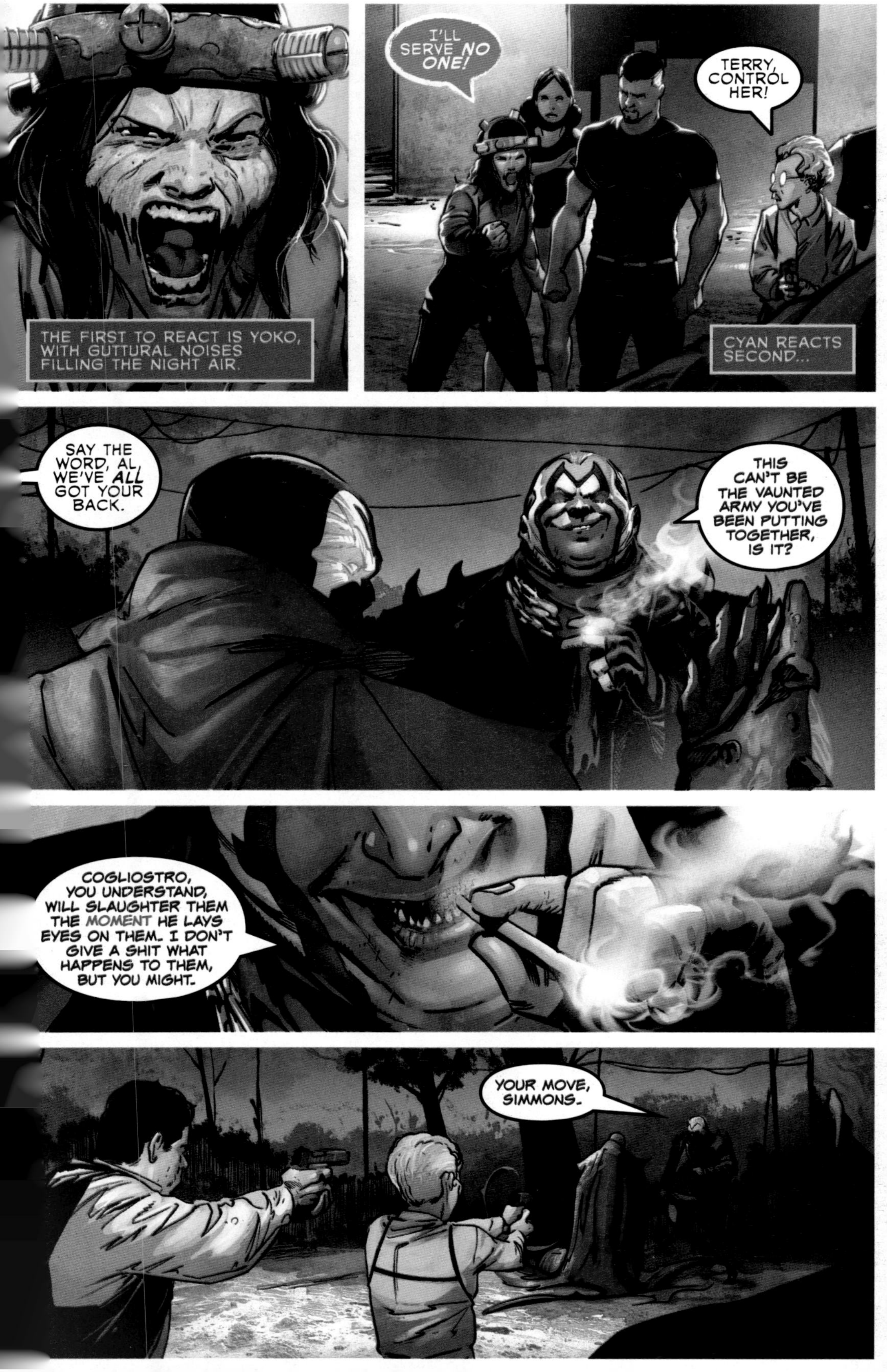
THE FIRST TO REACT IS YOKO, WITH GUTTURAL NOISES FILLING THE NIGHT AIR.
I'LL SERVE NO ONE!
TERRY, CONTROL HER!
CYAN REACTS SECOND...
SAY THE WORD, AL, WE'VE ALL GOT YOUR BACK.
THIS CAN'T BE THE VAUNTED ARMY YOU'VE BEEN PUTTING TOGETHER, IS IT?
COGLIOSTRO, YOU UNDERSTAND, WILL SLAUGHTER THEM THE MOMENT HE LAYS EYES ON THEM. I DON'T GIVE A SHIT WHAT HAPPENS TO THEM, BUT YOU MIGHT.
YOUR MOVE, SIMMONS.

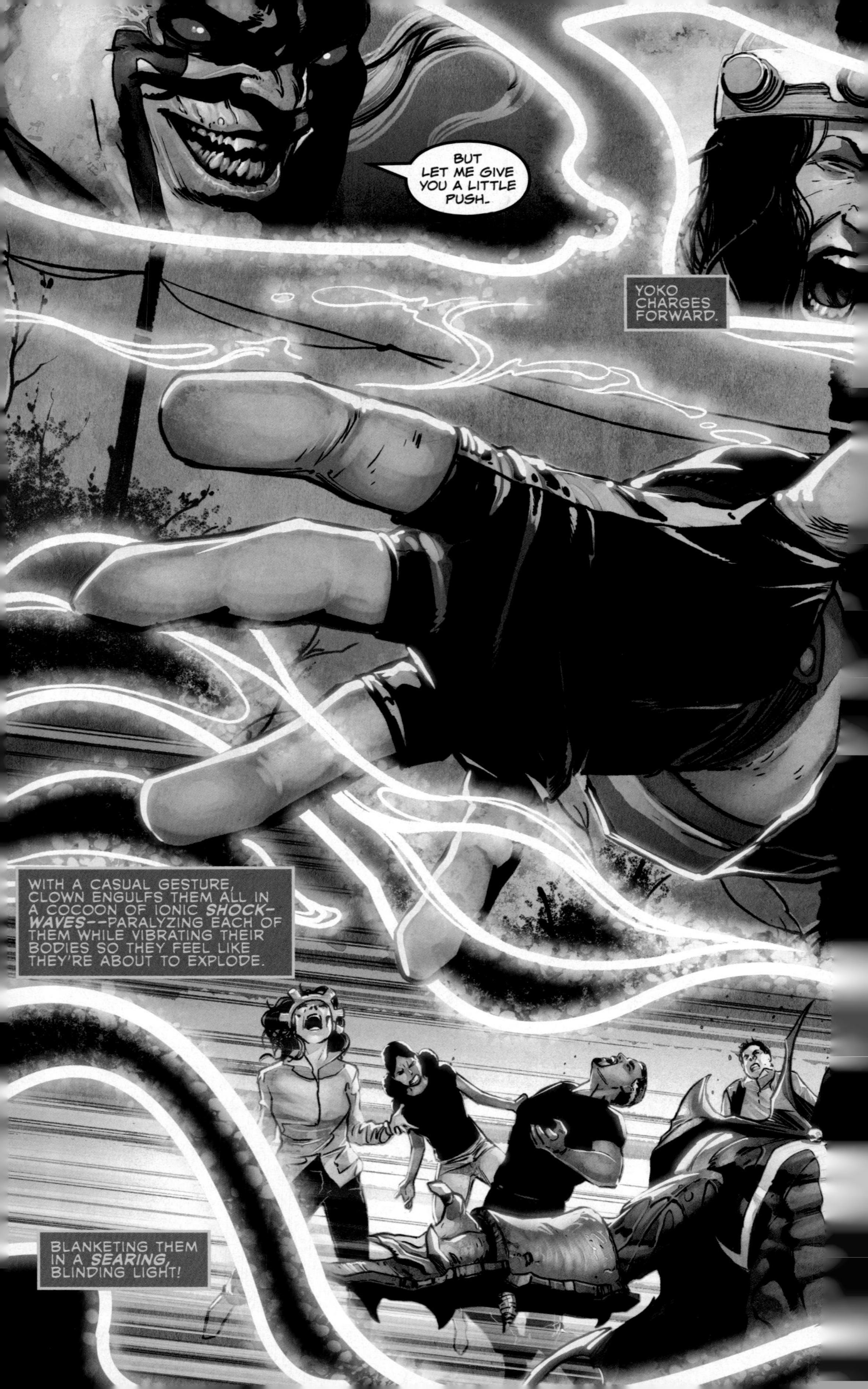

BUT LET ME GIVE YOU A LITTLE PUSH.
YOKO CHARGES FORWARD.
WITH A CASUAL GESTURE, CLOWN ENGULFS THEM ALL IN A COCOON OF IONIC *SHOCK-WAVES*--PARALYZING EACH OF THEM WHILE VIBRATING THEIR BODIES SO THEY FEEL LIKE THEY'RE ABOUT TO EXPLODE.
BLANKETING THEM IN A *SEARING*, BLINDING LIGHT!

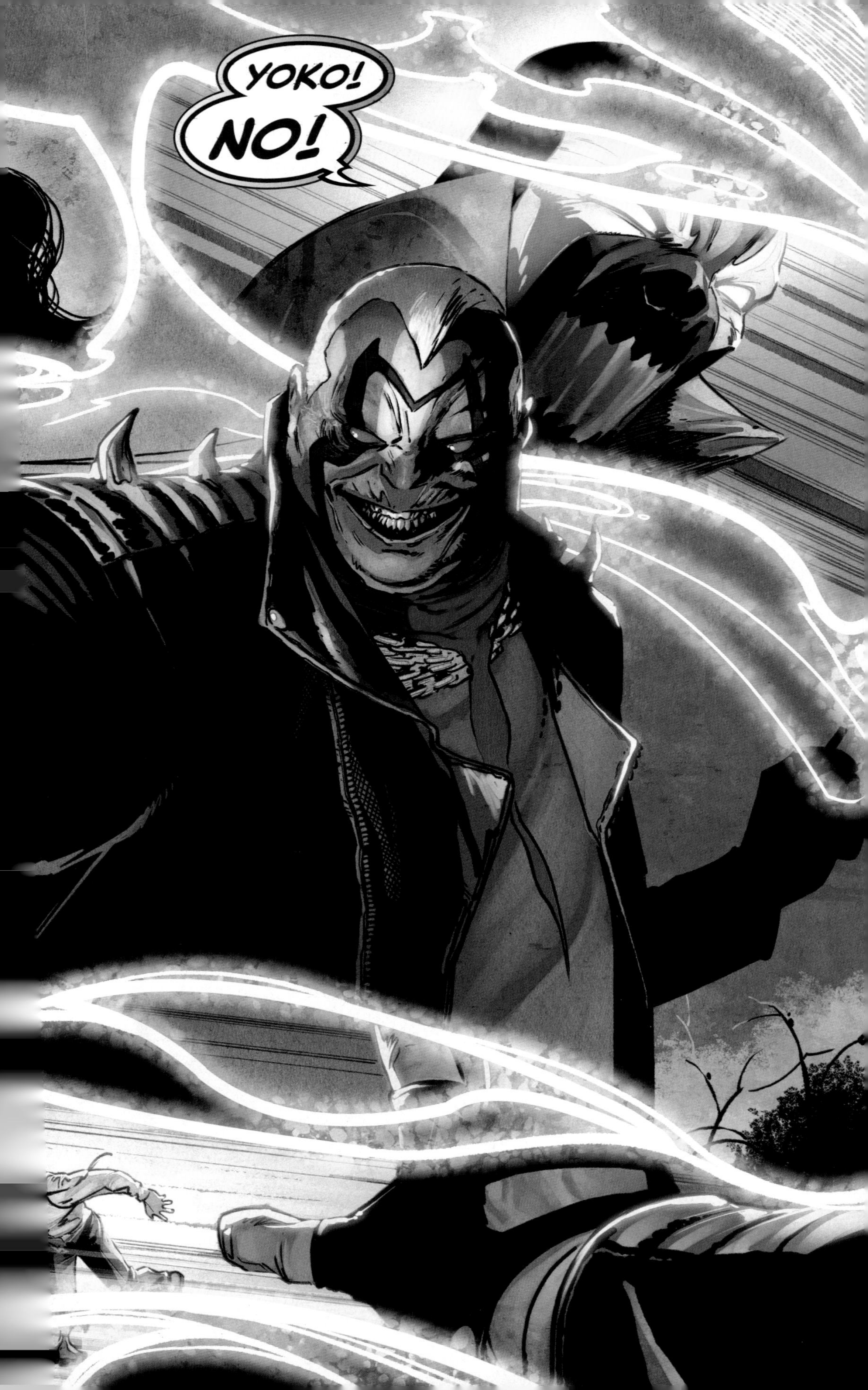
YOKO! NO!

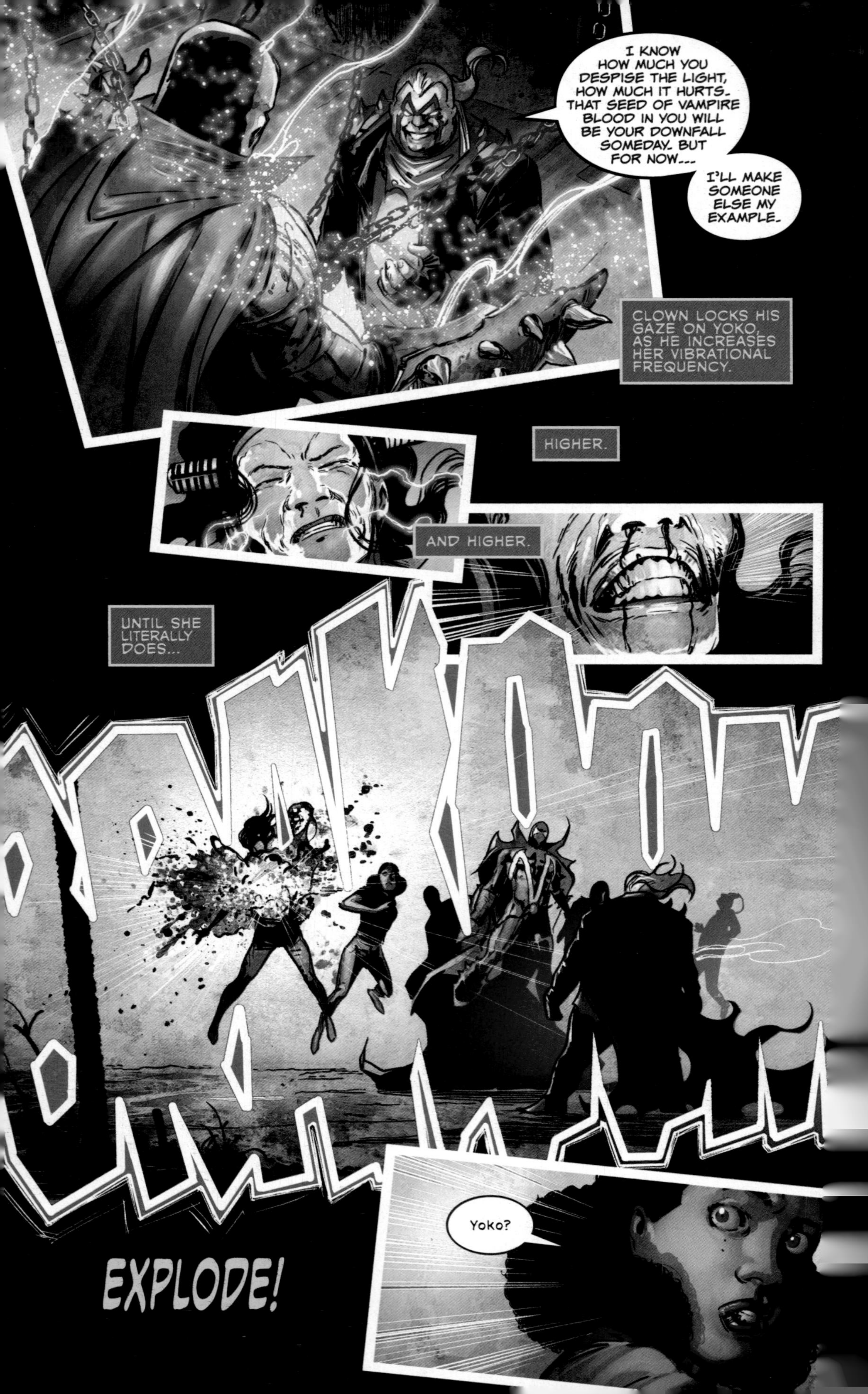
I KNOW HOW MUCH YOU DESPISE THE LIGHT, HOW MUCH IT HURTS. THAT SEED OF VAMPIRE BLOOD IN YOU WILL BE YOUR DOWNFALL SOMEDAY. BUT FOR NOW...
I'LL MAKE SOMEONE ELSE MY EXAMPLE.
CLOWN LOCKS HIS GAZE ON YOKO, AS HE INCREASES HER VIBRATIONAL FREQUENCY.
HIGHER.
AND HIGHER.
UNTIL SHE LITERALLY DOES...
EXPLODE!
Yoko?

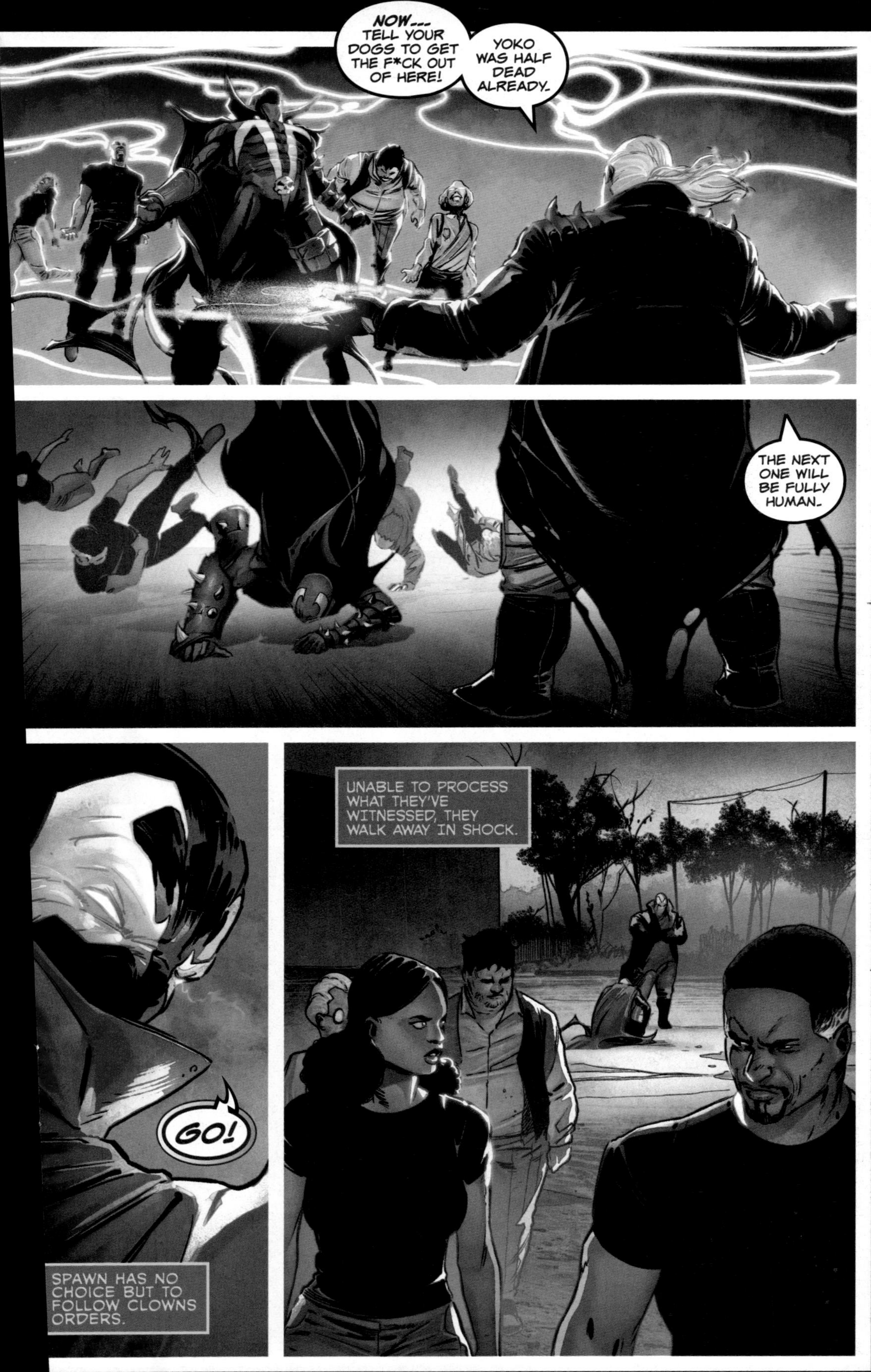
NOW... TELL YOUR DOGS TO GET THE F*CK OUT OF HERE!
YOKO WAS HALF DEAD ALREADY.
THE NEXT ONE WILL BE FULLY HUMAN.
GO!
SPAWN HAS NO CHOICE BUT TO FOLLOW CLOWNS ORDERS.
UNABLE TO PROCESS WHAT THEY'VE WITNESSED, THEY WALK AWAY IN SHOCK.

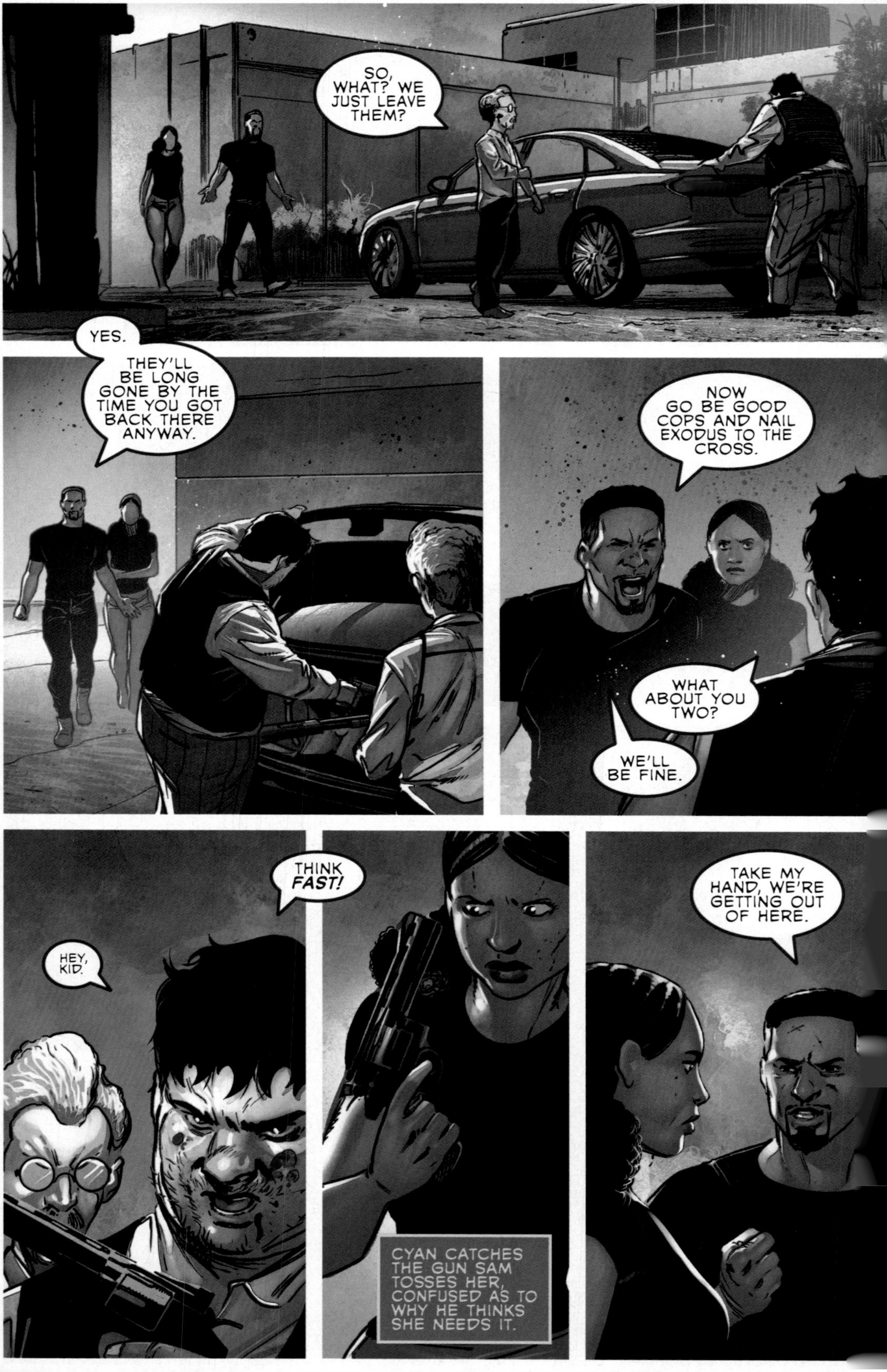
SO, WHAT? WE JUST LEAVE THEM?
YES.
THEY'LL BE LONG GONE BY THE TIME YOU GOT BACK THERE ANYWAY.
NOW GO BE GOOD COPS AND NAIL EXODUS TO THE CROSS.
WHAT ABOUT YOU TWO?
WE'LL BE FINE.
HEY, KID.
THINK *FAST!*
CYAN CATCHES THE GUN SAM TOSSES HER, CONFUSED AS TO WHY HE THINKS SHE NEEDS IT.
TAKE MY HAND, WE'RE GETTING OUT OF HERE.

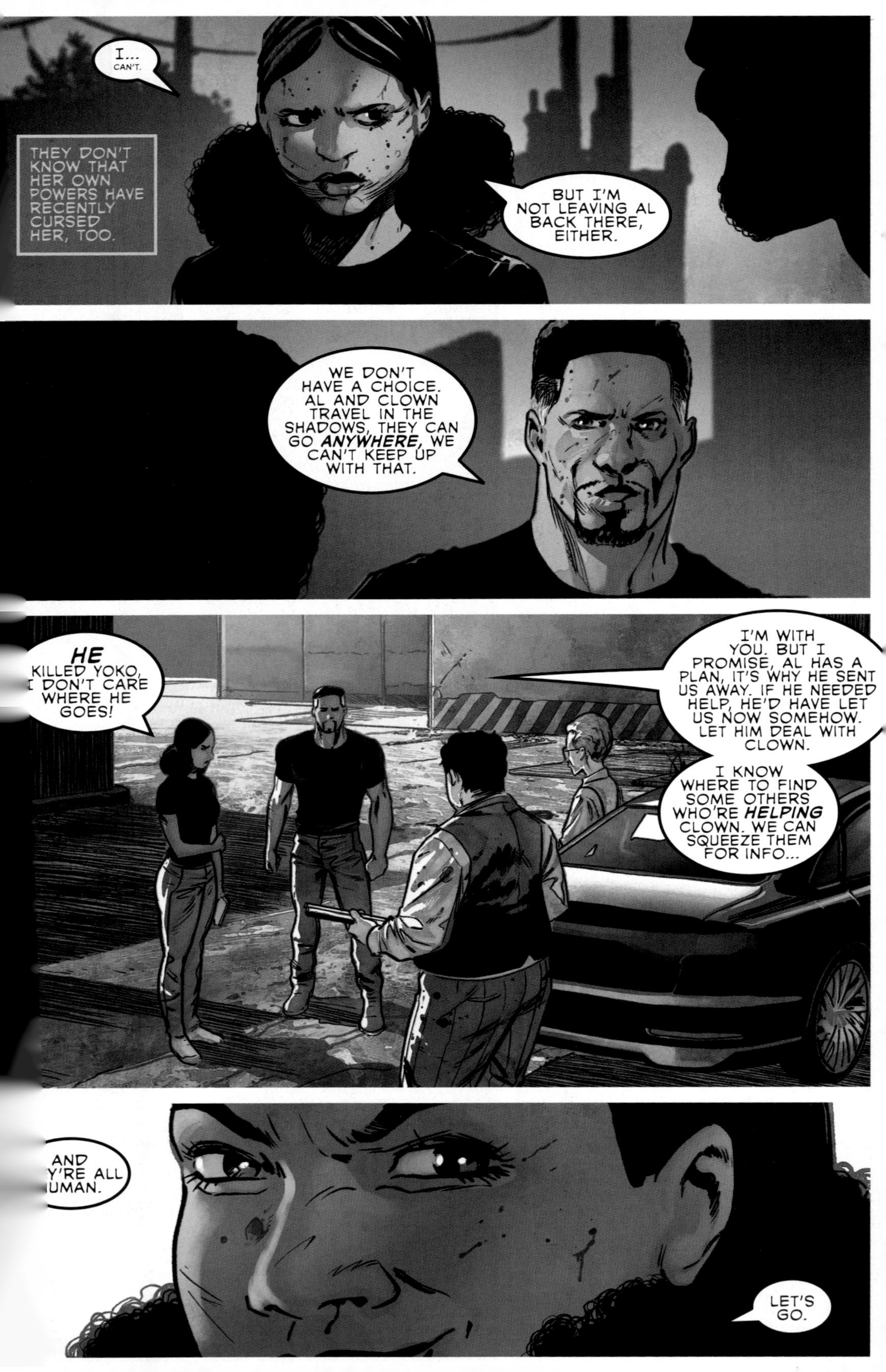

I... CAN'T.
THEY DON'T KNOW THAT HER OWN POWERS HAVE RECENTLY CURSED HER, TOO.
BUT I'M NOT LEAVING AL BACK THERE, EITHER.
WE DON'T HAVE A CHOICE. AL AND CLOWN TRAVEL IN THE SHADOWS, THEY CAN GO ANYWHERE, WE CAN'T KEEP UP WITH THAT.
HE KILLED YOKO, I DON'T CARE WHERE HE GOES!
I'M WITH YOU. BUT I PROMISE, AL HAS A PLAN, IT'S WHY HE SENT US AWAY. IF HE NEEDED HELP, HE'D HAVE LET US NOW SOMEHOW. LET HIM DEAL WITH CLOWN.
I KNOW WHERE TO FIND SOME OTHERS WHO'RE HELPING CLOWN. WE CAN SQUEEZE THEM FOR INFO...
AND Y'RE ALL UMAN.
LET'S GO.

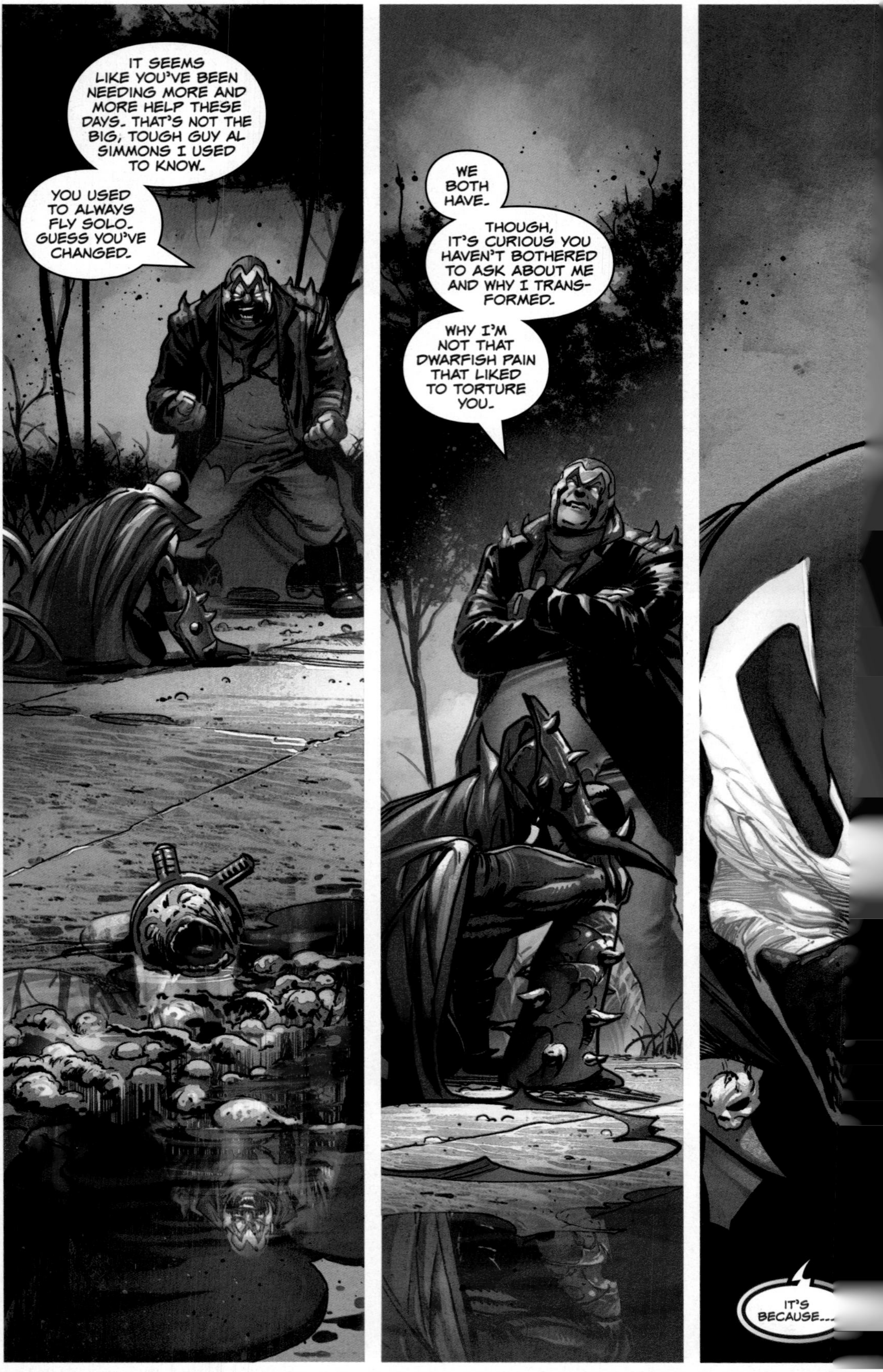
IT SEEMS LIKE YOU'VE BEEN NEEDING MORE AND MORE HELP THESE DAYS. THAT'S NOT THE BIG, TOUGH GUY AL SIMMONS I USED TO KNOW.
YOU USED TO ALWAYS FLY SOLO. GUESS YOU'VE CHANGED.
WE BOTH HAVE.
THOUGH, IT'S CURIOUS YOU HAVEN'T BOTHERED TO ASK ABOUT ME AND WHY I TRANS-FORMED.
WHY I'M NOT THAT DWARFISH PAIN THAT LIKED TO TORTURE YOU.
IT'S BECAUSE...

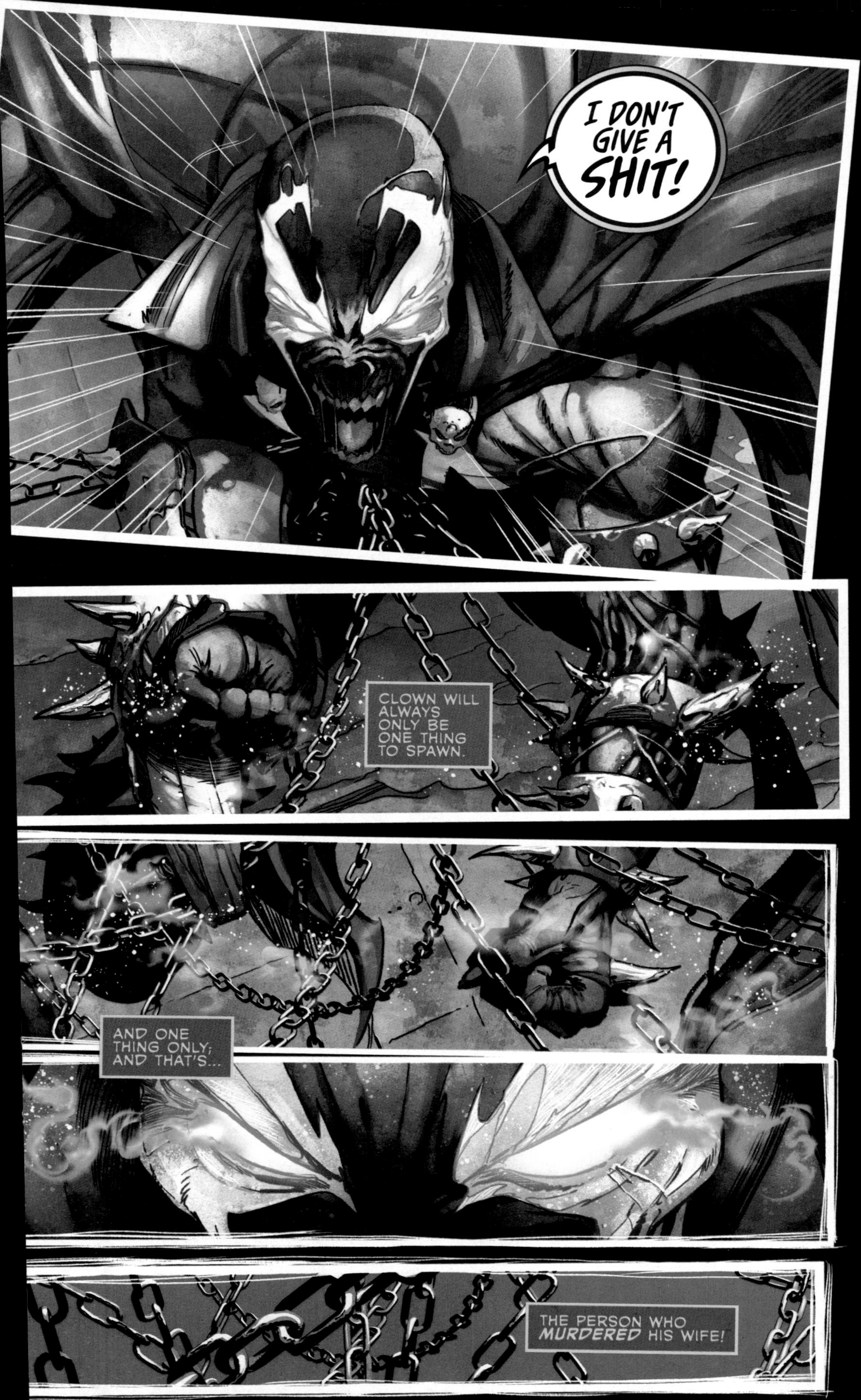
I DON'T GIVE A SHIT!
CLOWN WILL ALWAYS ONLY BE ONE THING TO SPAWN.
AND ONE THING ONLY; AND THAT'S...
THE PERSON WHO *MURDERED* HIS WIFE!

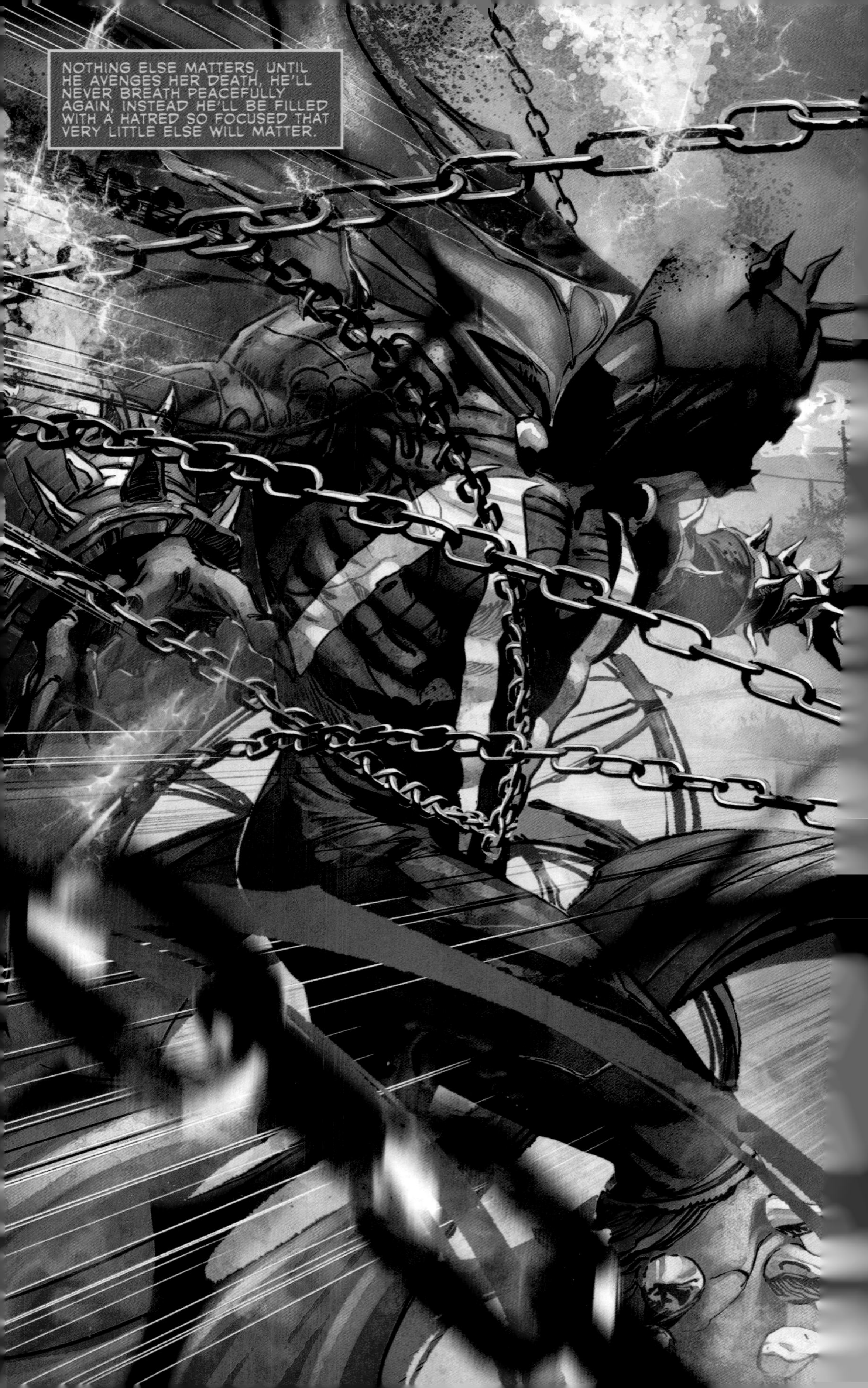
NOTHING ELSE MATTERS, UNTIL HE AVENGES HER DEATH, HE'LL NEVER BREATH PEACEFULLY AGAIN, INSTEAD HE'LL BE FILLED WITH A HATRED SO FOCUSED THAT VERY LITTLE ELSE WILL MATTER.

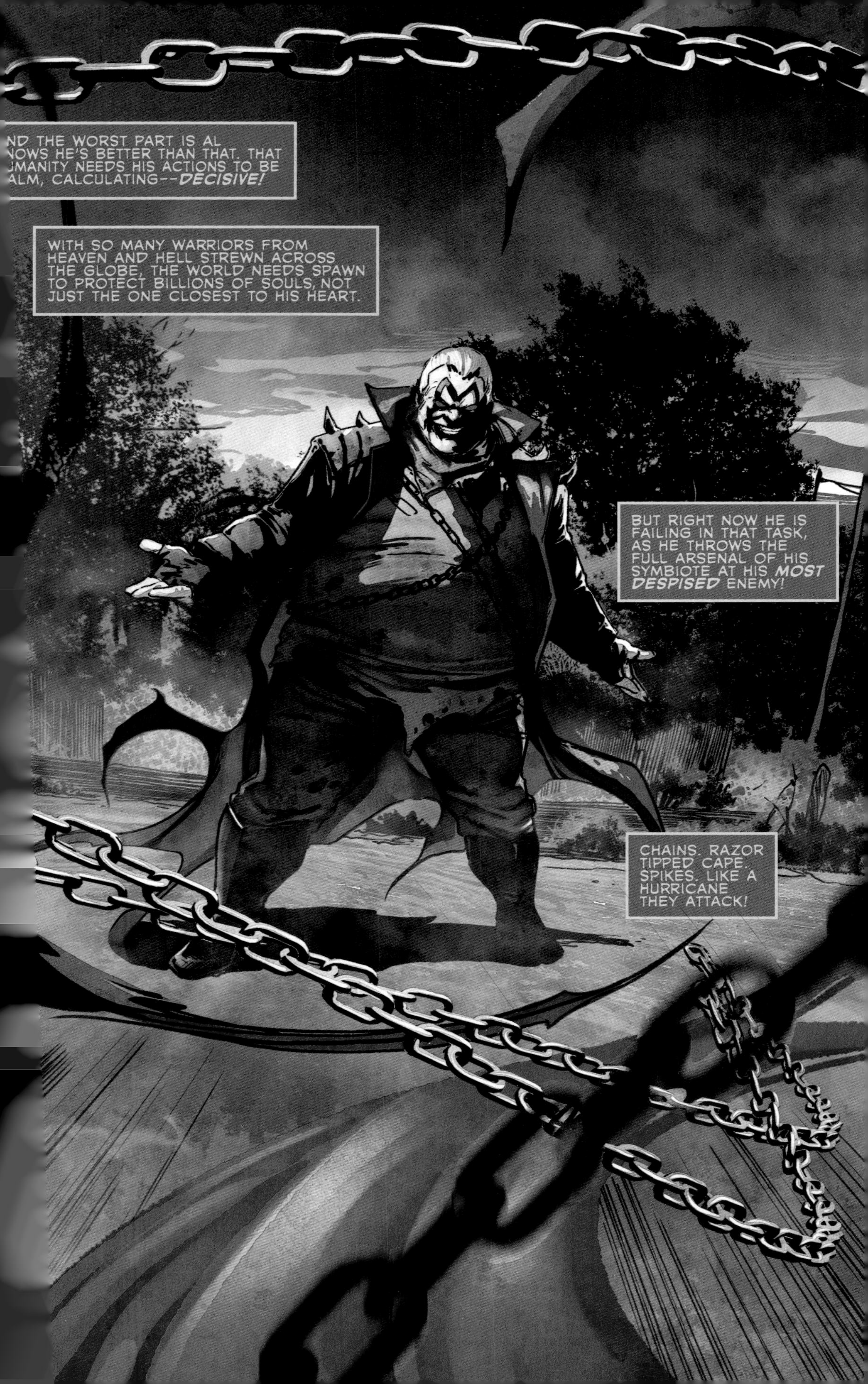
ND THE WORST PART IS AL NOWS HE'S BETTER THAN THAT. THAT UMANITY NEEDS HIS ACTIONS TO BE ALM, CALCULATING--DECISIVE!
WITH SO MANY WARRIORS FROM HEAVEN AND HELL STREWN ACROSS THE GLOBE, THE WORLD NEEDS SPAWN TO PROTECT BILLIONS OF SOULS, NOT JUST THE ONE CLOSEST TO HIS HEART.
BUT RIGHT NOW HE IS FAILING IN THAT TASK, AS HE THROWS THE FULL ARSENAL OF HIS SYMBIOTE AT HIS MOST DESPISED ENEMY!
CHAINS. RAZOR TIPPED CAPE. SPIKES. LIKE A HURRICANE THEY ATTACK!

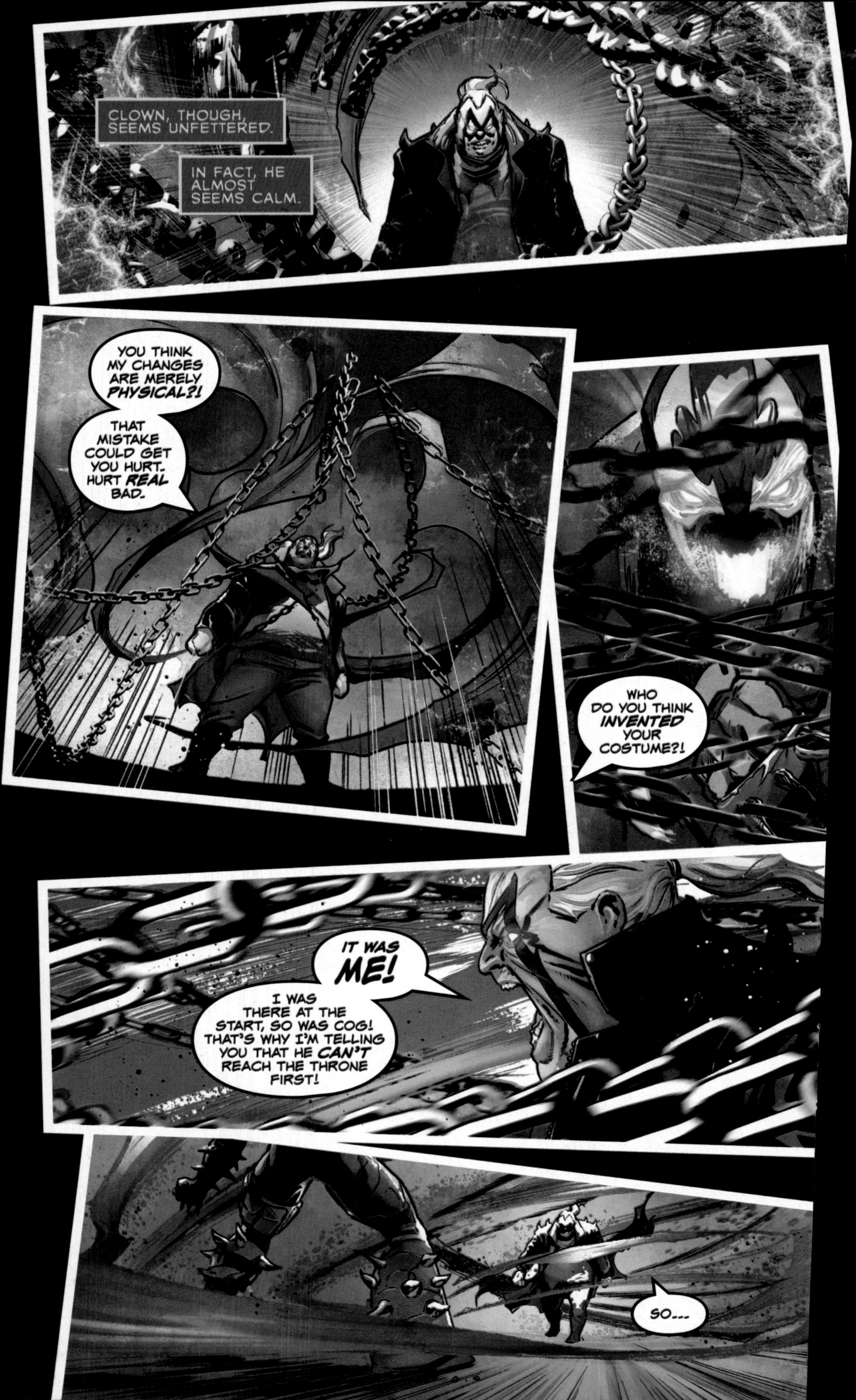
CLOWN, THOUGH, SEEMS UNFETTERED.
IN FACT, HE ALMOST SEEMS CALM.
YOU THINK MY CHANGES ARE MERELY PHYSICAL?!
THAT MISTAKE COULD GET YOU HURT. HURT REAL BAD.
WHO DO YOU THINK INVENTED YOUR COSTUME?!
IT WAS ME!
I WAS THERE AT THE START, SO WAS COG! THAT'S WHY I'M TELLING YOU THAT HE CAN'T REACH THE THRONE FIRST!
SO...

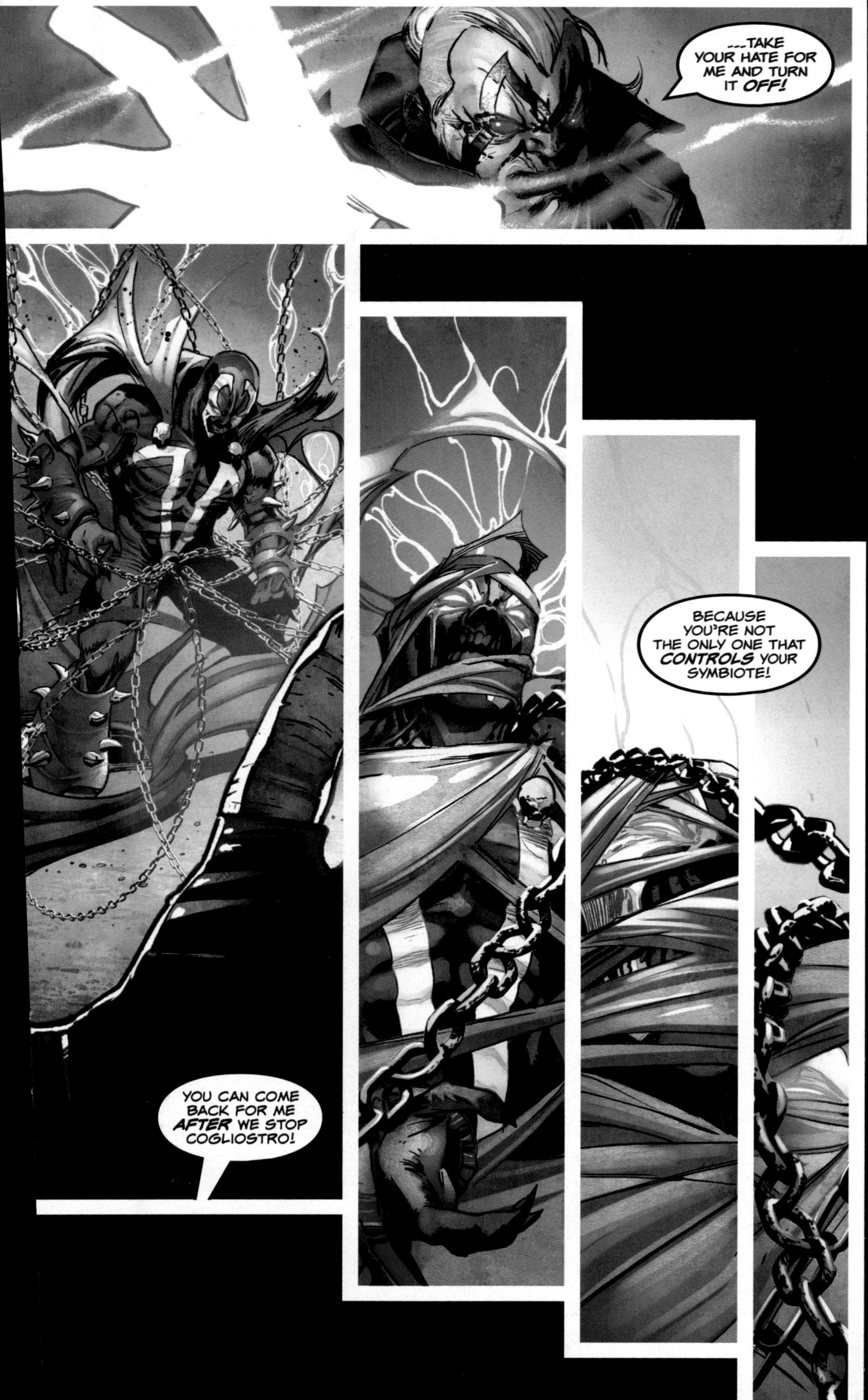
---TAKE YOUR HATE FOR ME AND TURN IT OFF!
YOU CAN COME BACK FOR ME AFTER WE STOP COGLIOSTRO!
BECAUSE YOU'RE NOT THE ONLY ONE THAT CONTROLS YOUR SYMBIOTE!

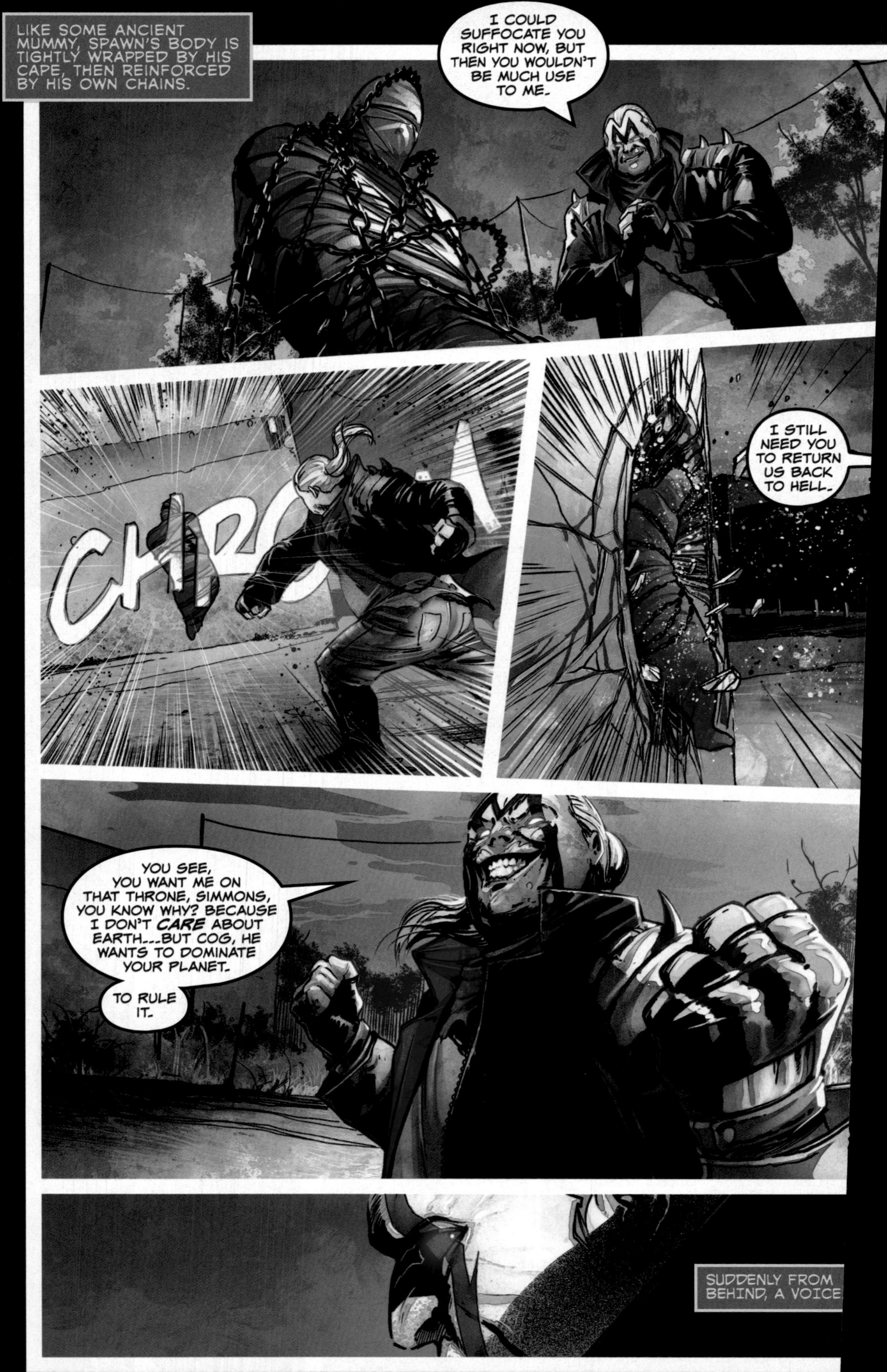
LIKE SOME ANCIENT MUMMY, SPAWN'S BODY IS TIGHTLY WRAPPED BY HIS CAPE, THEN REINFORCED BY HIS OWN CHAINS.
I COULD SUFFOCATE YOU RIGHT NOW, BUT THEN YOU WOULDN'T BE MUCH USE TO ME.
CHRO
I STILL NEED YOU TO RETURN US BACK TO HELL.
YOU SEE, YOU WANT ME ON THAT THRONE, SIMMONS, YOU KNOW WHY? BECAUSE I DON'T *CARE* ABOUT EARTH...BUT COG, HE WANTS TO DOMINATE YOUR PLANET.
TO RULE IT.
SUDDENLY FROM BEHIND, A VOICE

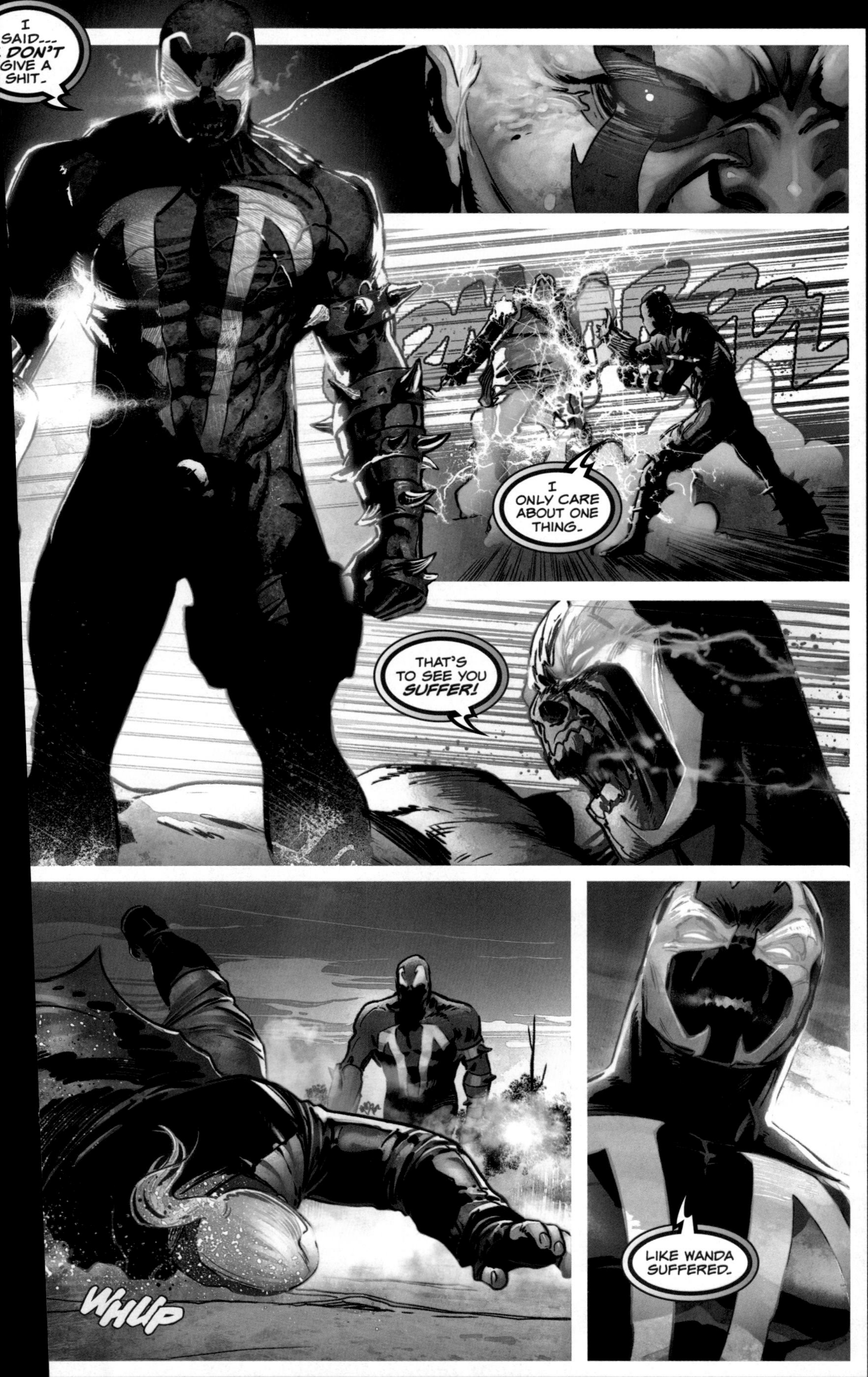
I SAID... I DON'T GIVE A SHIT.
I ONLY CARE ABOUT ONE THING.
THAT'S TO SEE YOU SUFFER!
WHUP
LIKE WANDA SUFFERED.

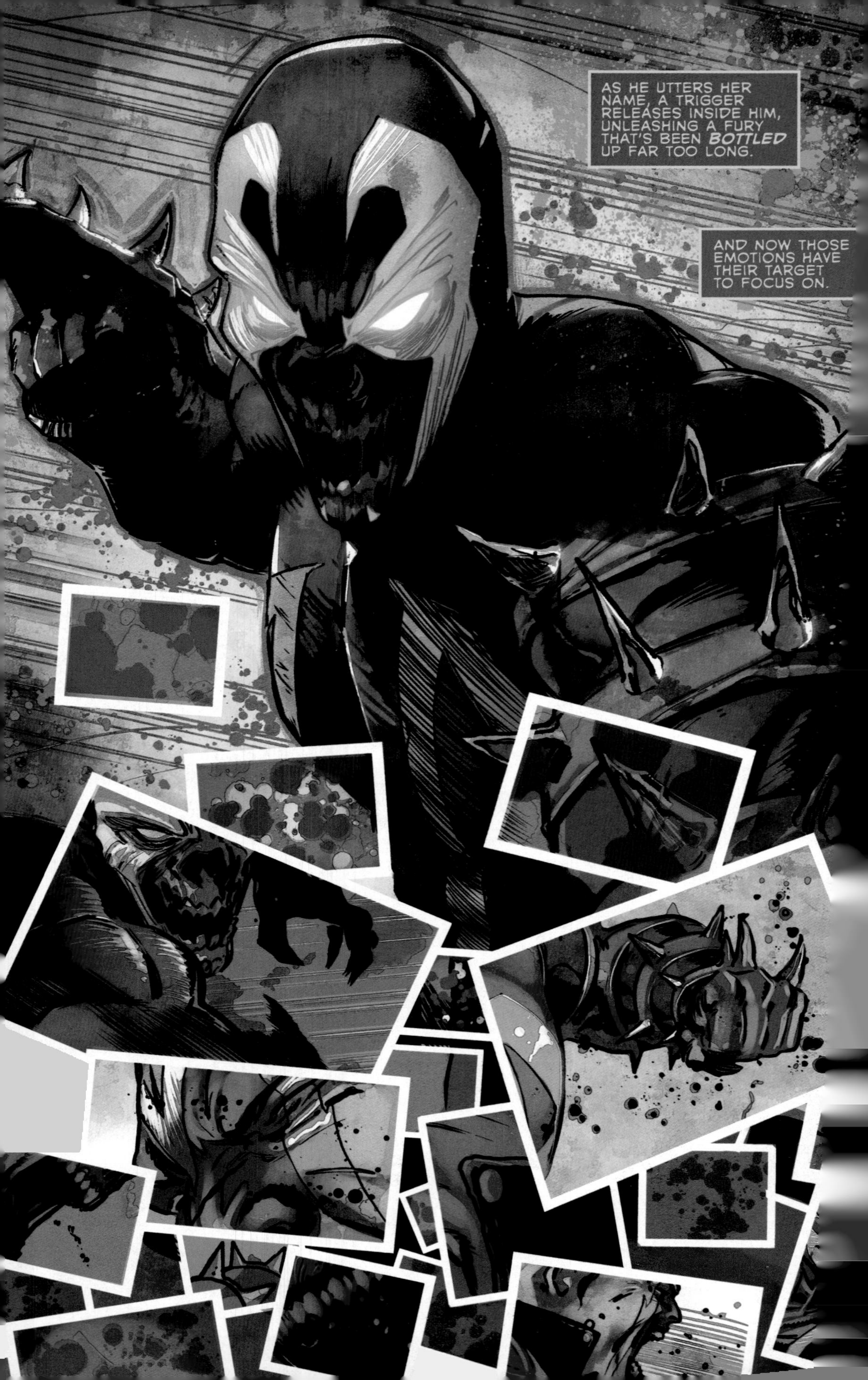
AS HE UTTERS HER NAME, A TRIGGER RELEASES INSIDE HIM, UNLEASHING A FURY THAT'S BEEN *BOTTLED* UP FAR TOO LONG.
AND NOW THOSE EMOTIONS HAVE THEIR TARGET TO FOCUS ON.

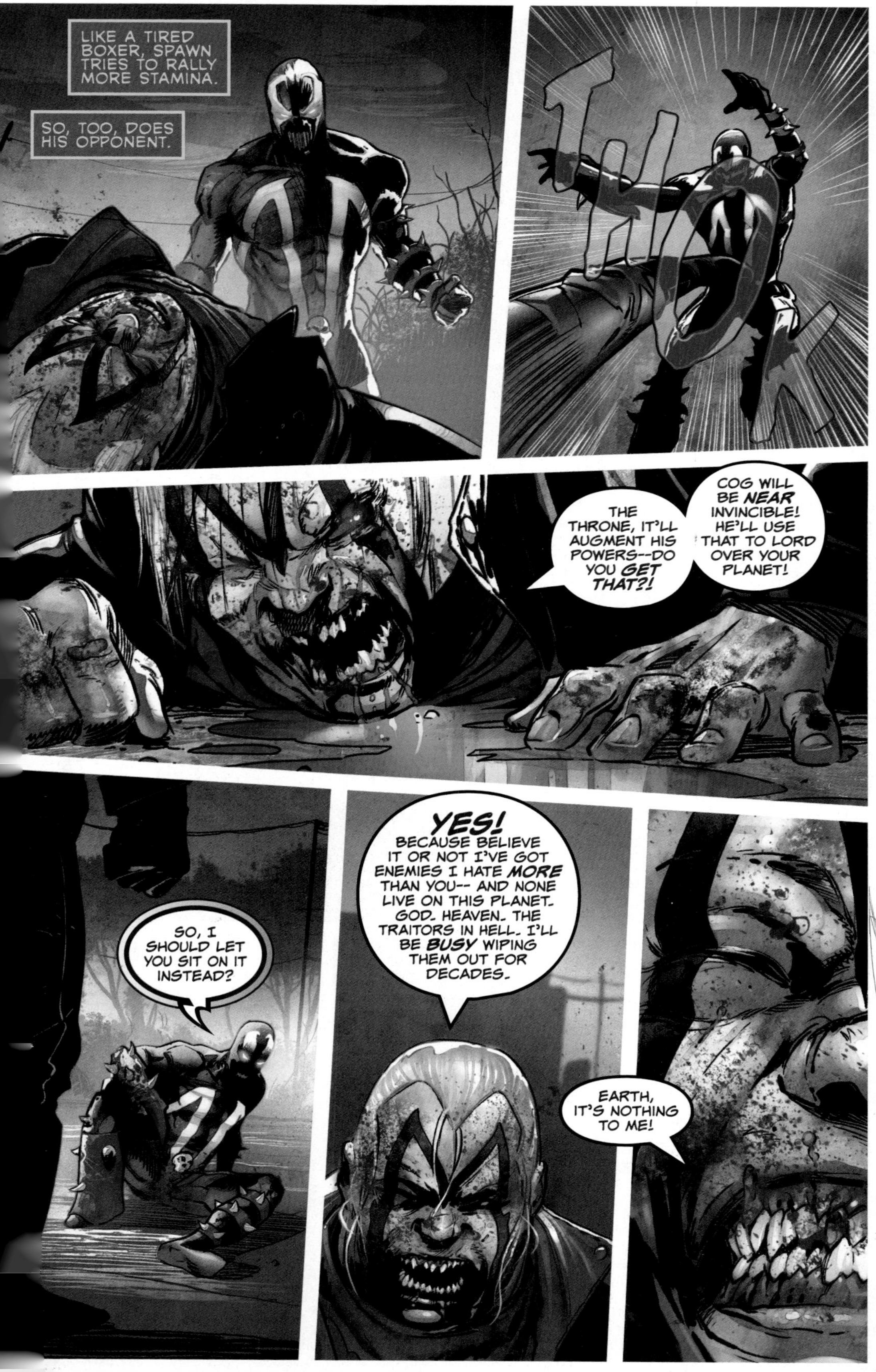
LIKE A TIRED BOXER, SPAWN TRIES TO RALLY MORE STAMINA.
SO, TOO, DOES HIS OPPONENT.
THOK
THE THRONE, IT'LL AUGMENT HIS POWERS--DO YOU GET THAT?!
COG WILL BE NEAR INVINCIBLE! HE'LL USE THAT TO LORD OVER YOUR PLANET!
SO, I SHOULD LET YOU SIT ON IT INSTEAD?
YES! BECAUSE BELIEVE IT OR NOT I'VE GOT ENEMIES I HATE MORE THAN YOU-- AND NONE LIVE ON THIS PLANET. GOD. HEAVEN. THE TRAITORS IN HELL. I'LL BE BUSY WIPING THEM OUT FOR DECADES.
EARTH, IT'S NOTHING TO ME!

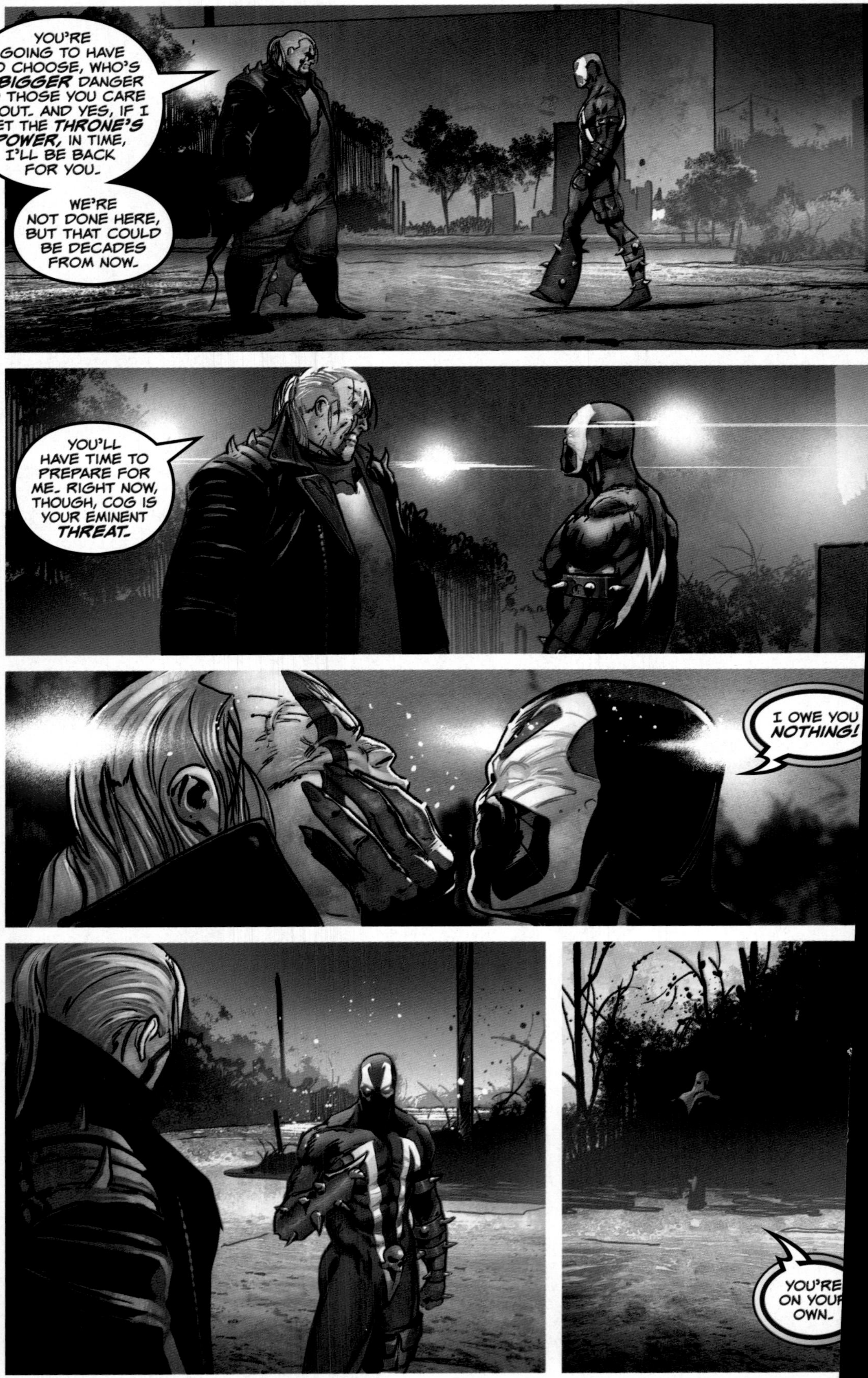
YOU'RE GOING TO HAVE TO CHOOSE, WHO'S A BIGGER DANGER TO THOSE YOU CARE ABOUT. AND YES, IF I GET THE THRONE'S POWER, IN TIME, I'LL BE BACK FOR YOU.
WE'RE NOT DONE HERE, BUT THAT COULD BE DECADES FROM NOW.
YOU'LL HAVE TIME TO PREPARE FOR ME. RIGHT NOW, THOUGH, COG IS YOUR EMINENT THREAT.
I OWE YOU NOTHING!
YOU'RE ON YOUR OWN.

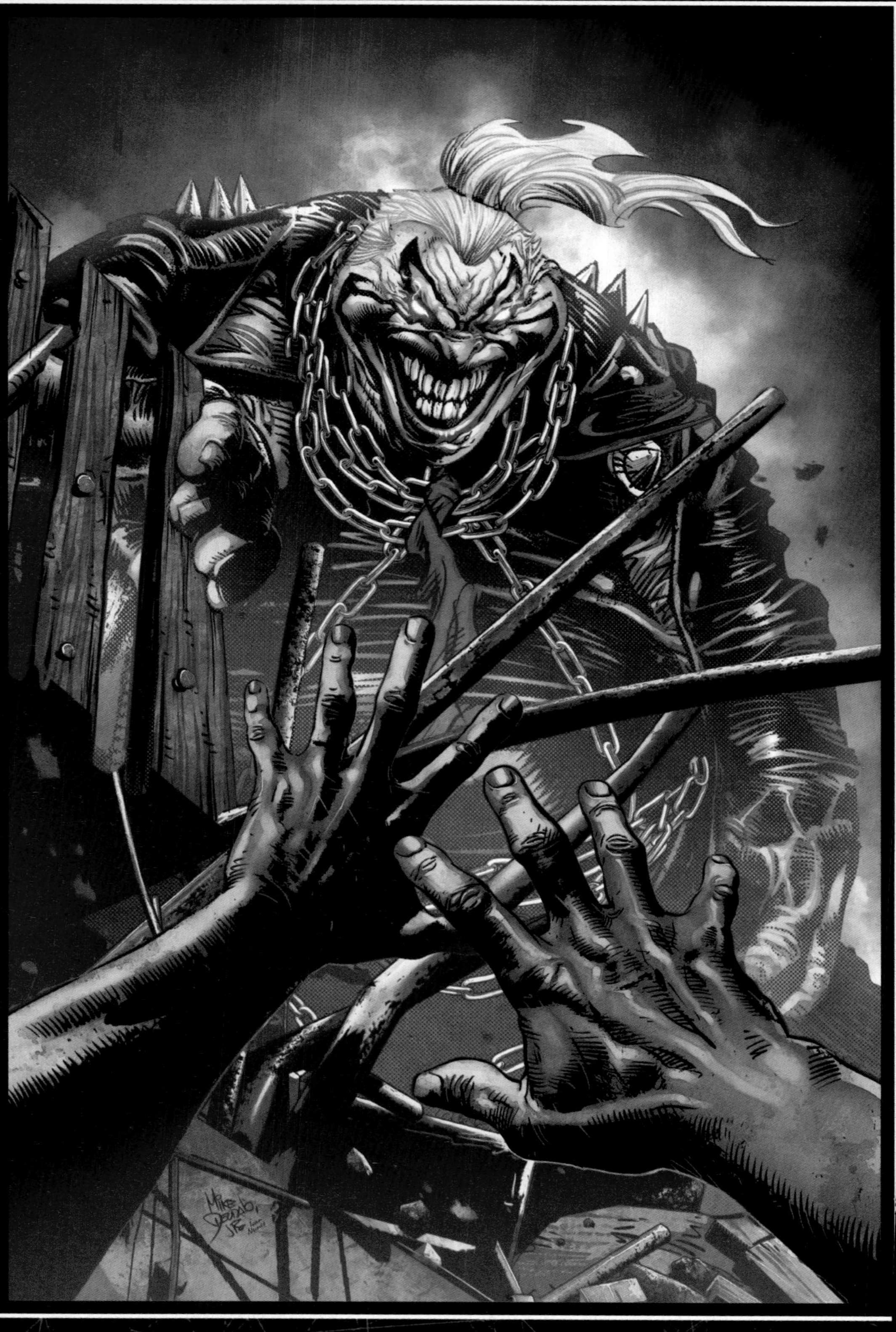

King Spawn #26 Cover by Mike Deodato Jr.

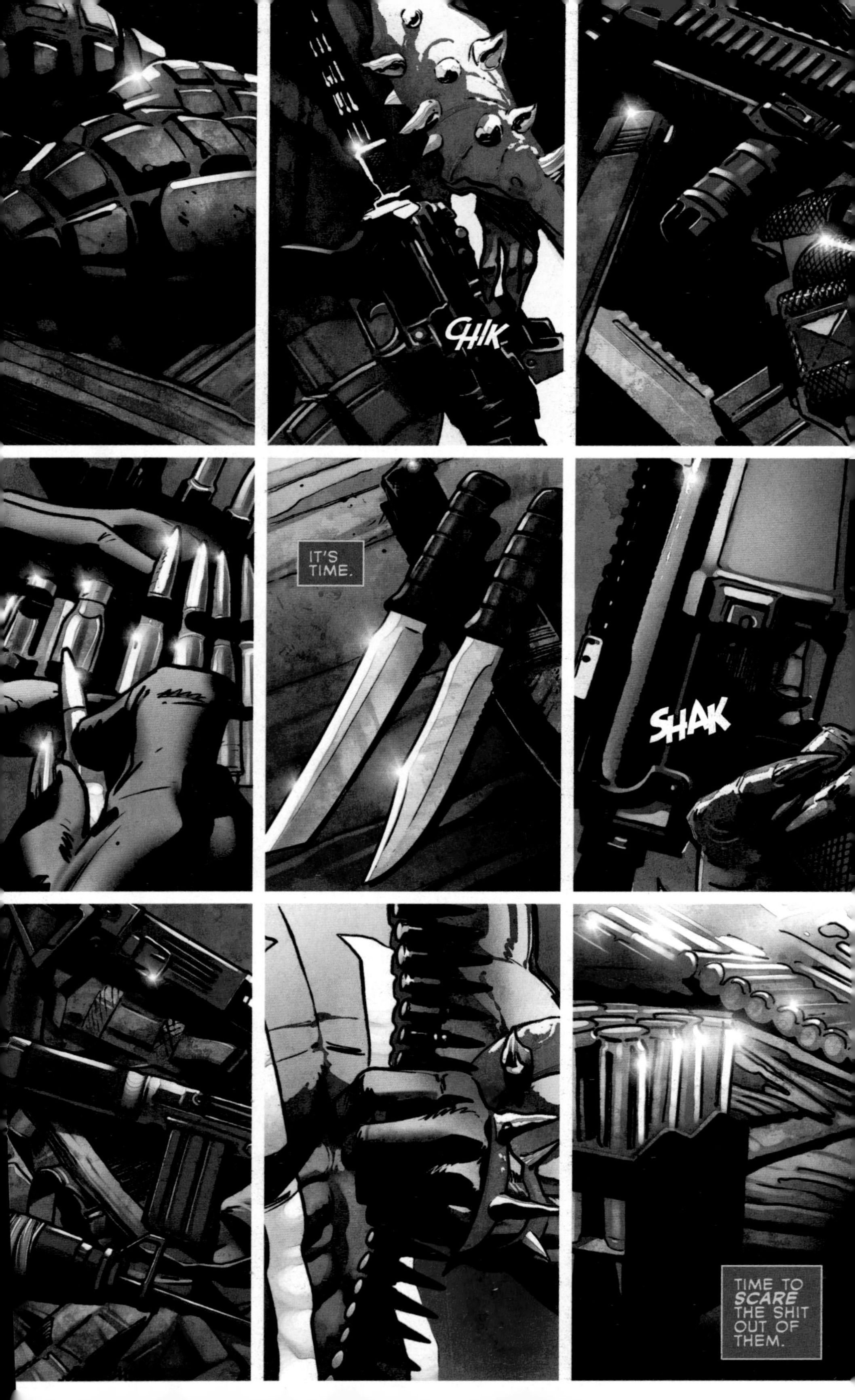
CHIK
IT'S TIME.
SHAK
TIME TO SCARE THE SHIT OUT OF THEM.

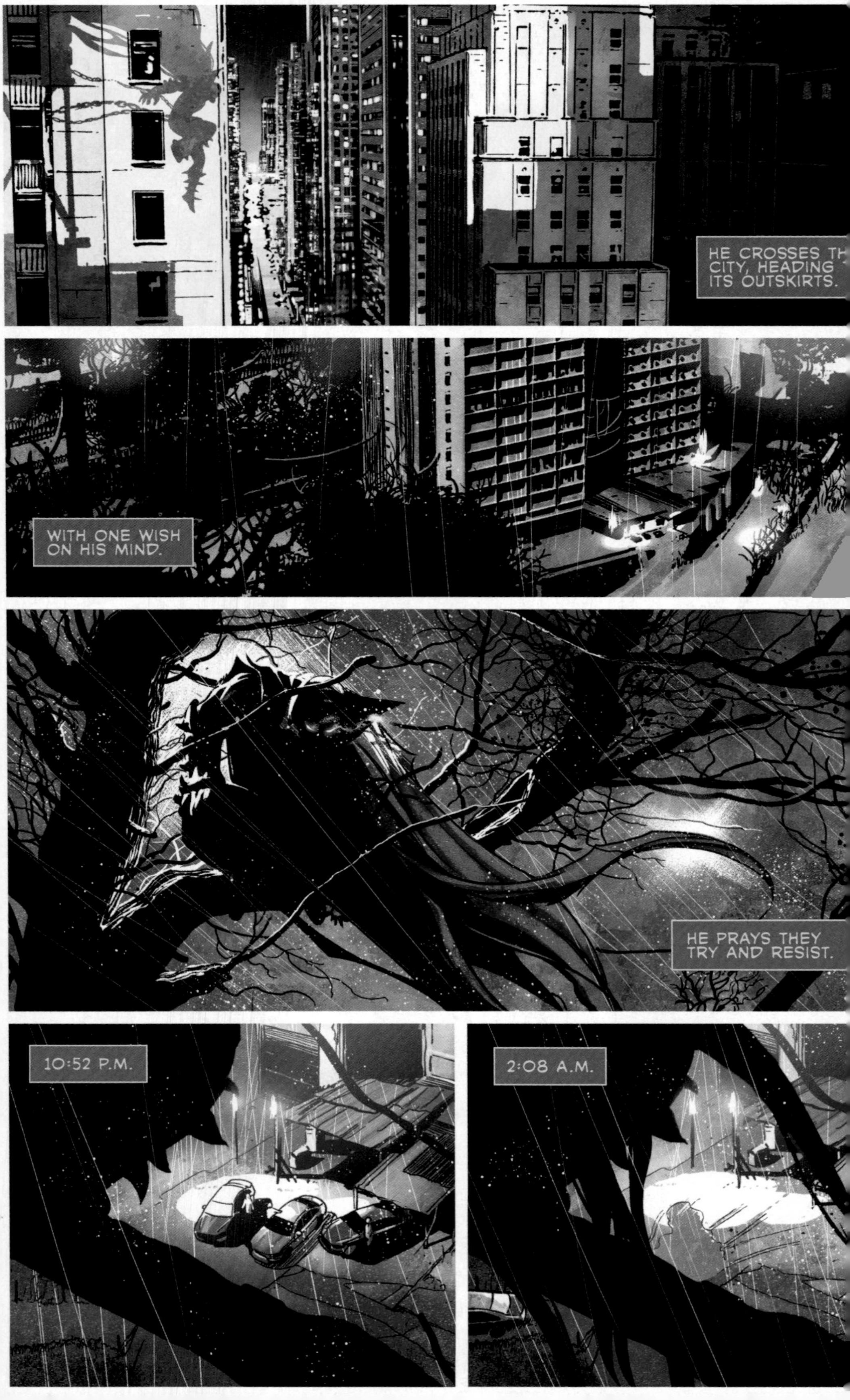
HE CROSSES TH
CITY, HEADING
ITS OUTSKIRTS.
WITH ONE WISH
ON HIS MIND.
HE PRAYS THEY
TRY AND RESIST.
10:52 P.M.
2:08 A.M.

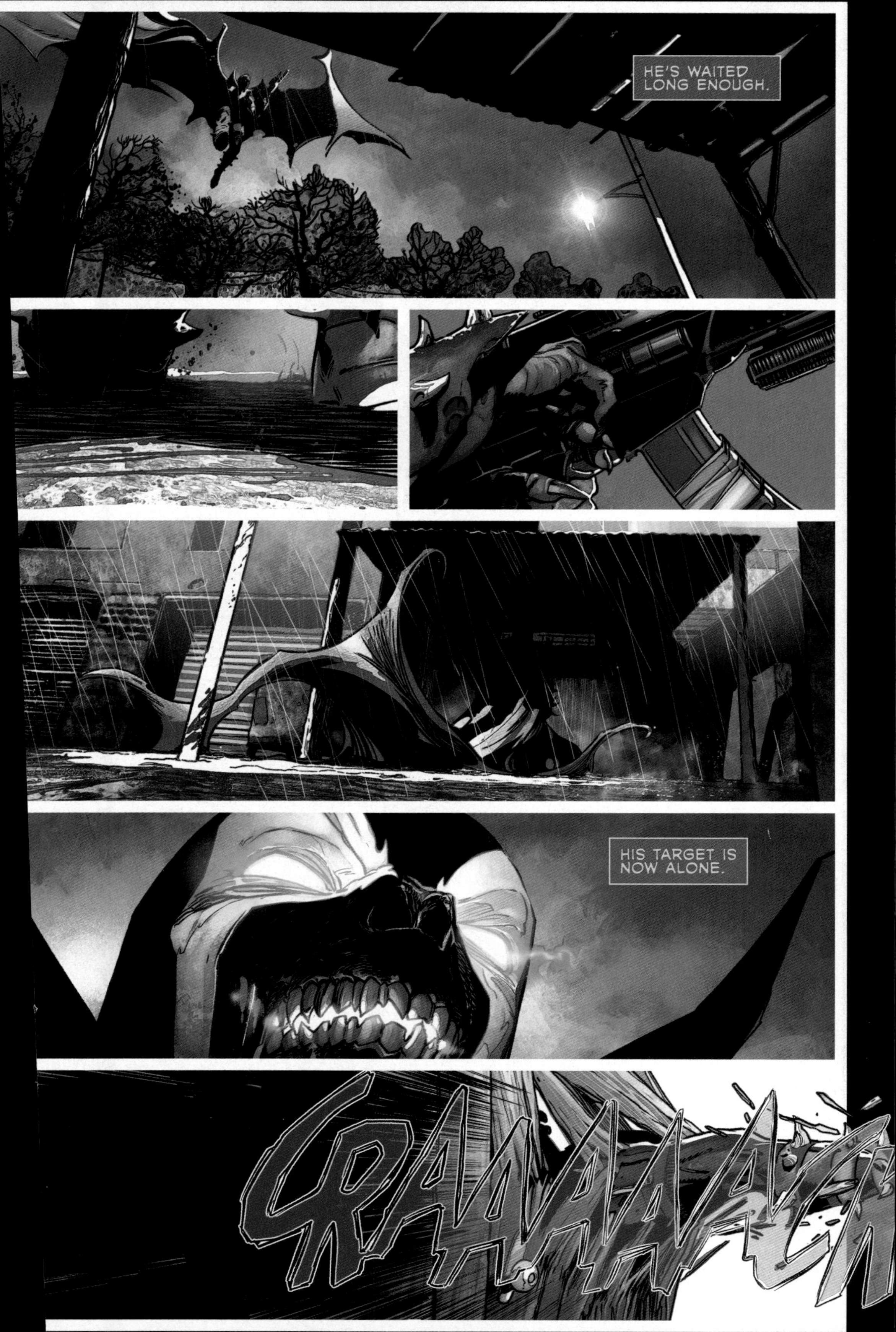
HE'S WAITED LONG ENOUGH.
HIS TARGET IS NOW ALONE.
CRAAAAAACK

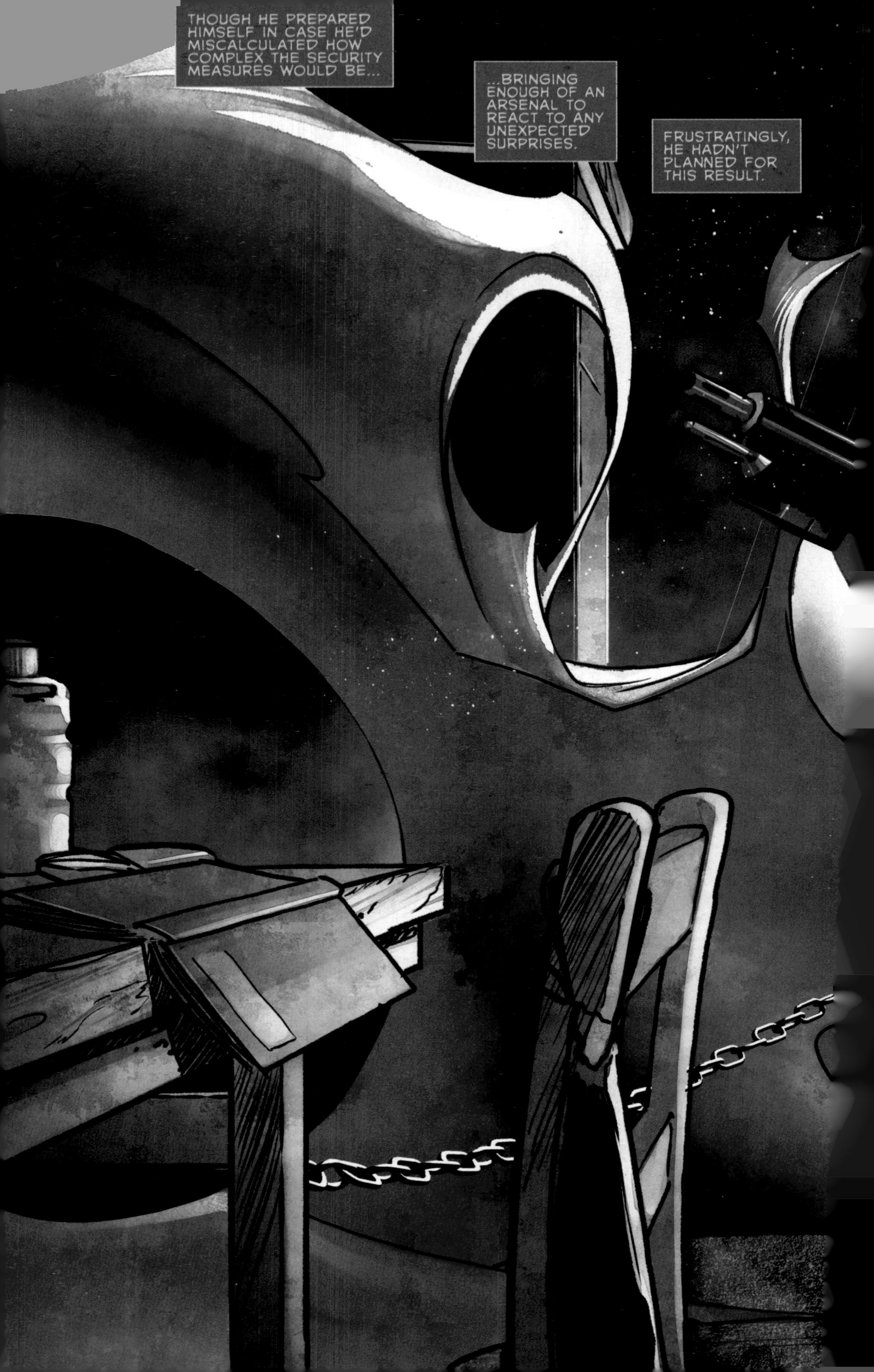
THOUGH HE PREPARED HIMSELF IN CASE HE'D MISCALCULATED HOW COMPLEX THE SECURITY MEASURES WOULD BE...
...BRINGING ENOUGH OF AN ARSENAL TO REACT TO ANY UNEXPECTED SURPRISES.
FRUSTRATINGLY, HE HADN'T PLANNED FOR THIS RESULT.

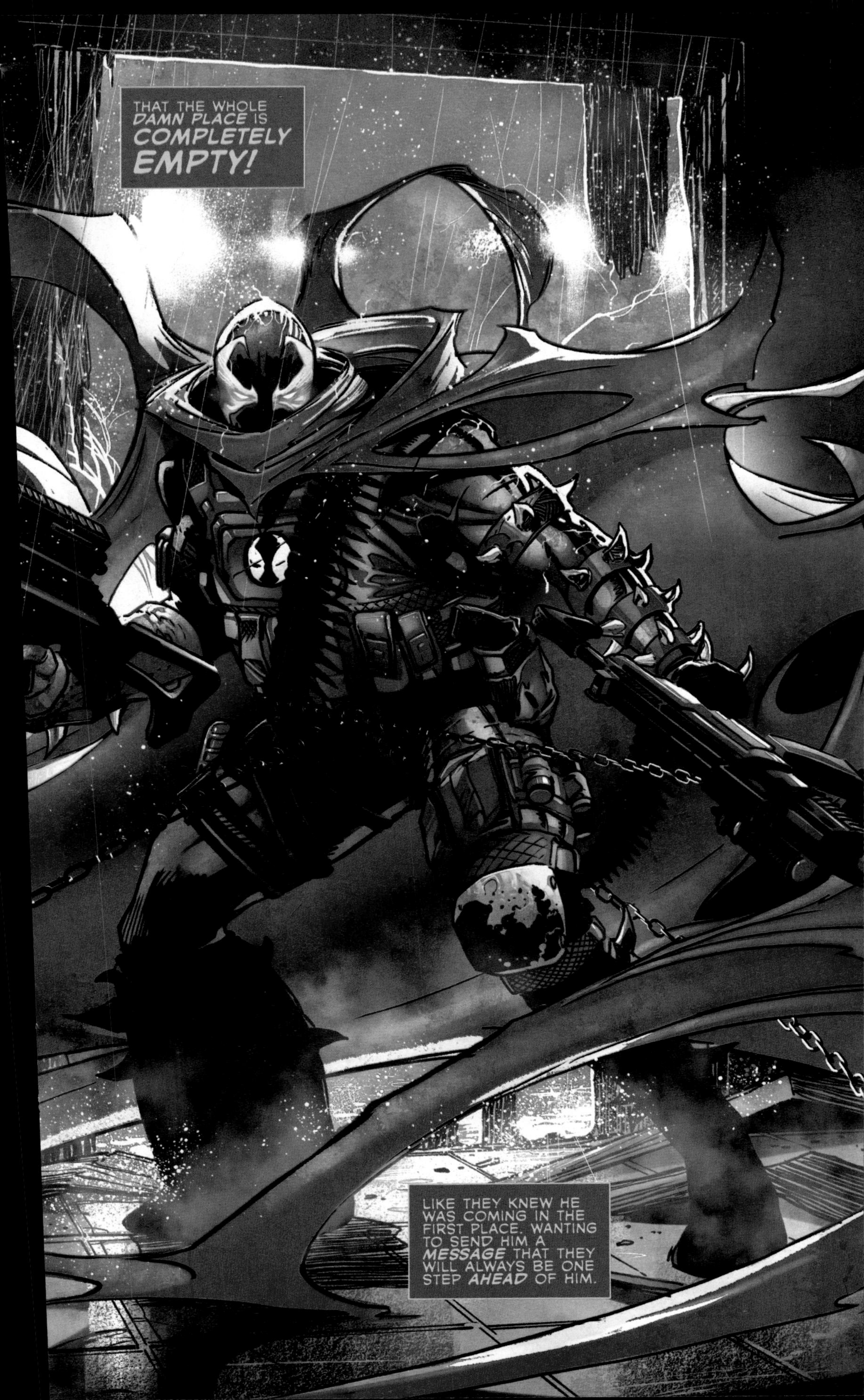
THAT THE WHOLE *DAMN PLACE* IS **COMPLETELY EMPTY!**
LIKE THEY KNEW HE WAS COMING IN THE FIRST PLACE. WANTING TO SEND HIM A ***MESSAGE*** THAT THEY WILL ALWAYS BE ONE STEP ***AHEAD*** OF HIM.

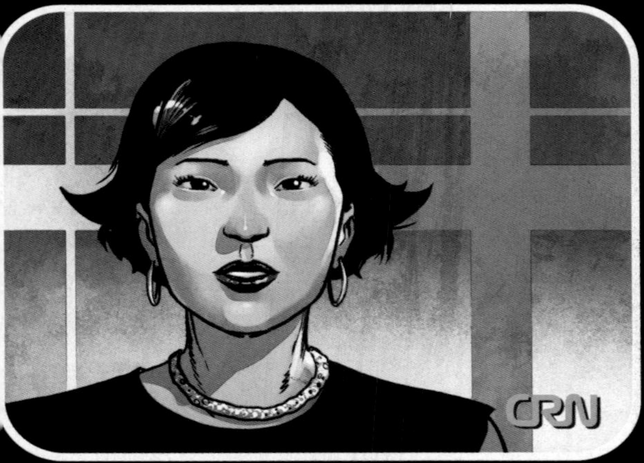
CRN

ANOTHER WEATHER ALERT IS BEING GIVEN THIS TIME FOR RESIDENTS ALONG THE GULF OF MEXICO, AS AN UNSEASONABLY STRONG HURRICANE HAS BEEN BUILDING OFF THE SOUTHERN COAST NEAR LOUISIANA, AND ALONG THE COASTLINE TO FLORIDA. EMERGENCY PRECAUTIONS HAVE BEGUN TO TAKE PLACE AS INCOMING WINDS HAVE BEEN REGISTERED AS STRONG AS 90 MILES PER HOUR.

THIS IS NOW THE THIRTEENTH NATURAL DISASTER TO LAND UPON THE SHORES OF AMERICA IN THE PAST NINE MONTHS, WITH ANOTHER TWENTY-FIVE SIMILAR INCIDENT SCATTERED ACROSS THE REST OF THE GLOBE. WITH LAST WEEK'S STORM IN SPA TAKING THE LIVES OF OVER 180 PEOPLE. THOUGH MANY ARE TALKING ABOUT GLOB WARMING, SOME EXPERTS HAVE BECOME FAR MORE CYNICAL AND BELIEVE THAT W ARE SEEING THE HAND OF GOD MAKING PRESENCE KNOWN.

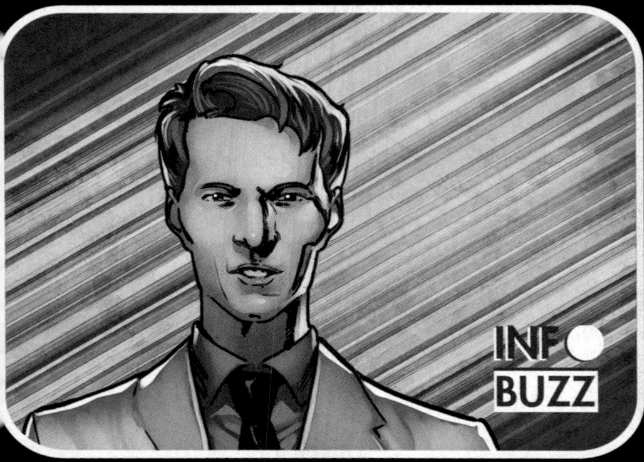
INFO
BUZZ

TO ADD FURTHER CONCERNS TO EVERYTHING ELSE, THE SHEER NUMBER OF ***'COSTUMED SIGHTINGS'*** IN THOSE SAME NINE MONTHS HAS INCREASED SIGNIFICANTLY. SOME OFFICIALS IN GOVERNMENT ARE SPECULATING THAT THERE IS A POSSIBLE CONNECTION BETWEEN THE TWO AND THAT MAYBE TH COSTUMED PEOPLE AND THEIR MOSTLY, AS OF TODAY, ***UNKNOWN*** POWERS ARE POSSIBLY THE CAUSE OF OUR WEATHER PATTERNS SHIFTING.

SOME SCIENTISTS ARE LIKENING IT TO THE GRAVITATIONAL PULLS OF THE MOO HAVING A DIRECT CAUSE ON THE OCEA TIDE'S EBB AND FLOW ON OUR PLANET BUT SINCE THESE NEWLY SIGHTED BEINGS ARE STILL MOSTLY A MYSTERY TO US, ANGER HAS BEGUN TO GROW FOR OUR GOVERNMENT LEADERS TO STEP UP AND DO SOMETHING ABOUT ALL THIS DESTRUCTION OUR WEATHER IS CAUSING.

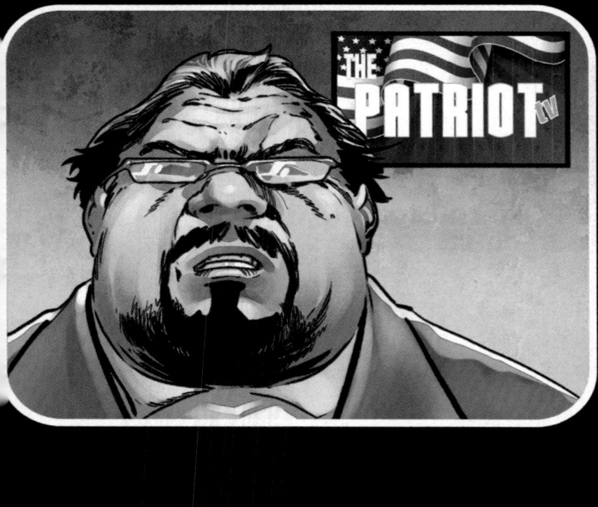
THE PATRIOT TV

IT'S ***ALL*** SOME ***MASTER PLAN*** CONCO BY THE DEEP STATE THAT'S TRYING TO SURE THAT THE PATRIOTIC STATES ALO OUR SOUTHERN BORDERS AND OCEAN ARE **CONVIENIENTLY** IN A ST OF CHAOS JUST AS SOME VERY CRUC PRIMARY ELECTIONS ARE SUPPOSED T TAKING PLACE. **WHY?!** ***BECAUSE AFRAID OF US!!!*** AFRAID WE'LL HAVE POWER TO REIGN IN THESE SO-CALLE ***"SUPER-HEROES"*** AND PROVE ONCE FOR ALL THAT THIS WHOLE DEBATE O GLOBAL WARMING IS A **HOAX**.

THE RADICAL LEFT SAY IT HAS TO DO FOSSIL FUEL AND MAN-MADE GASES WELL, I'M TELLIN' YOU IT'S NOT ***GOD*** DOING THIS.--THOUGH HE HAS PLENT BE PISSED OFF ABOUT--IT IS THE FA THESE **COSTUMED MEN** THA MADE THIS!!! NOT MAN... ***COSTUMED*** ARE THE CULPRITS!!!

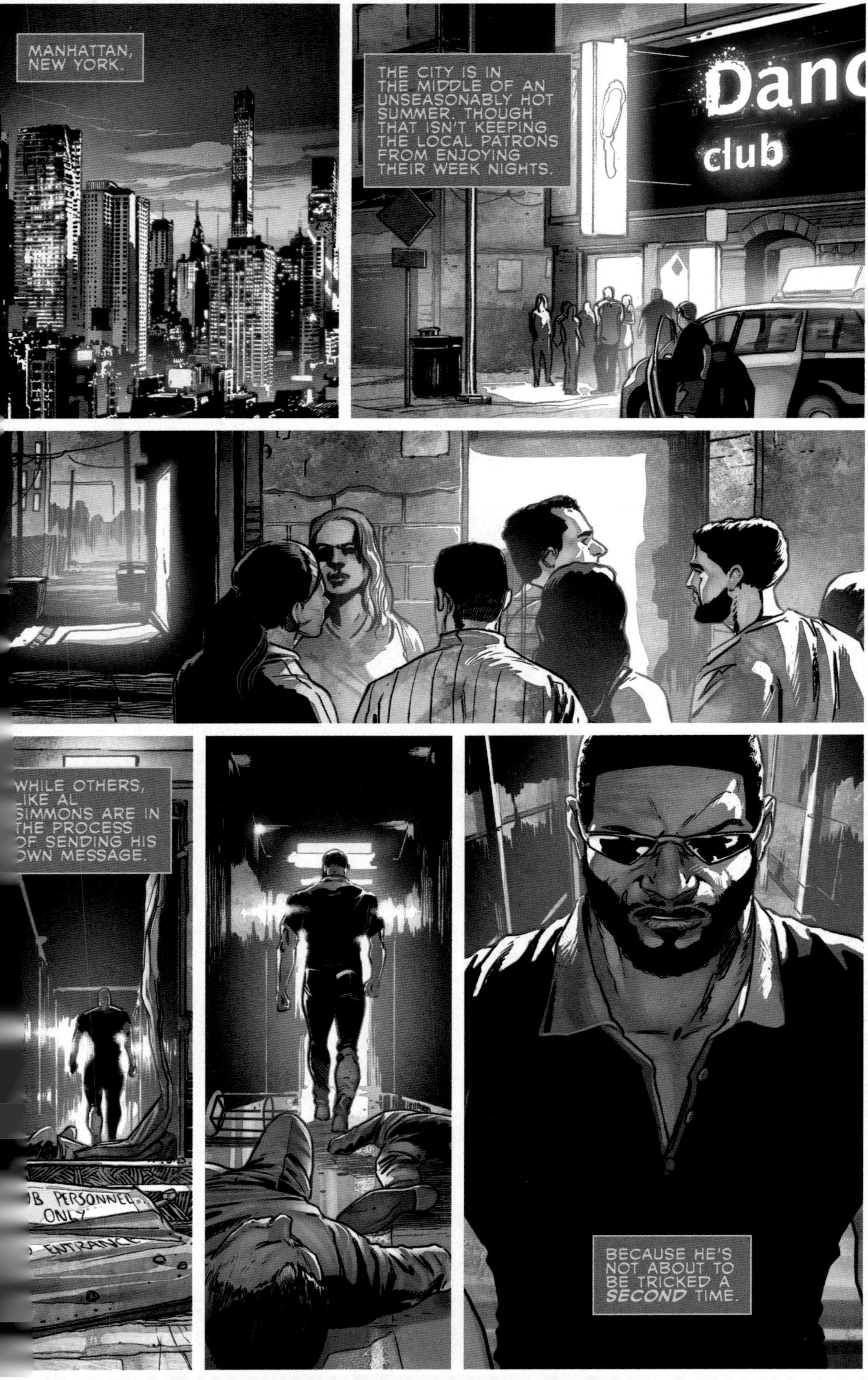
MANHATTAN, NEW YORK.
THE CITY IS IN THE MIDDLE OF AN UNSEASONABLY HOT SUMMER. THOUGH THAT ISN'T KEEPING THE LOCAL PATRONS FROM ENJOYING THEIR WEEK NIGHTS.
Danc
club
WHILE OTHERS, LIKE AL SIMMONS ARE IN THE PROCESS OF SENDING HIS OWN MESSAGE.
B PERSONNEL ONLY
ENTRANCE
BECAUSE HE'S NOT ABOUT TO BE TRICKED A *SECOND* TIME.

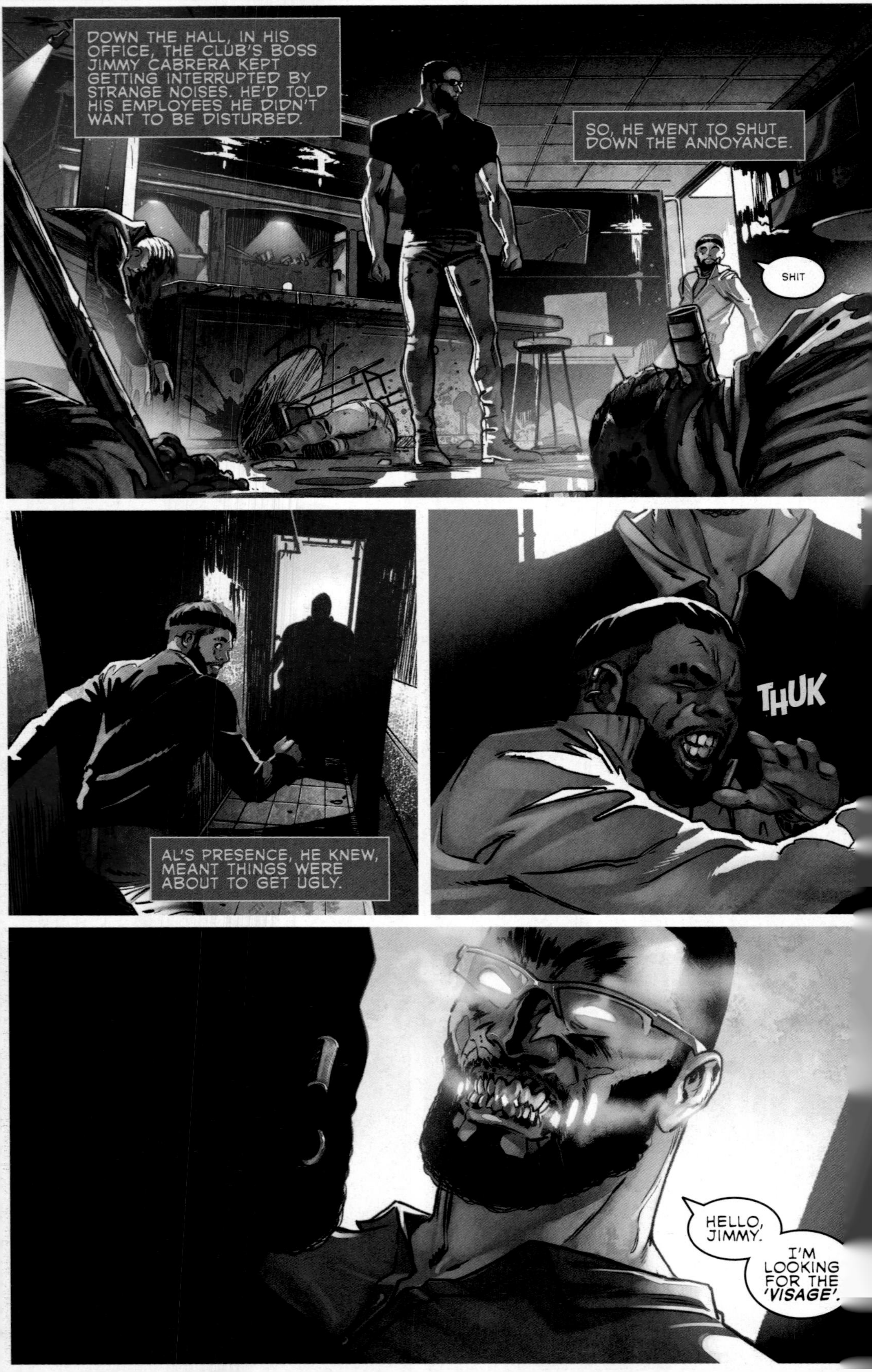
DOWN THE HALL, IN HIS OFFICE, THE CLUB'S BOSS JIMMY CABRERA KEPT GETTING INTERRUPTED BY STRANGE NOISES. HE'D TOLD HIS EMPLOYEES HE DIDN'T WANT TO BE DISTURBED.
SO, HE WENT TO SHUT DOWN THE ANNOYANCE.
SHIT
AL'S PRESENCE, HE KNEW, MEANT THINGS WERE ABOUT TO GET UGLY.
THUK
HELLO, JIMMY.
I'M LOOKING FOR THE 'VISAGE'.

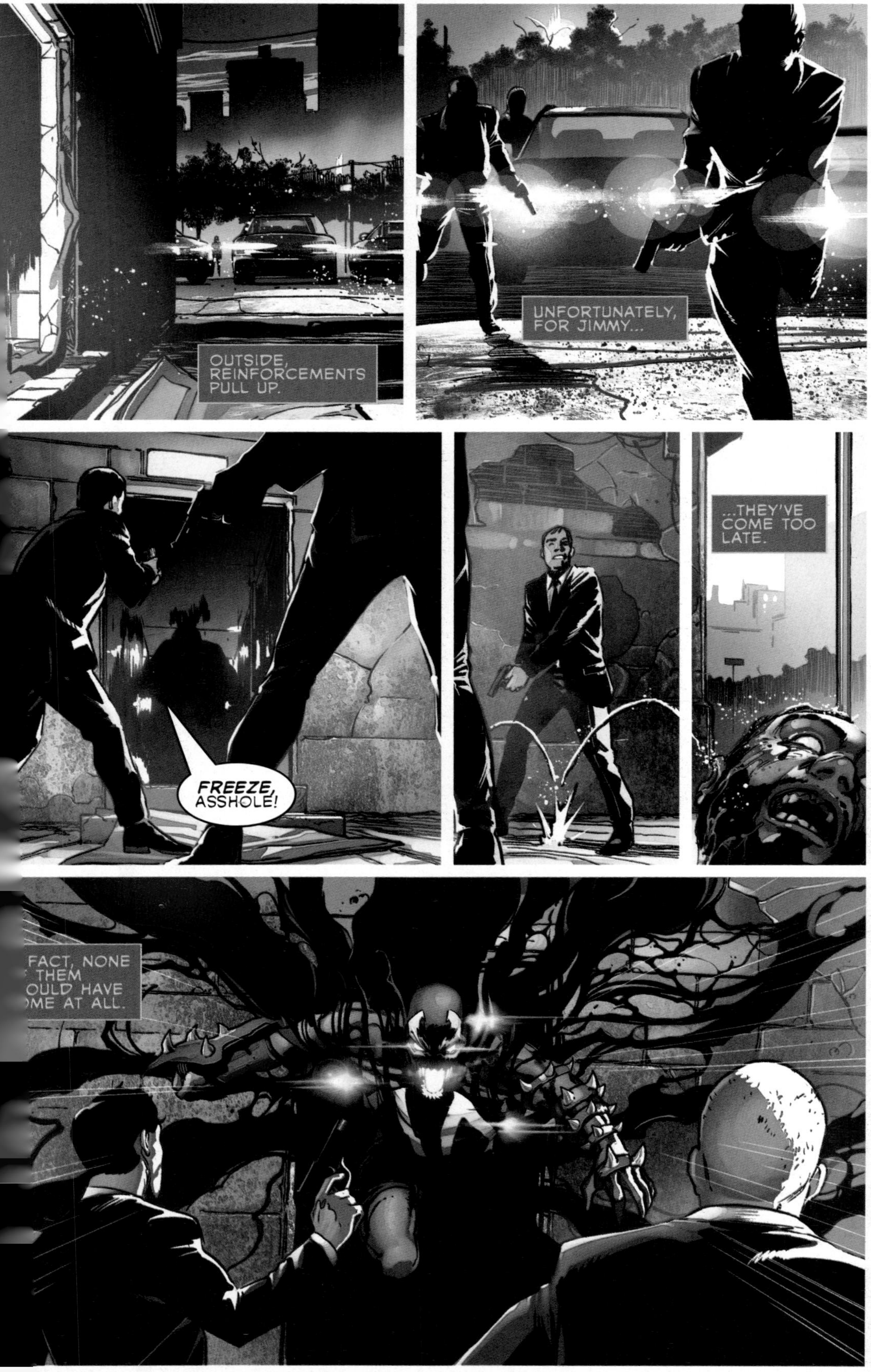
OUTSIDE, REINFORCEMENTS PULL UP.
UNFORTUNATELY, FOR JIMMY...
FREEZE, ASSHOLE!
...THEY'VE COME TOO LATE.
FACT, NONE
THEM
OULD HAVE
OME AT ALL.

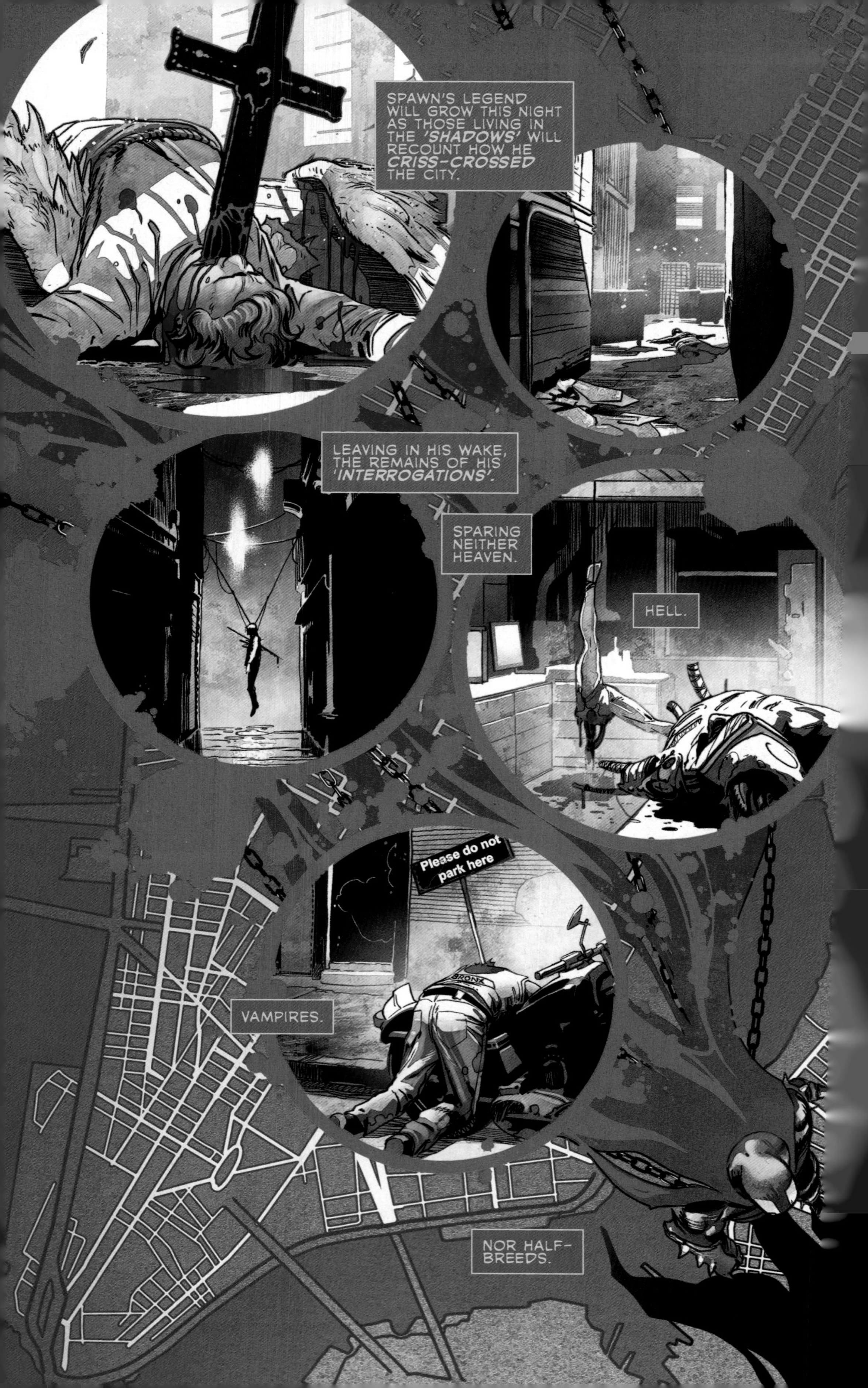
SPAWN'S LEGEND WILL GROW THIS NIGHT AS THOSE LIVING IN THE 'SHADOWS' WILL RECOUNT HOW HE CRISS-CROSSED THE CITY.
LEAVING IN HIS WAKE, THE REMAINS OF HIS 'INTERROGATIONS'.
SPARING NEITHER HEAVEN.
HELL.
Please do not park here
VAMPIRES.
NOR HALF-BREEDS.

BY THE SECOND NIGHT, THEY WERE ALL RUNNING SCARED.

SOME CONVINCED THEY ONLY NEEDED TO GO *DEEPER* IN THE SHADOWS FOR PROTECTION.

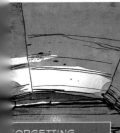

ORGETTING, OMEHOW, THAT HE BEAST UNTING THEM *REW* STRONGER S THE DARKNESS ETS BLACKER.

THE 'VISAGE'--

WHERE IS SHE?

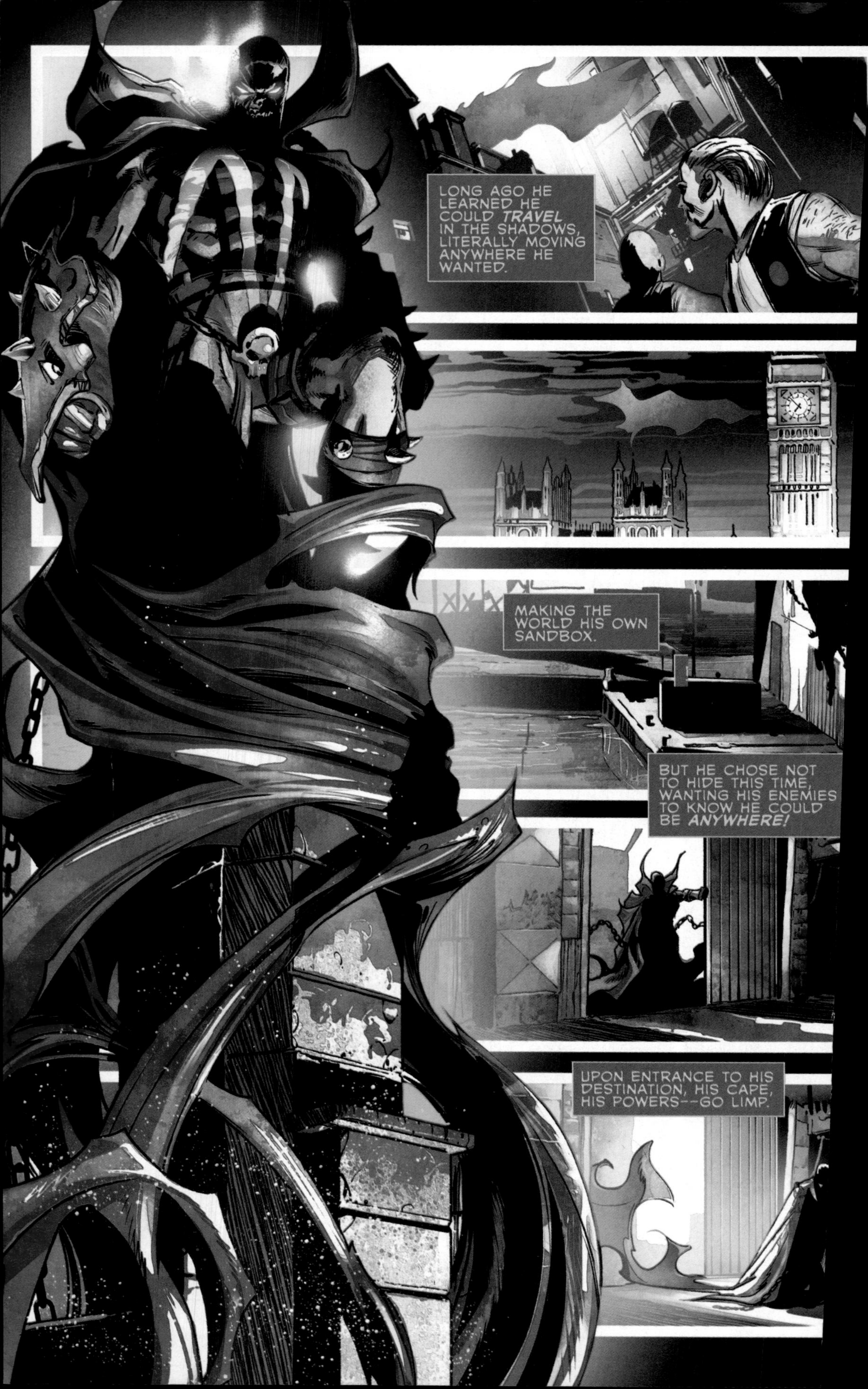
LONG AGO HE LEARNED HE COULD TRAVEL IN THE SHADOWS, LITERALLY MOVING ANYWHERE HE WANTED.
MAKING THE WORLD HIS OWN SANDBOX.
BUT HE CHOSE NOT TO HIDE THIS TIME, WANTING HIS ENEMIES TO KNOW HE COULD BE ANYWHERE!
UPON ENTRANCE TO HIS DESTINATION, HIS CAPE, HIS POWERS--GO LIMP.

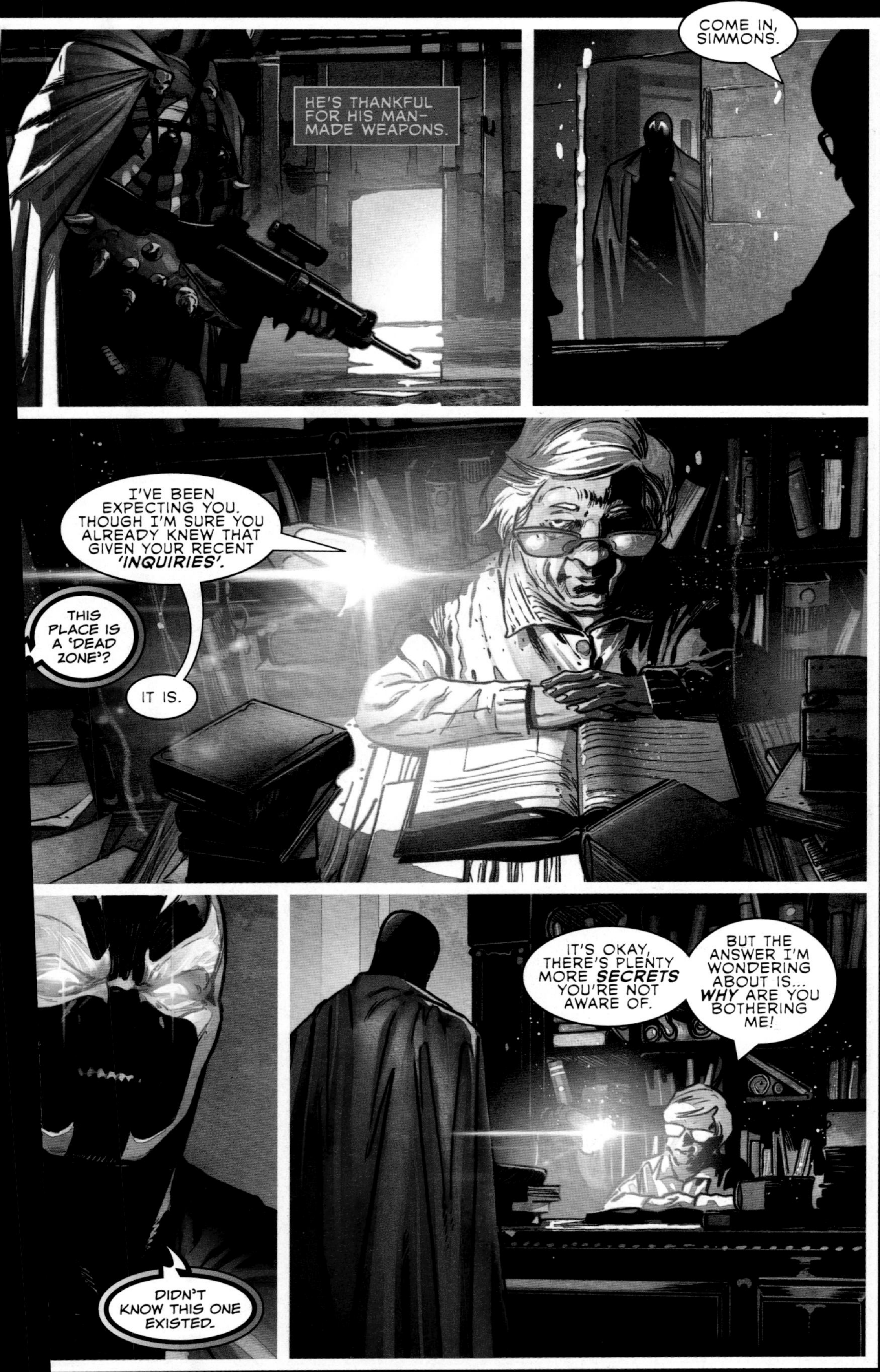
HE'S THANKFUL FOR HIS MAN-MADE WEAPONS.
COME IN, SIMMONS.
I'VE BEEN EXPECTING YOU. THOUGH I'M SURE YOU ALREADY KNEW THAT GIVEN YOUR RECENT **'INQUIRIES'**.
THIS PLACE IS A 'DEAD ZONE'?
IT IS.
DIDN'T KNOW THIS ONE EXISTED.
IT'S OKAY, THERE'S PLENTY MORE **SECRETS** YOU'RE NOT AWARE OF.
BUT THE ANSWER I'M WONDERING ABOUT IS... **WHY** ARE YOU BOTHERING ME!

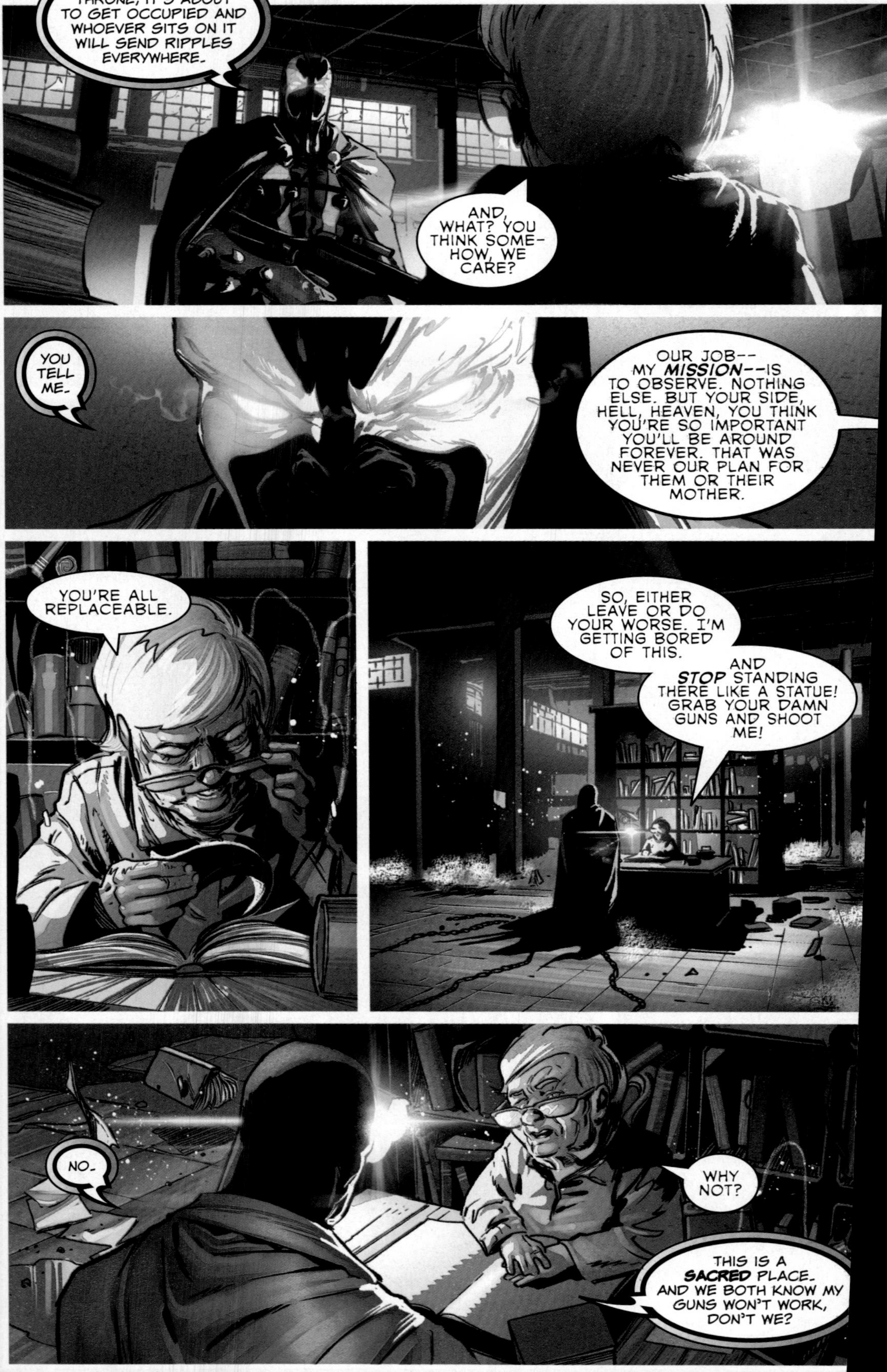
HELL'S THRONE, IT'S ABOUT TO GET OCCUPIED AND WHOEVER SITS ON IT WILL SEND RIPPLES EVERYWHERE.
AND, WHAT? YOU THINK SOME-HOW, WE CARE?
YOU TELL ME.
OUR JOB-- MY MISSION--IS TO OBSERVE. NOTHING ELSE. BUT YOUR SIDE, HELL, HEAVEN, YOU THINK YOU'RE SO IMPORTANT YOU'LL BE AROUND FOREVER. THAT WAS NEVER OUR PLAN FOR THEM OR THEIR MOTHER.
YOU'RE ALL REPLACEABLE.
SO, EITHER LEAVE OR DO YOUR WORSE. I'M GETTING BORED OF THIS.
AND STOP STANDING THERE LIKE A STATUE! GRAB YOUR DAMN GUNS AND SHOOT ME!
NO.
WHY NOT?
THIS IS A SACRED PLACE. AND WE BOTH KNOW MY GUNS WON'T WORK, DON'T WE?

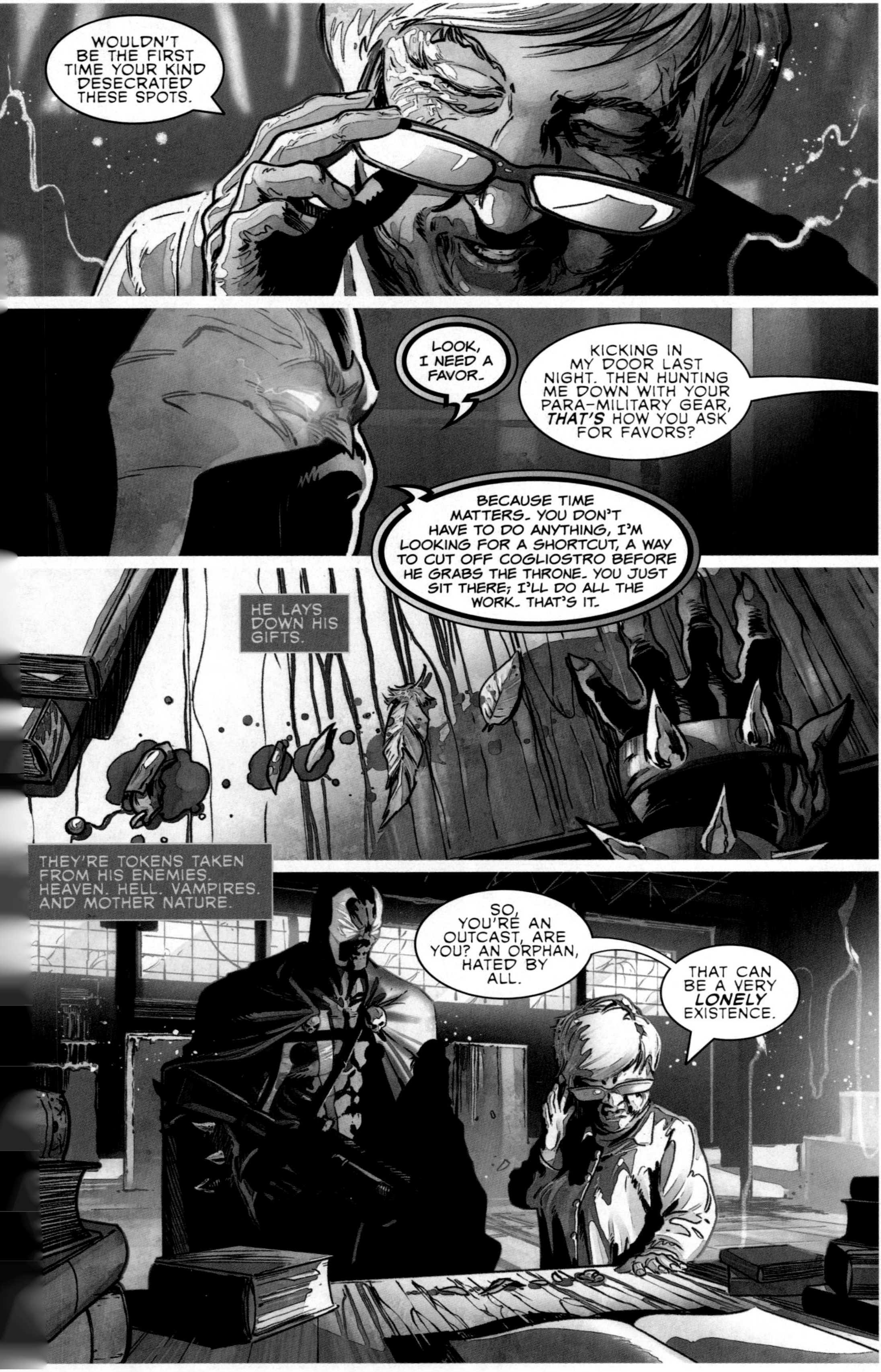
WOULDN'T BE THE FIRST TIME YOUR KIND DESECRATED THESE SPOTS.
LOOK, I NEED A FAVOR.
KICKING IN MY DOOR LAST NIGHT. THEN HUNTING ME DOWN WITH YOUR PARA-MILITARY GEAR, THAT'S HOW YOU ASK FOR FAVORS?
BECAUSE TIME MATTERS. YOU DON'T HAVE TO DO ANYTHING, I'M LOOKING FOR A SHORTCUT, A WAY TO CUT OFF COGLIOSTRO BEFORE HE GRABS THE THRONE. YOU JUST SIT THERE; I'LL DO ALL THE WORK. THAT'S IT.
HE LAYS DOWN HIS GIFTS.
THEY'RE TOKENS TAKEN FROM HIS ENEMIES. HEAVEN. HELL. VAMPIRES. AND MOTHER NATURE.
SO, YOU'RE AN OUTCAST, ARE YOU? AN ORPHAN, HATED BY ALL.
THAT CAN BE A VERY LONELY EXISTENCE.

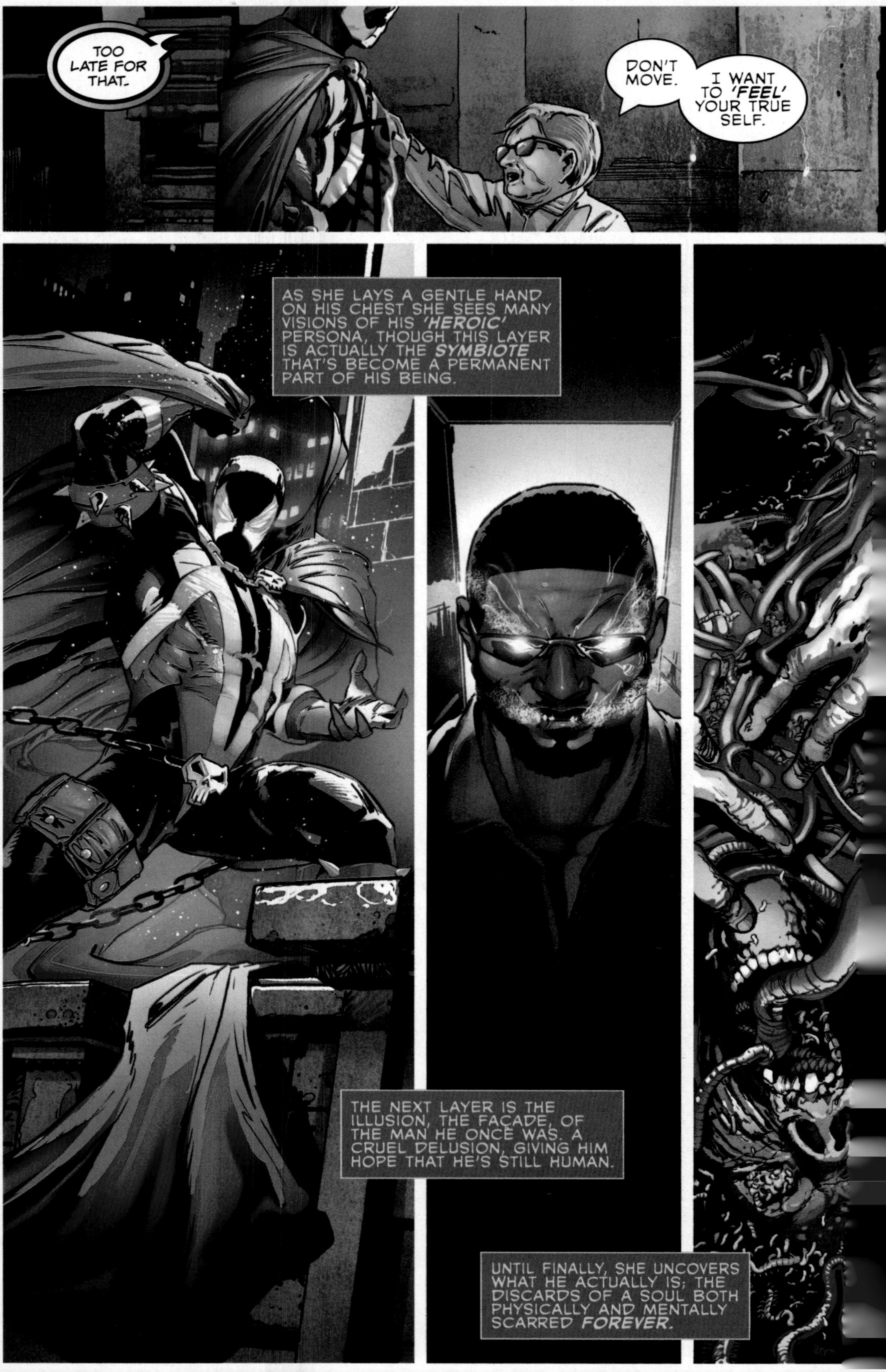
TOO LATE FOR THAT.
DON'T MOVE.
I WANT TO 'FEEL' YOUR TRUE SELF.
AS SHE LAYS A GENTLE HAND ON HIS CHEST SHE SEES MANY VISIONS OF HIS 'HEROIC' PERSONA, THOUGH THIS LAYER IS ACTUALLY THE SYMBIOTE THAT'S BECOME A PERMANENT PART OF HIS BEING.
THE NEXT LAYER IS THE ILLUSION, THE FAÇADE, OF THE MAN HE ONCE WAS. A CRUEL DELUSION, GIVING HIM HOPE THAT HE'S STILL HUMAN.
UNTIL FINALLY, SHE UNCOVERS WHAT HE ACTUALLY IS; THE DISCARDS OF A SOUL BOTH PHYSICALLY AND MENTALLY SCARRED FOREVER.

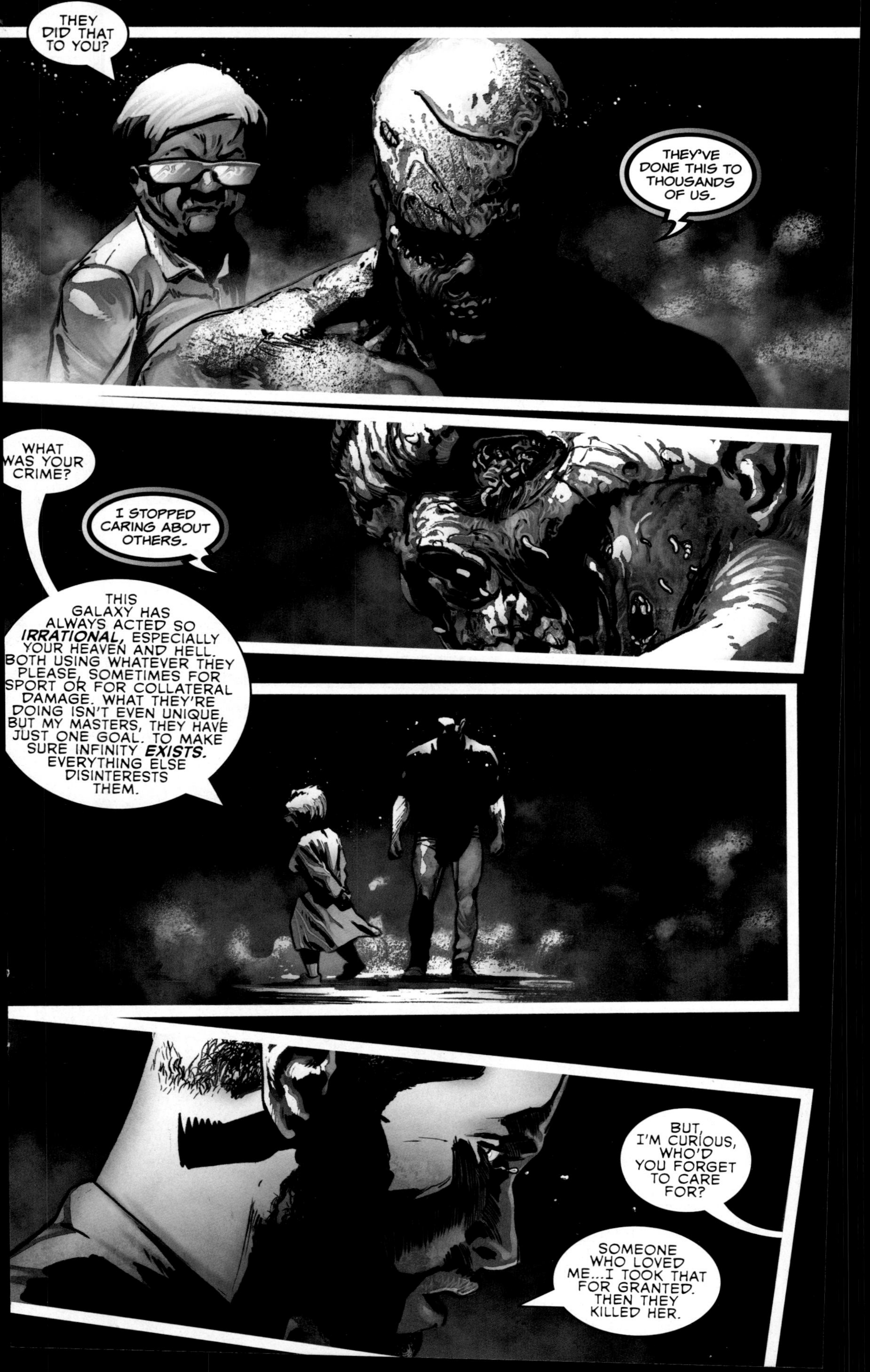

THEY DID THAT TO YOU?
THEY'VE DONE THIS TO THOUSANDS OF US.
WHAT WAS YOUR CRIME?
I STOPPED CARING ABOUT OTHERS.
THIS GALAXY HAS ALWAYS ACTED SO IRRATIONAL, ESPECIALLY YOUR HEAVEN AND HELL. BOTH USING WHATEVER THEY PLEASE, SOMETIMES FOR SPORT OR FOR COLLATERAL DAMAGE. WHAT THEY'RE DOING ISN'T EVEN UNIQUE, BUT MY MASTERS, THEY HAVE JUST ONE GOAL. TO MAKE SURE INFINITY EXISTS. EVERYTHING ELSE DISINTERESTS THEM.
BUT, I'M CURIOUS, WHO'D YOU FORGET TO CARE FOR?
SOMEONE WHO LOVED ME...I TOOK THAT FOR GRANTED. THEN THEY KILLED HER.

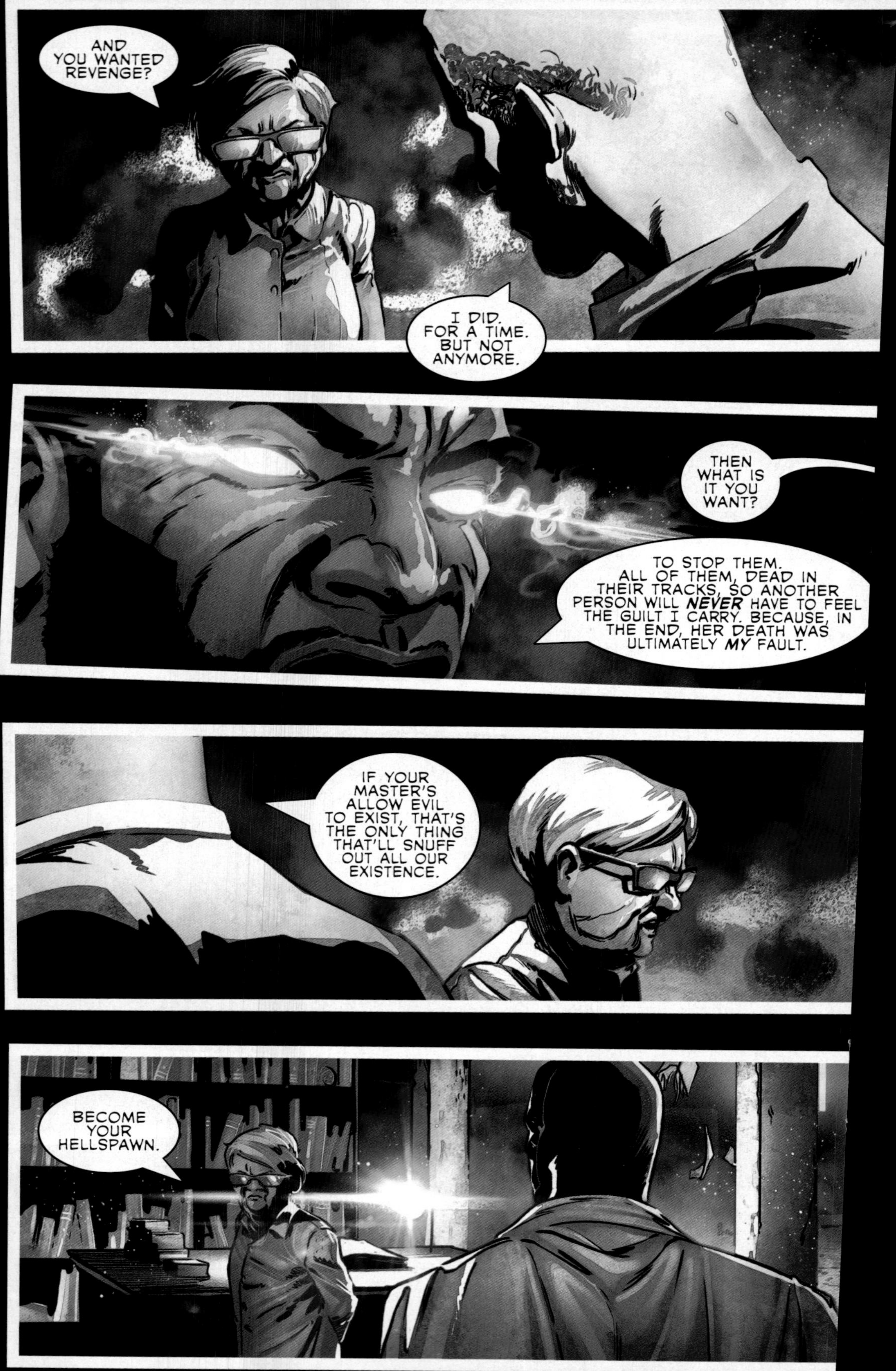
AND YOU WANTED REVENGE?
I DID. FOR A TIME. BUT NOT ANYMORE.
THEN WHAT IS IT YOU WANT?
TO STOP THEM. ALL OF THEM, DEAD IN THEIR TRACKS, SO ANOTHER PERSON WILL NEVER HAVE TO FEEL THE GUILT I CARRY. BECAUSE, IN THE END, HER DEATH WAS ULTIMATELY MY FAULT.
IF YOUR MASTER'S ALLOW EVIL TO EXIST, THAT'S THE ONLY THING THAT'LL SNUFF OUT ALL OUR EXISTENCE.
BECOME YOUR HELLSPAWN.

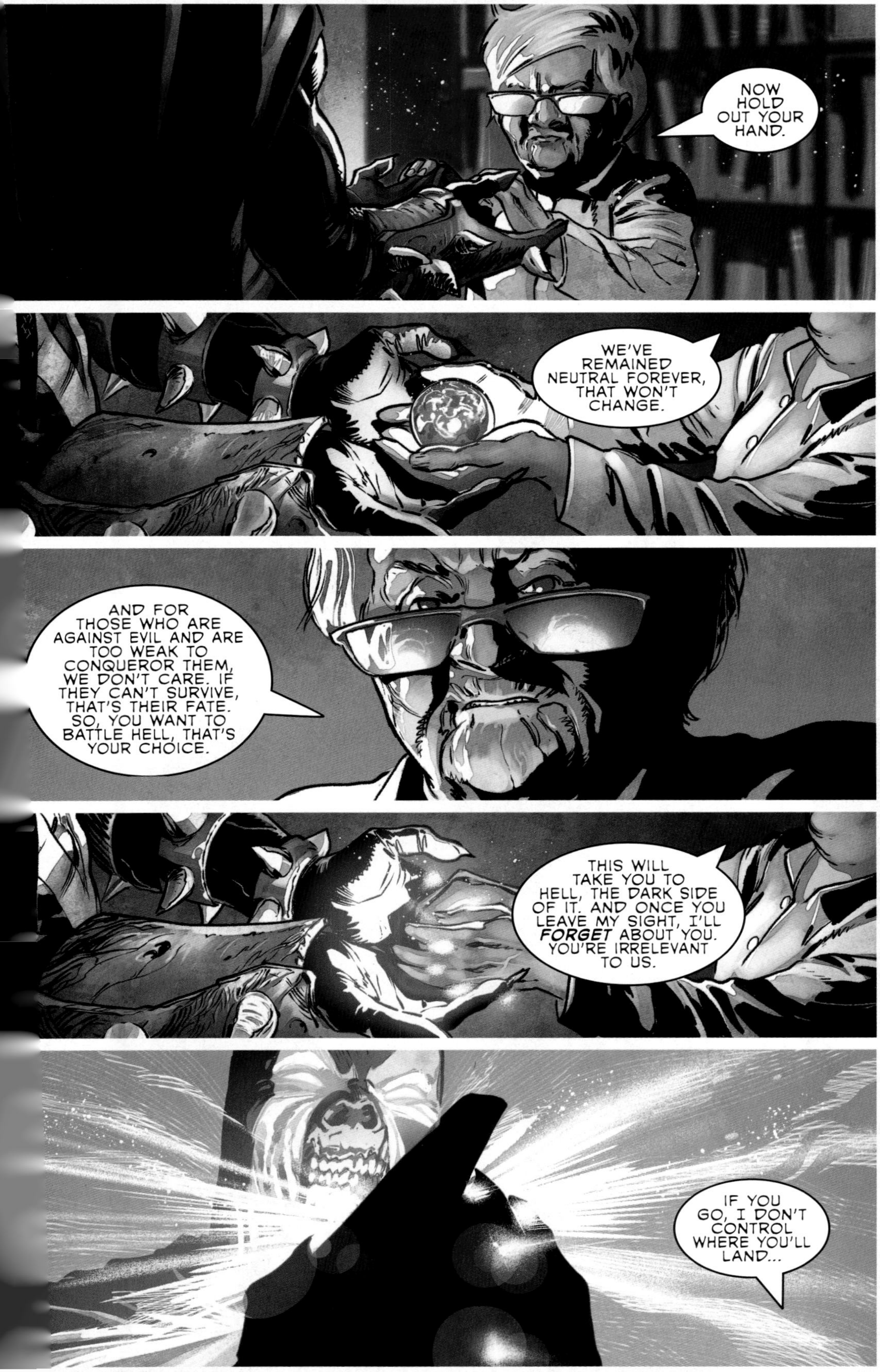
NOW HOLD OUT YOUR HAND.
WE'VE REMAINED NEUTRAL FOREVER, THAT WON'T CHANGE.
AND FOR THOSE WHO ARE AGAINST EVIL AND ARE TOO WEAK TO CONQUEROR THEM, WE DON'T CARE. IF THEY CAN'T SURVIVE, THAT'S THEIR FATE. SO, YOU WANT TO BATTLE HELL, THAT'S YOUR CHOICE.
THIS WILL TAKE YOU TO HELL, THE DARK SIDE OF IT. AND ONCE YOU LEAVE MY SIGHT, I'LL *FORGET* ABOUT YOU. YOU'RE IRRELEVANT TO US.
IF YOU GO, I DON'T CONTROL WHERE YOU'LL LAND...

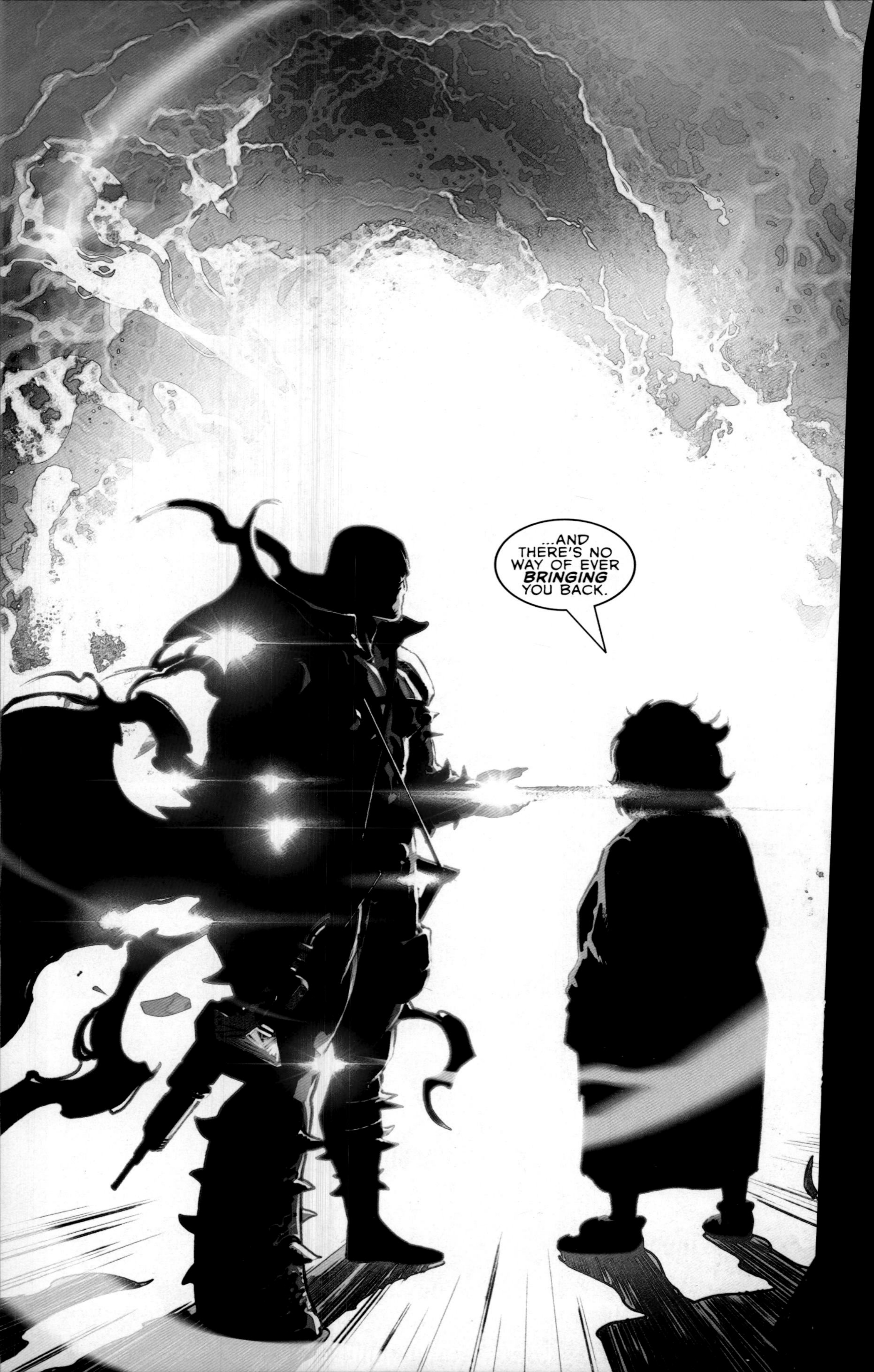
...AND THERE'S NO WAY OF EVER BRINGING YOU BACK.

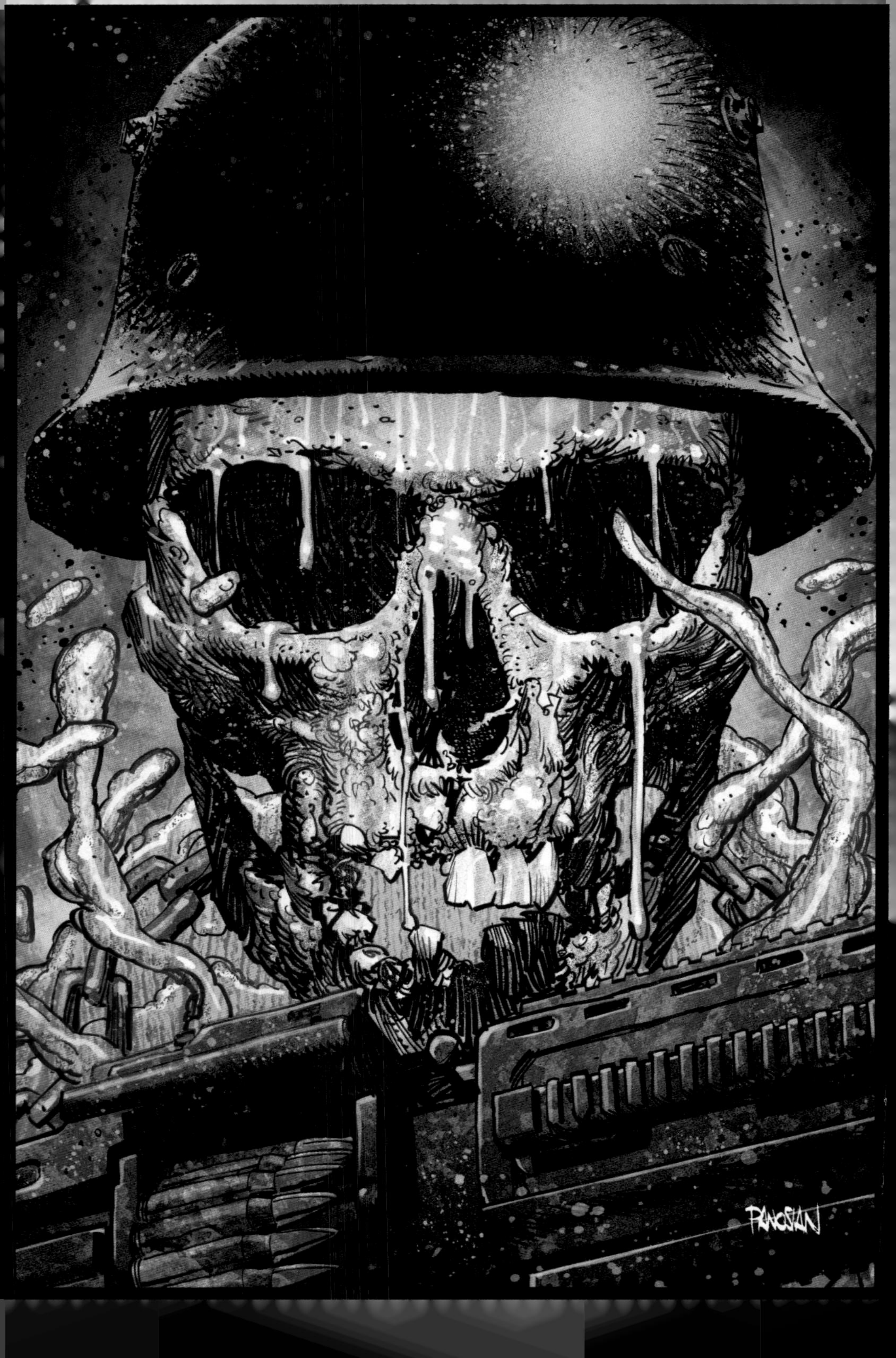
PANOSIAN

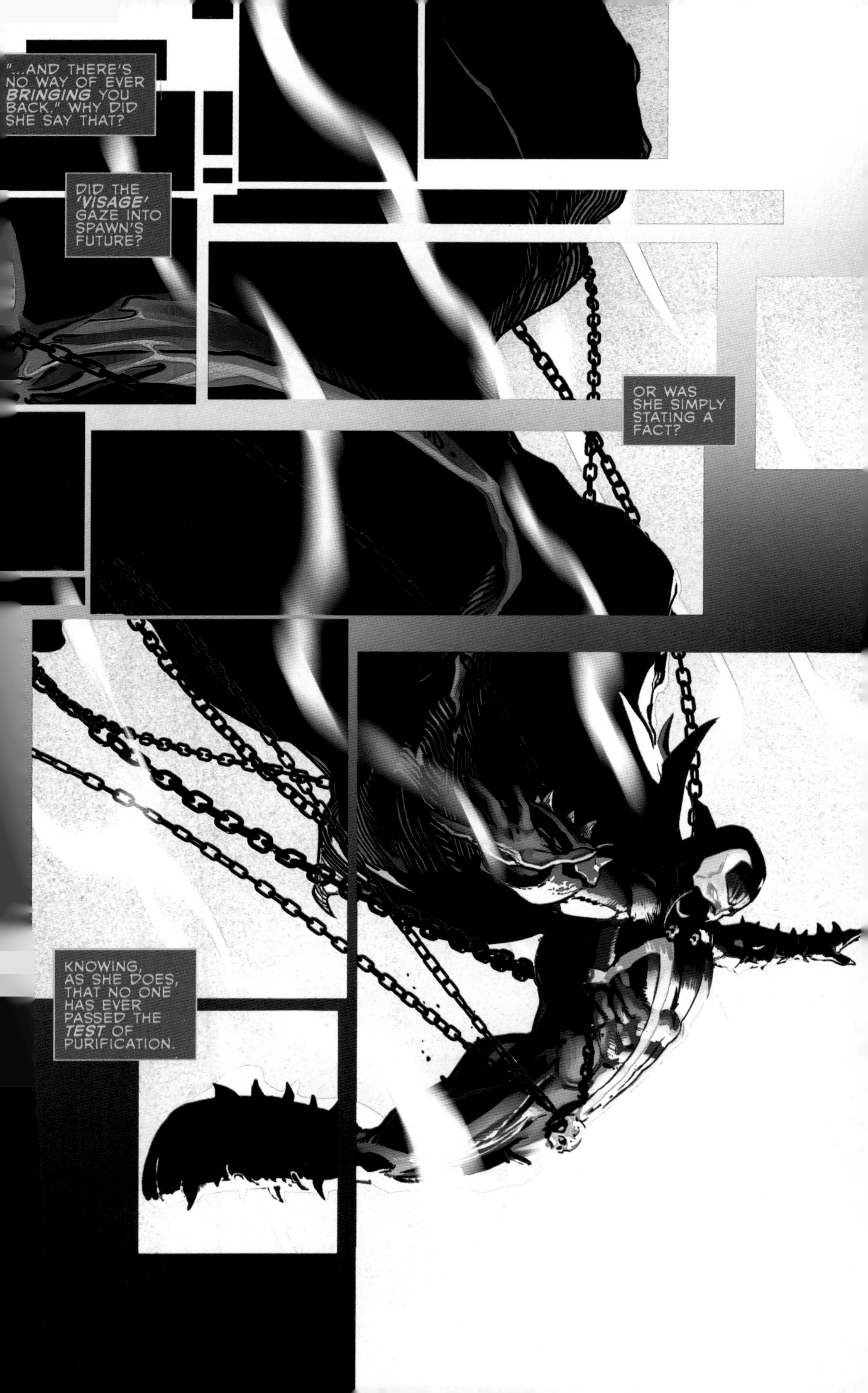
"...AND THERE'S NO WAY OF EVER BRINGING YOU BACK." WHY DID SHE SAY THAT?
DID THE 'VISAGE' GAZE INTO SPAWN'S FUTURE?
OR WAS SHE SIMPLY STATING A FACT?
KNOWING, AS SHE DOES, THAT NO ONE HAS EVER PASSED THE TEST OF PURIFICATION.

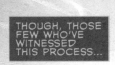
THOUGH, THOSE FEW WHO'VE WITNESSED THIS PROCESS...

...HAVE NEVER CALLED IT A TEST.

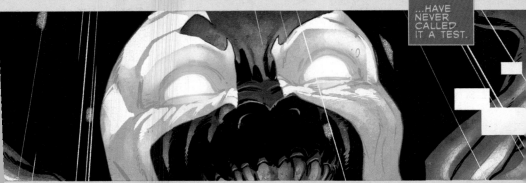

THEY KNOW IT'S ACTUAL PUNISHMEN

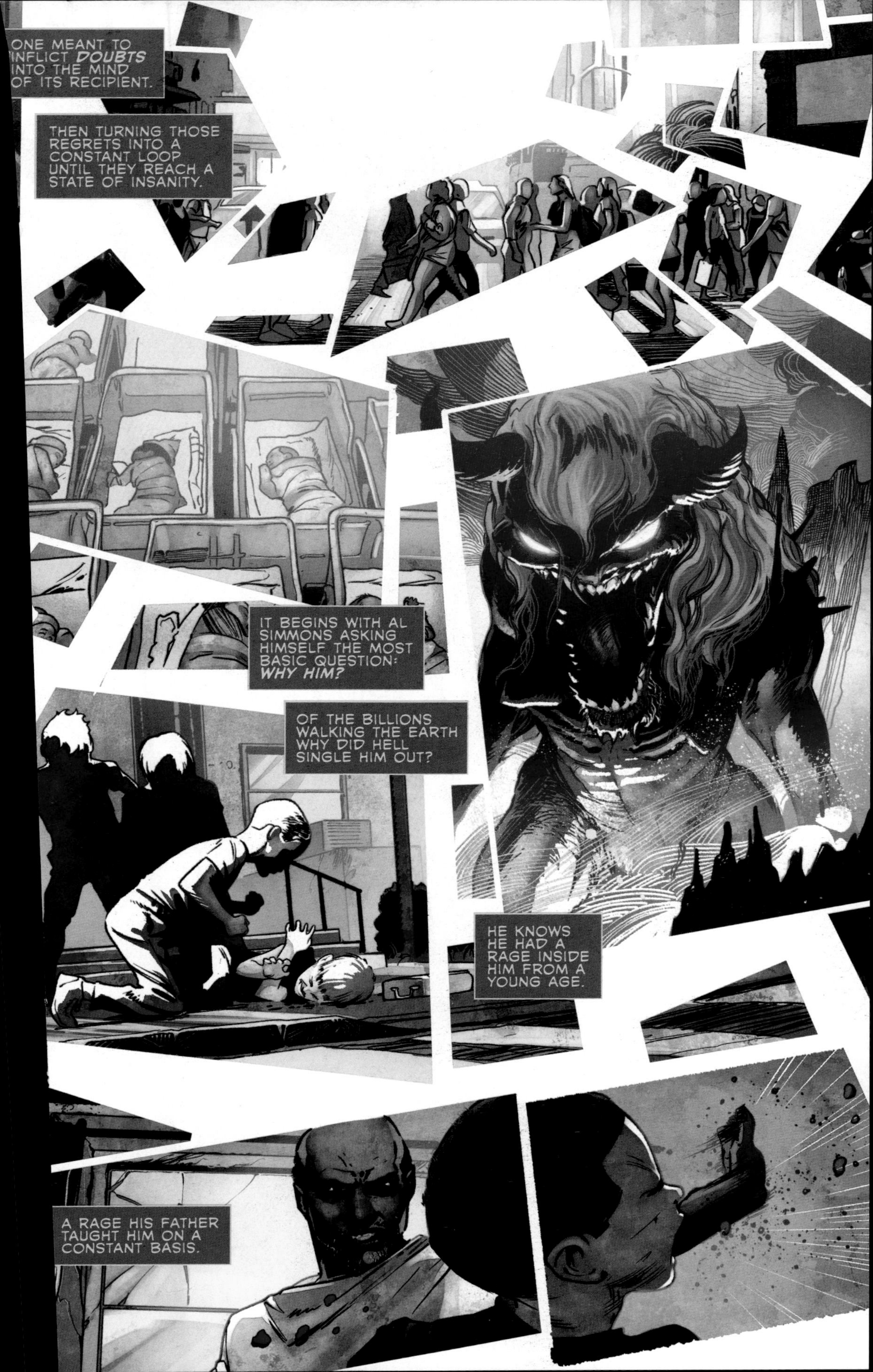

ONE MEANT TO INFLICT DOUBTS INTO THE MIND OF ITS RECIPIENT.
THEN TURNING THOSE REGRETS INTO A CONSTANT LOOP UNTIL THEY REACH A STATE OF INSANITY.
IT BEGINS WITH AL SIMMONS ASKING HIMSELF THE MOST BASIC QUESTION: WHY HIM?
OF THE BILLIONS WALKING THE EARTH WHY DID HELL SINGLE HIM OUT?
HE KNOWS HE HAD A RAGE INSIDE HIM FROM A YOUNG AGE.
A RAGE HIS FATHER TAUGHT HIM ON A CONSTANT BASIS.

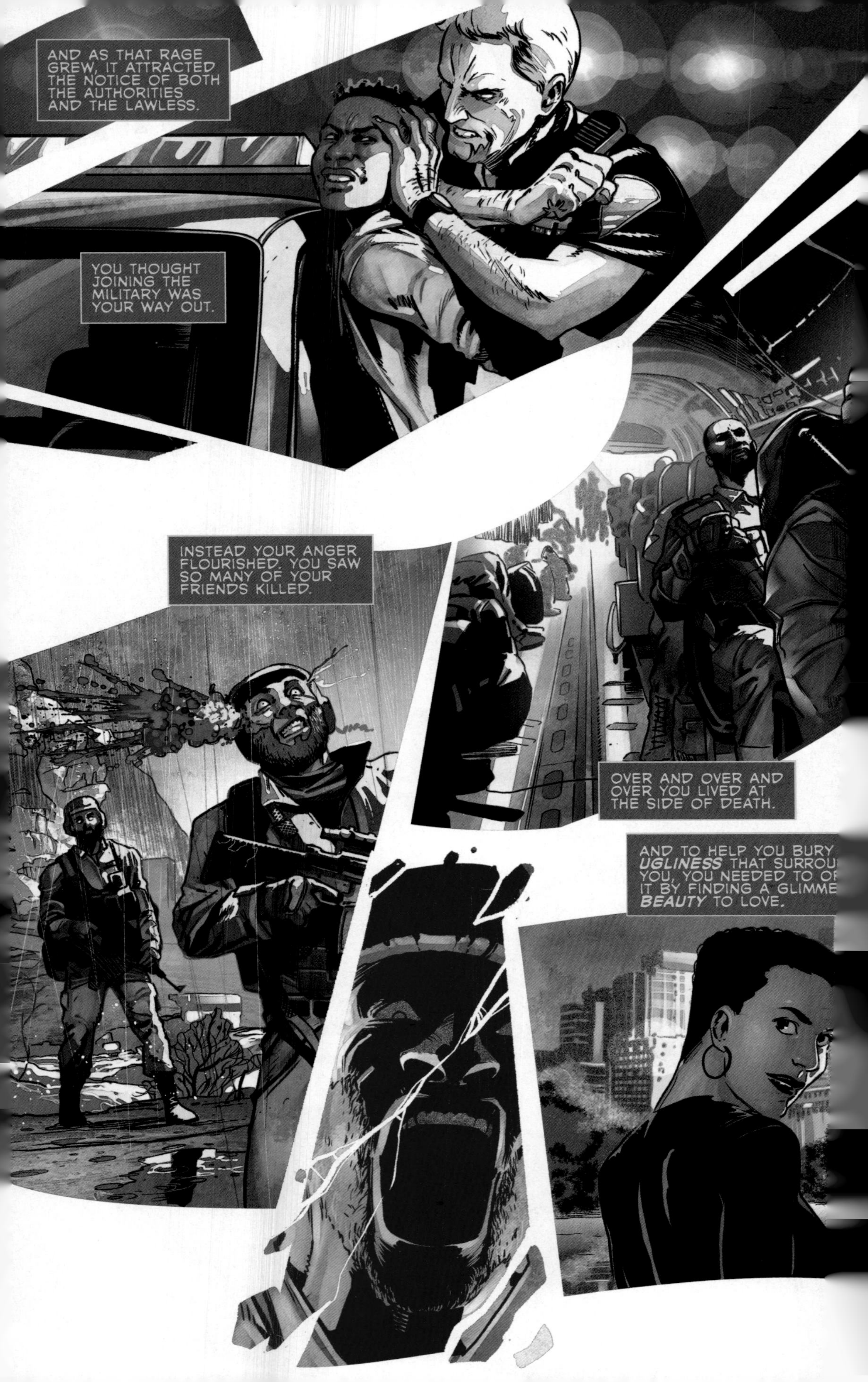
AND AS THAT RAGE GREW, IT ATTRACTED THE NOTICE OF BOTH THE AUTHORITIES AND THE LAWLESS.
YOU THOUGHT JOINING THE MILITARY WAS YOUR WAY OUT.
INSTEAD YOUR ANGER FLOURISHED. YOU SAW SO MANY OF YOUR FRIENDS KILLED.
OVER AND OVER AND OVER YOU LIVED AT THE SIDE OF DEATH.
AND TO HELP YOU BURY UGLINESS THAT SURROU YOU, YOU NEEDED TO O IT BY FINDING A GLIMME BEAUTY TO LOVE.

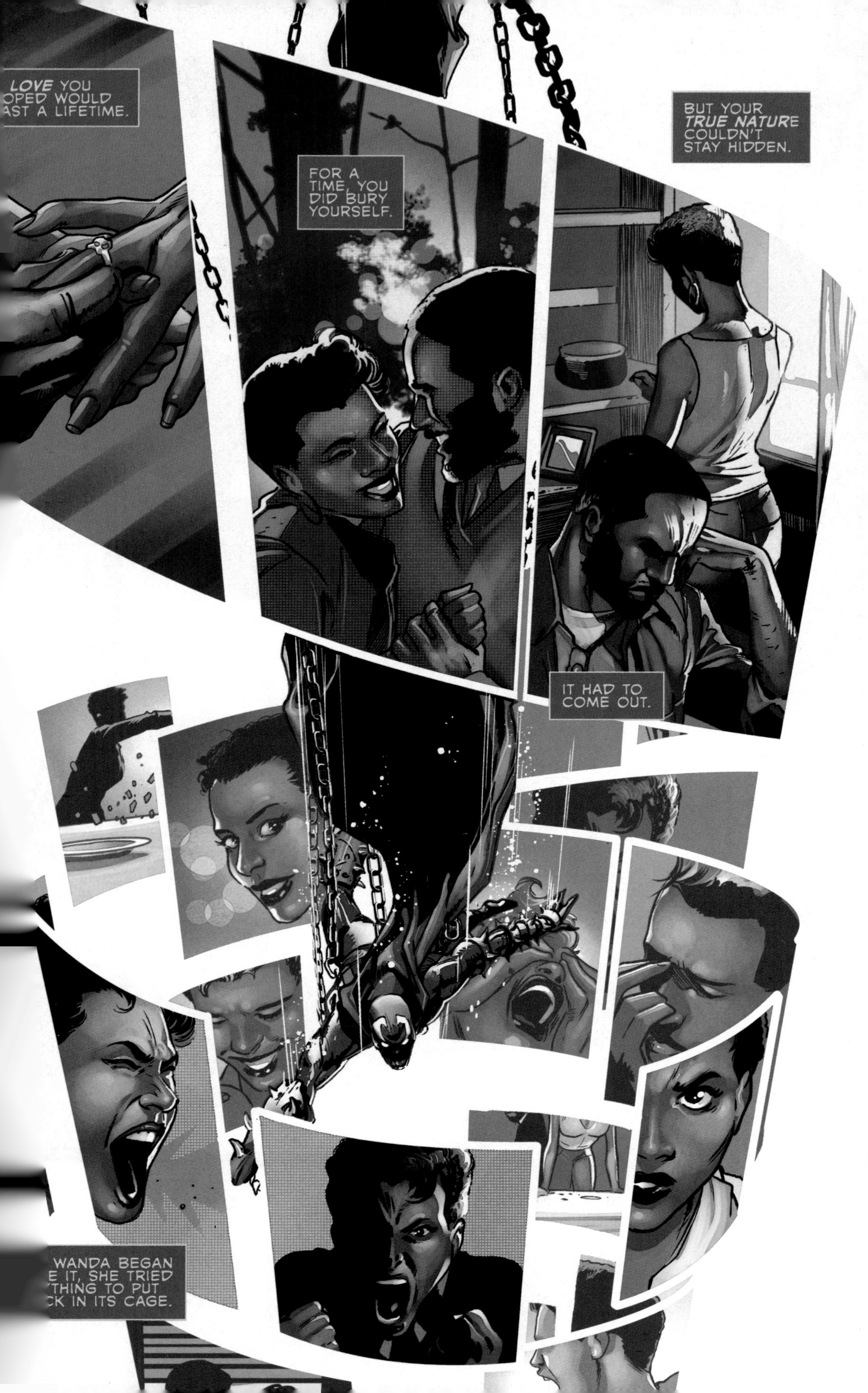
LOVE YOU
OPED WOULD
AST A LIFETIME.
FOR A
TIME, YOU
DID BURY
YOURSELF.
BUT YOUR
TRUE NATURE
COULDN'T
STAY HIDDEN.
IT HAD TO
COME OUT.
WANDA BEGAN
E IT, SHE TRIED
THING TO PUT
CK IN ITS CAGE.

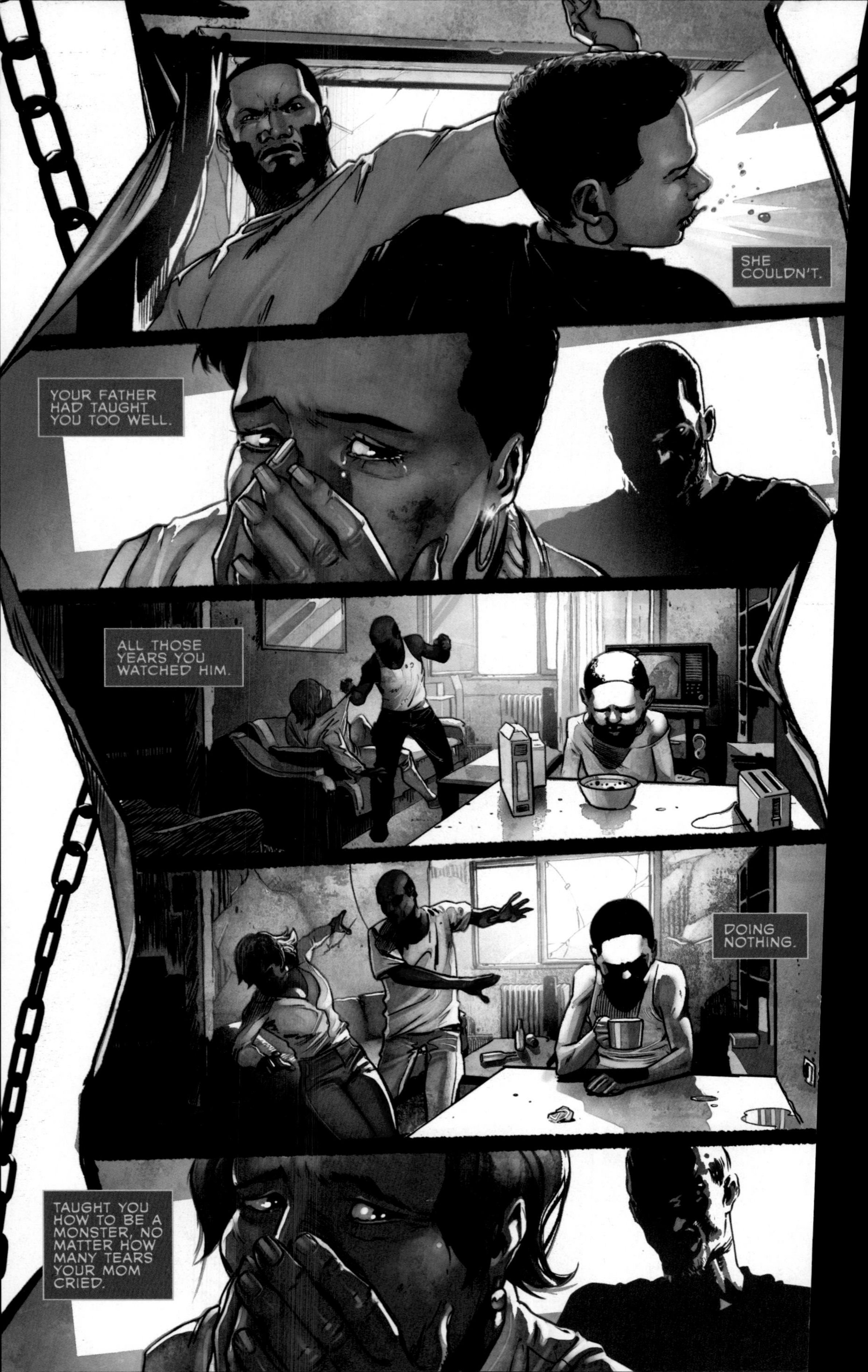
SHE COULDN'T.
YOUR FATHER HAD TAUGHT YOU TOO WELL.
ALL THOSE YEARS YOU WATCHED HIM.
DOING NOTHING.
TAUGHT YOU HOW TO BE A MONSTER, NO MATTER HOW MANY TEARS YOUR MOM CRIED.

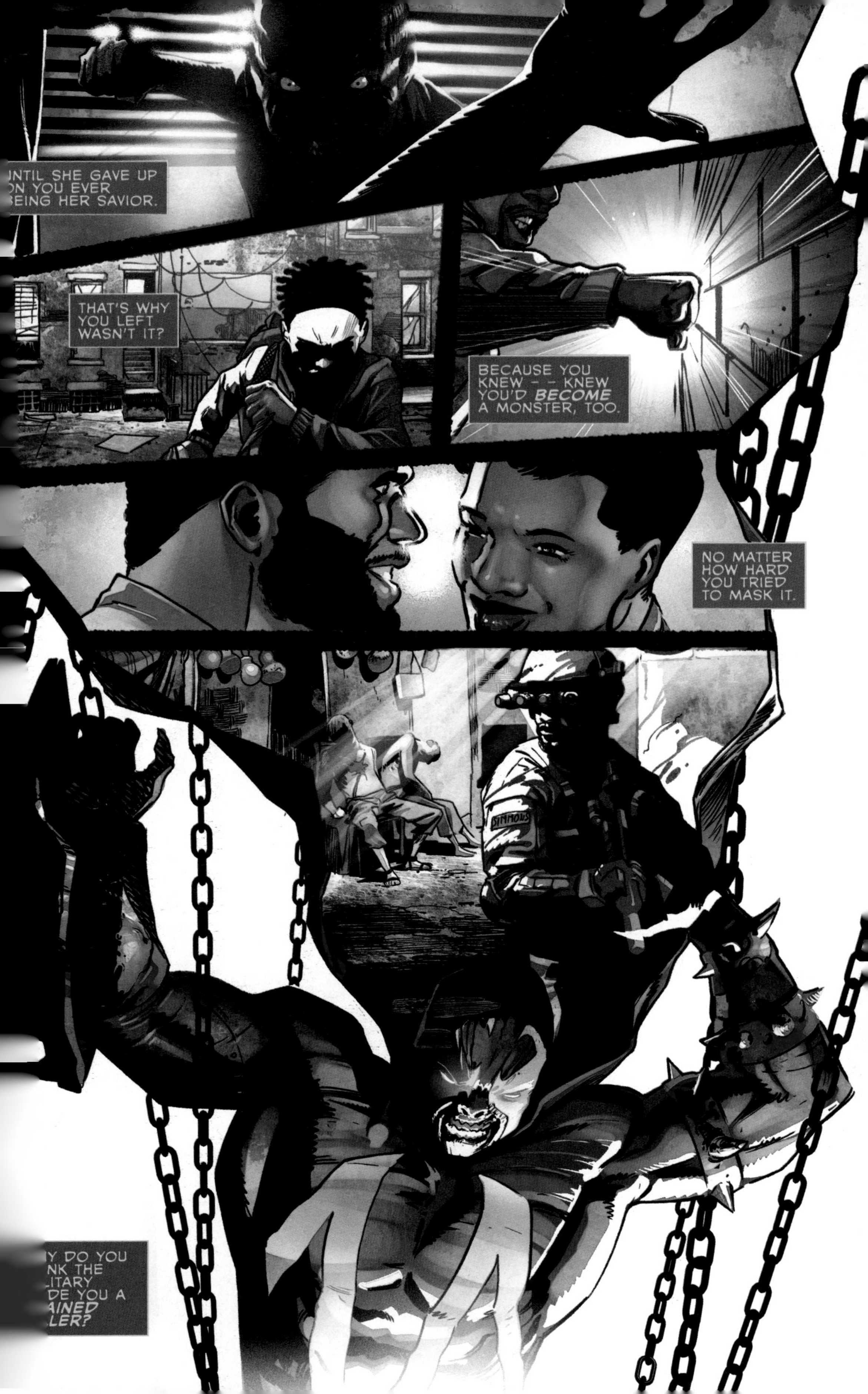
NTIL SHE GAVE UP ON YOU EVER EING HER SAVIOR.
THAT'S WHY YOU LEFT WASN'T IT?
BECAUSE YOU KNEW - - KNEW YOU'D *BECOME* A MONSTER, TOO.
NO MATTER HOW HARD YOU TRIED TO MASK IT.
Y DO YOU NK THE LITARY DE YOU A *AINED LER?*

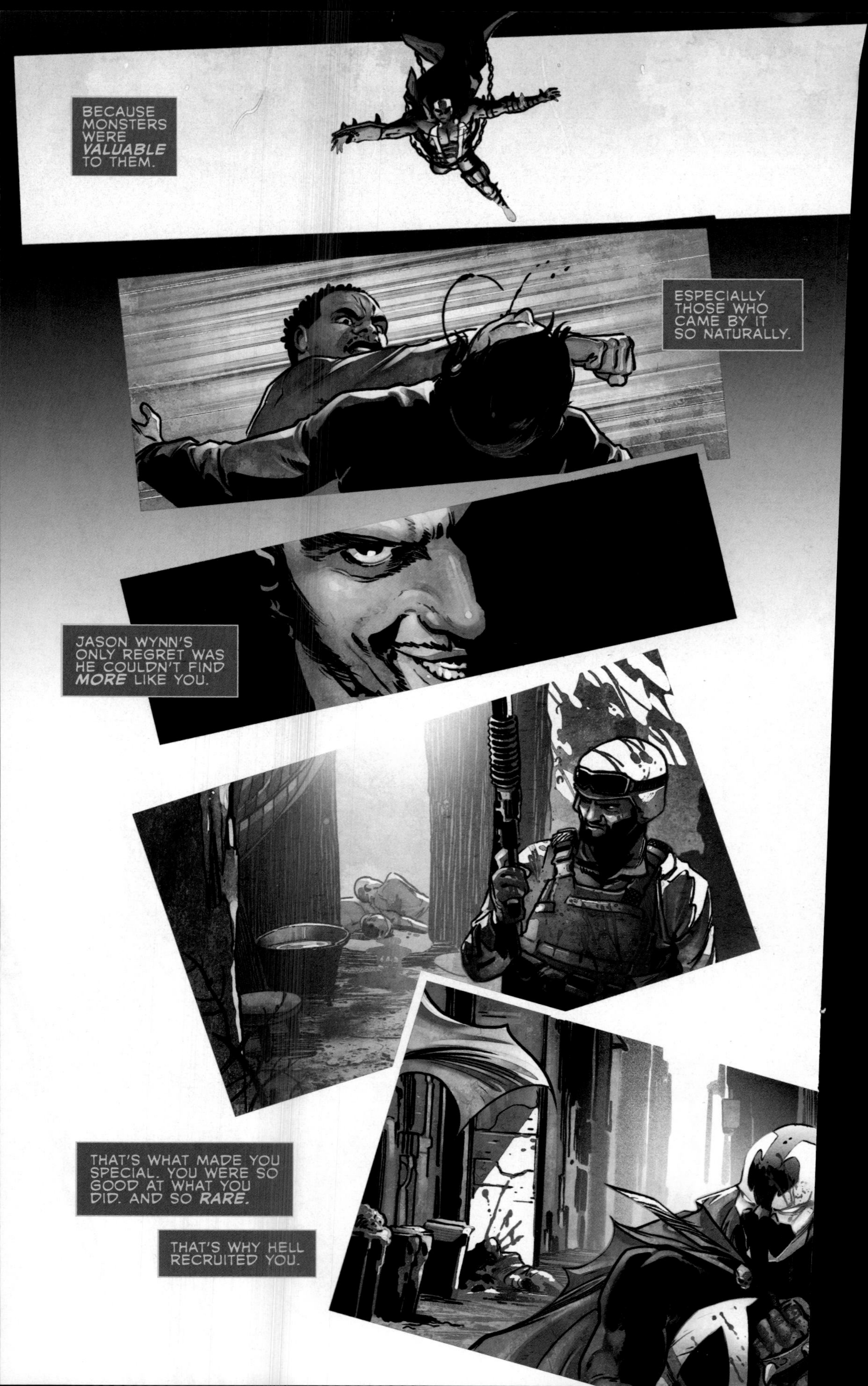
BECAUSE MONSTERS WERE *VALUABLE* TO THEM.
ESPECIALLY THOSE WHO CAME BY IT SO NATURALLY.
JASON WYNN'S ONLY REGRET WAS HE COULDN'T FIND *MORE* LIKE YOU.
THAT'S WHAT MADE YOU SPECIAL. YOU WERE SO GOOD AT WHAT YOU DID. AND SO *RARE.*
THAT'S WHY HELL RECRUITED YOU.

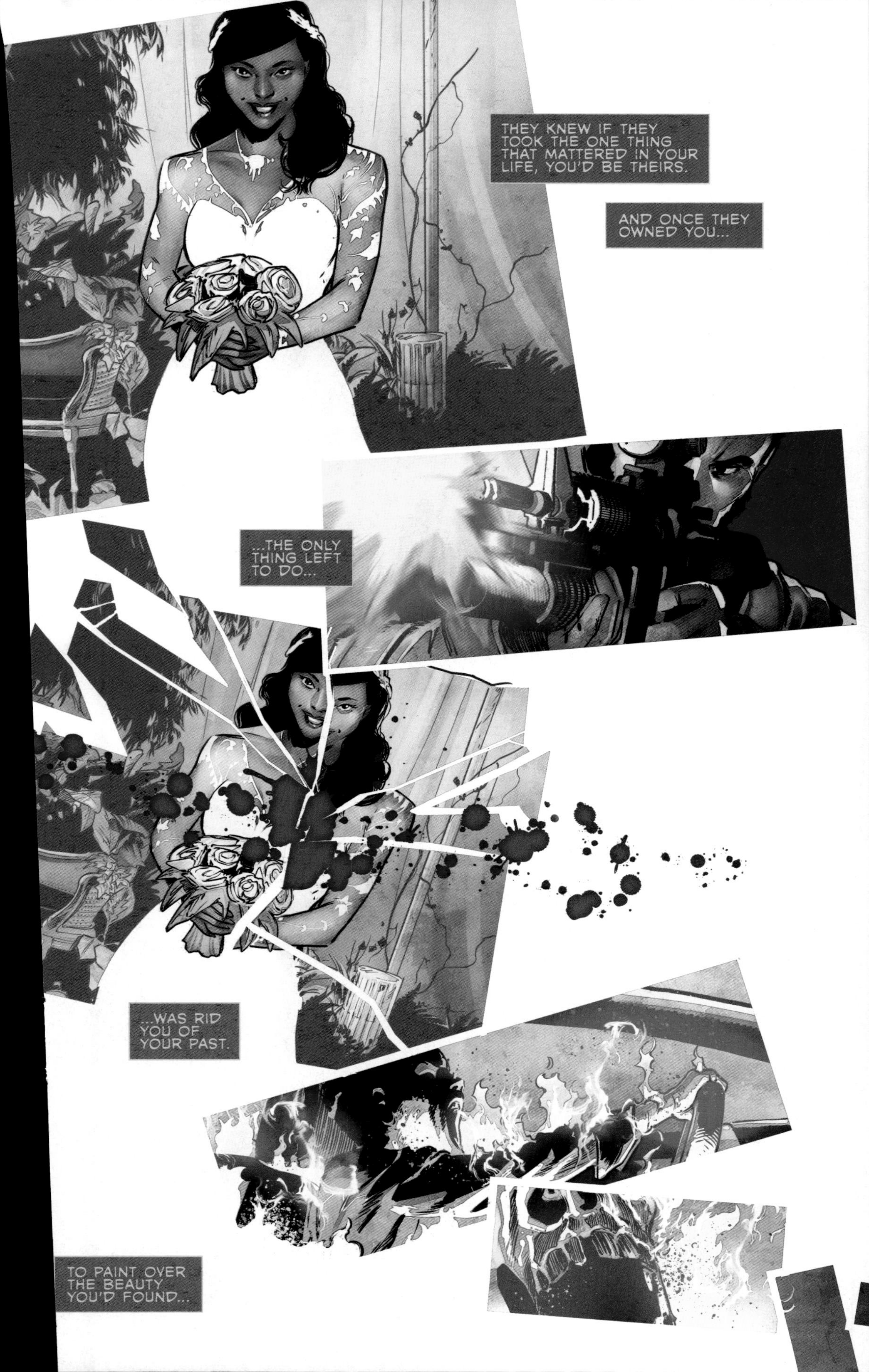
THEY KNEW IF THEY TOOK THE ONE THING THAT MATTERED IN YOUR LIFE, YOU'D BE THEIRS.
AND ONCE THEY OWNED YOU...
...THE ONLY THING LEFT TO DO...
...WAS RID YOU OF YOUR PAST.
TO PAINT OVER THE BEAUTY YOU'D FOUND...

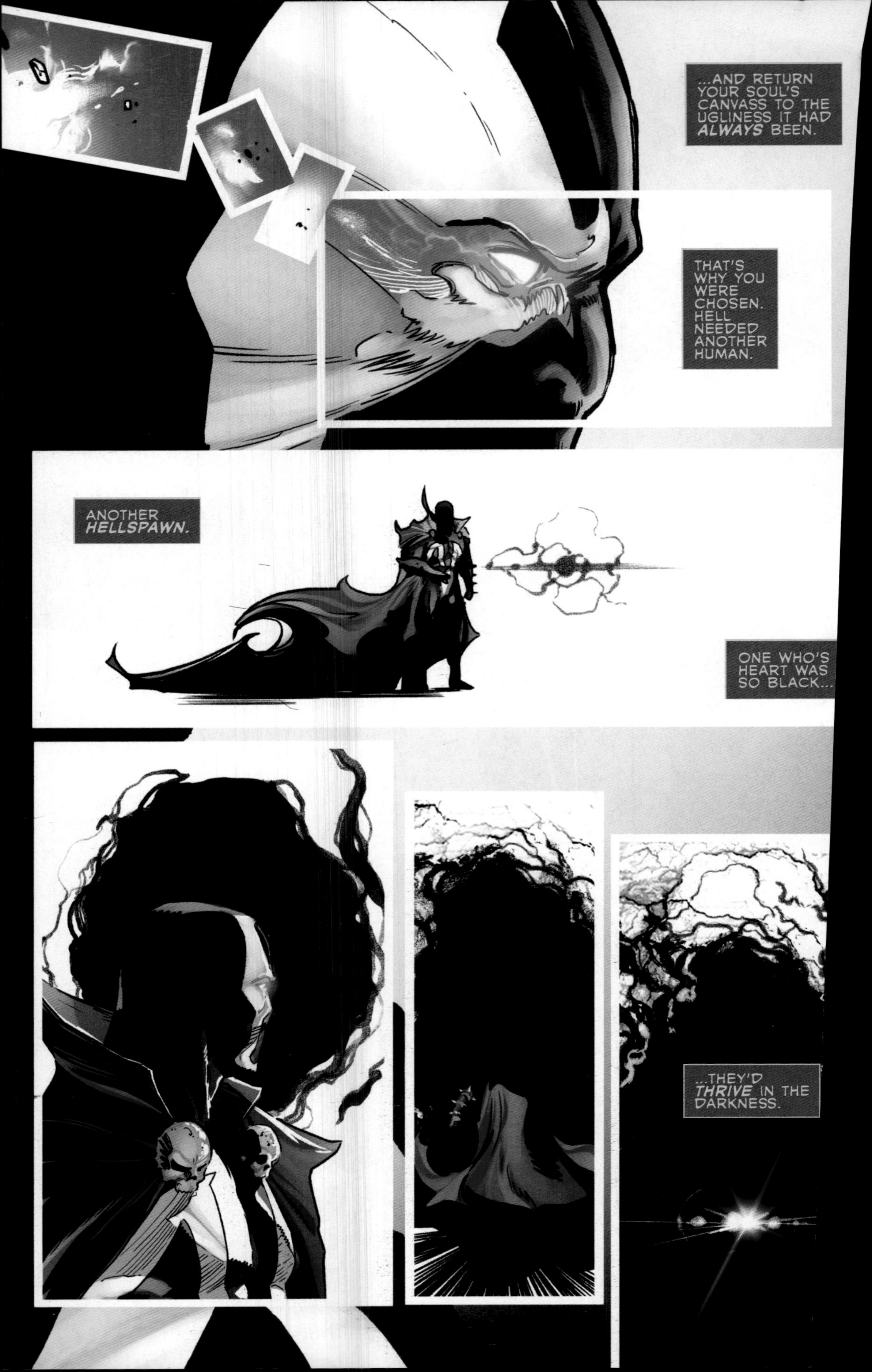

...AND RETURN YOUR SOUL'S CANVASS TO THE UGLINESS IT HAD *ALWAYS* BEEN.
THAT'S WHY YOU WERE CHOSEN. HELL NEEDED ANOTHER HUMAN.
ANOTHER *HELLSPAWN.*
ONE WHO'S HEART WAS SO BLACK...
...THEY'D *THRIVE* IN THE DARKNESS.

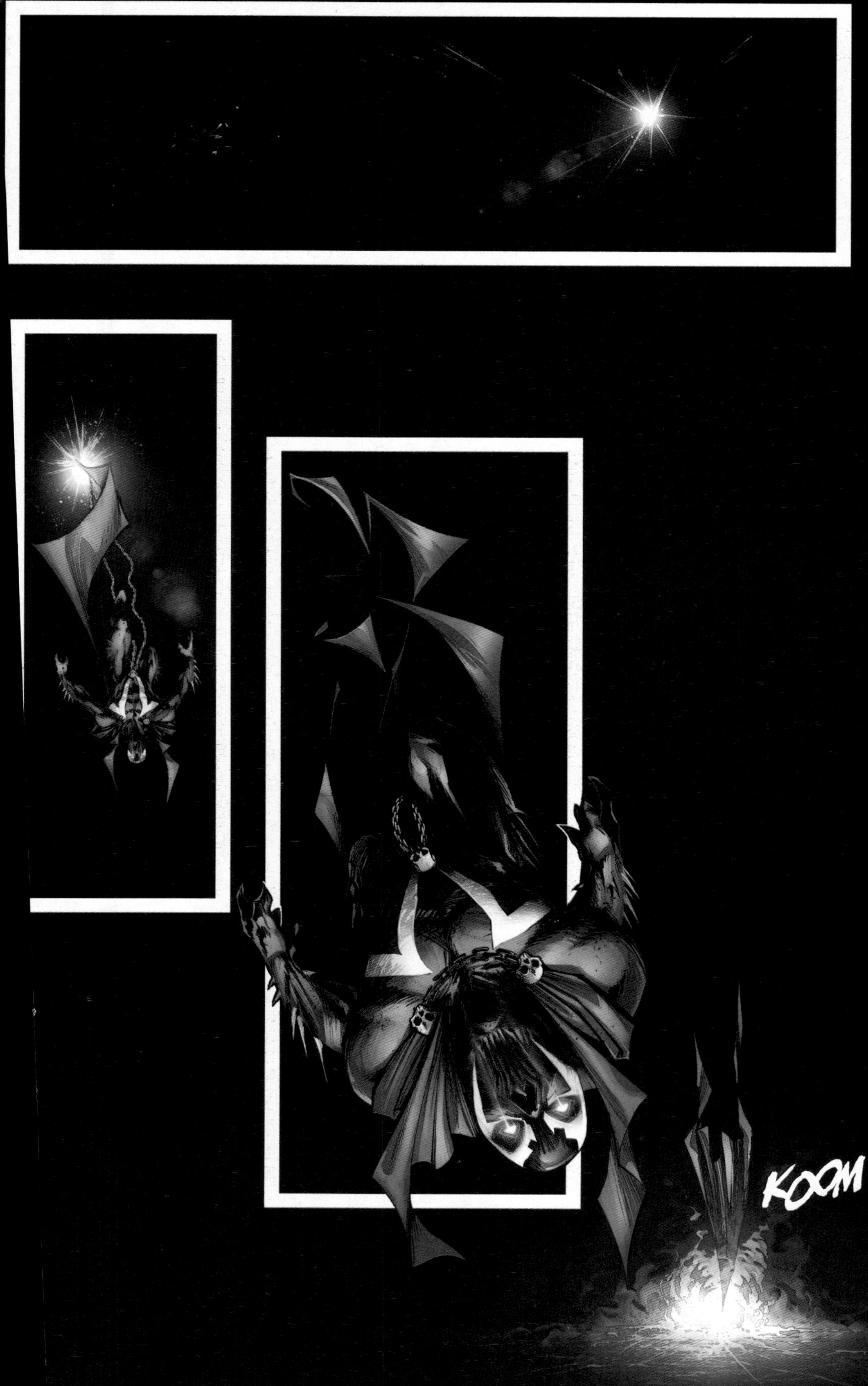
KOOM

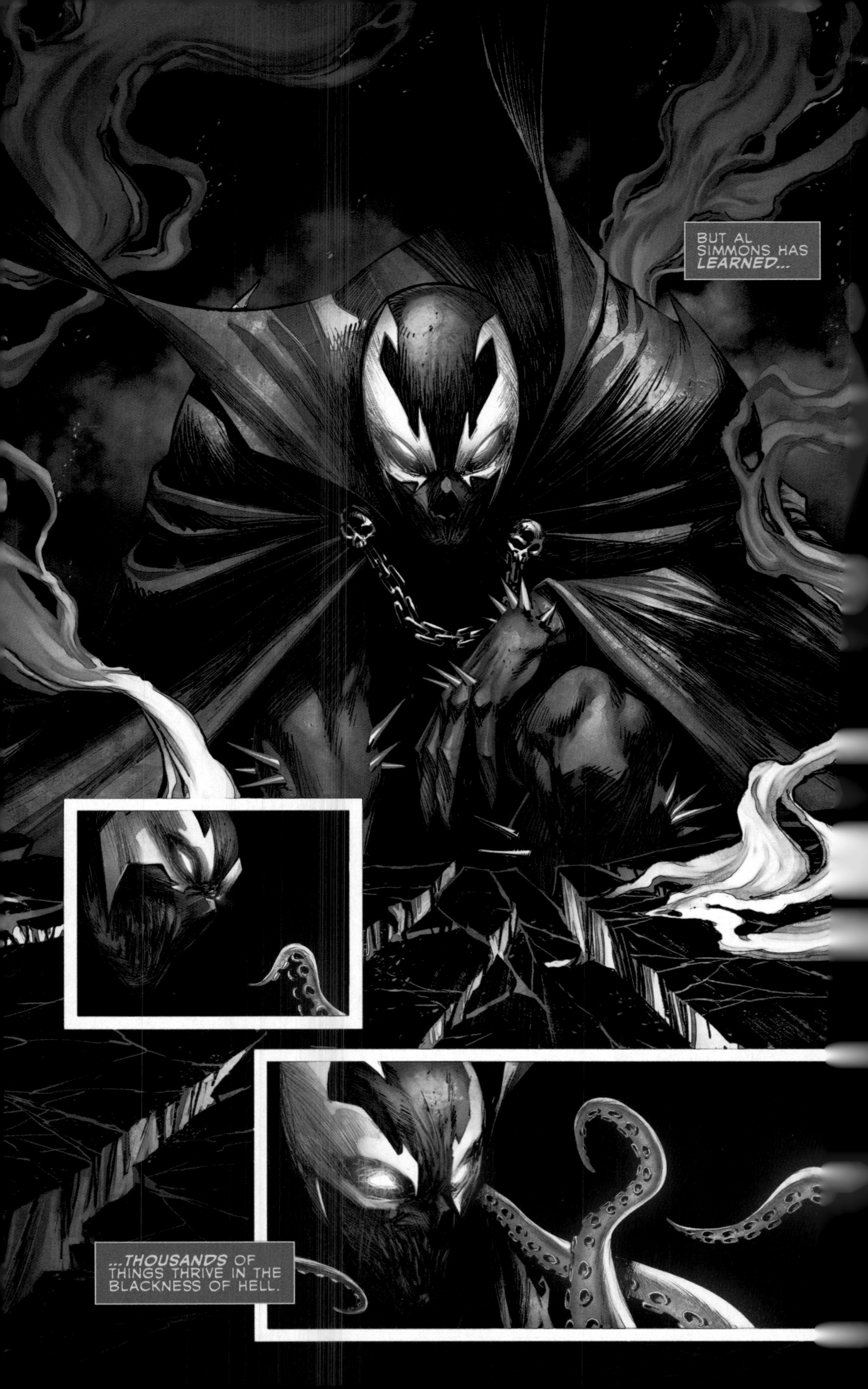
BUT AL SIMMONS HAS *LEARNED...*
...*THOUSANDS* OF THINGS THRIVE IN THE BLACKNESS OF HELL.

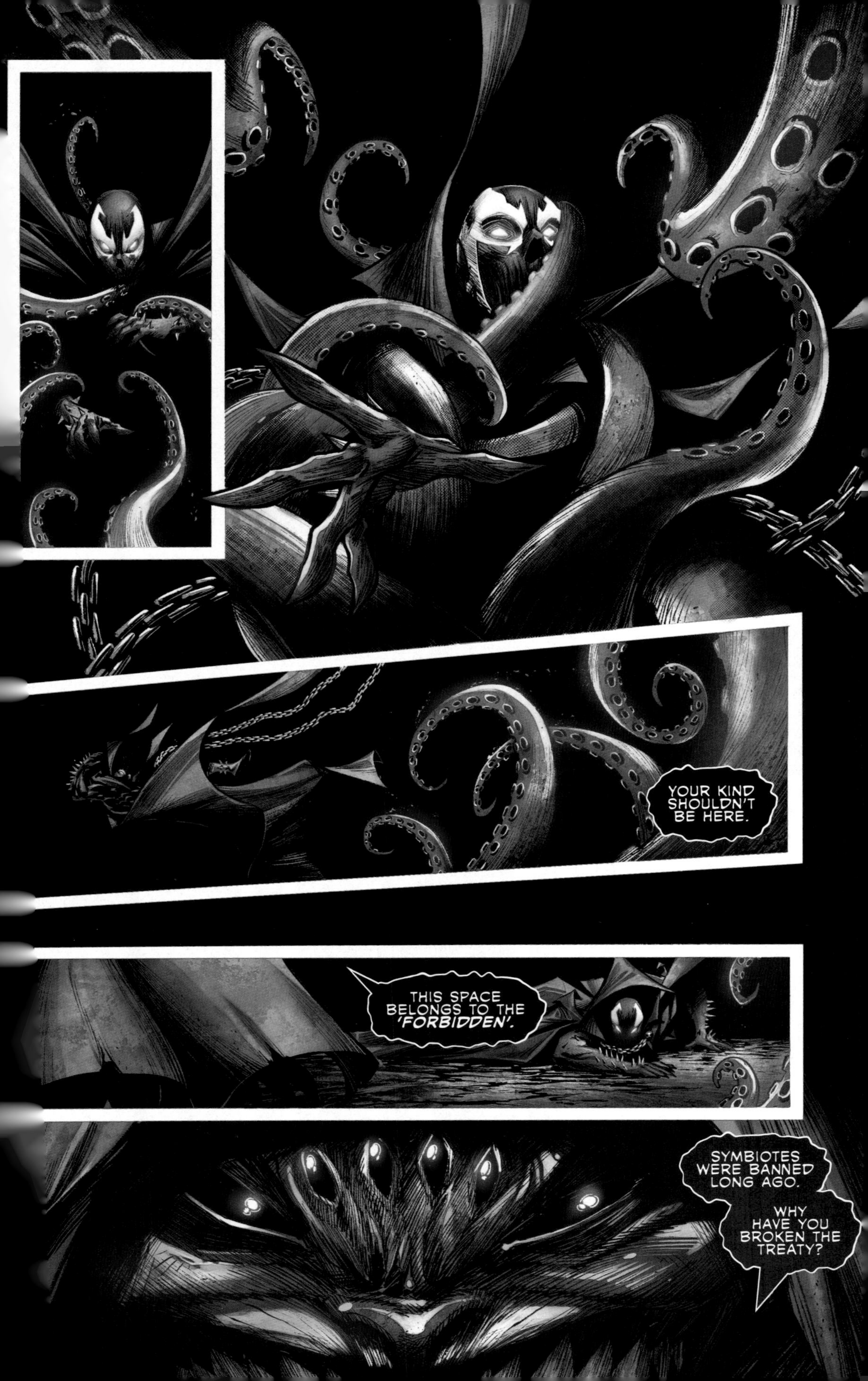
YOUR KIND SHOULDN'T BE HERE.
THIS SPACE BELONGS TO THE 'FORBIDDEN'.
SYMBIOTES WERE BANNED LONG AGO.
WHY HAVE YOU BROKEN THE TREATY?

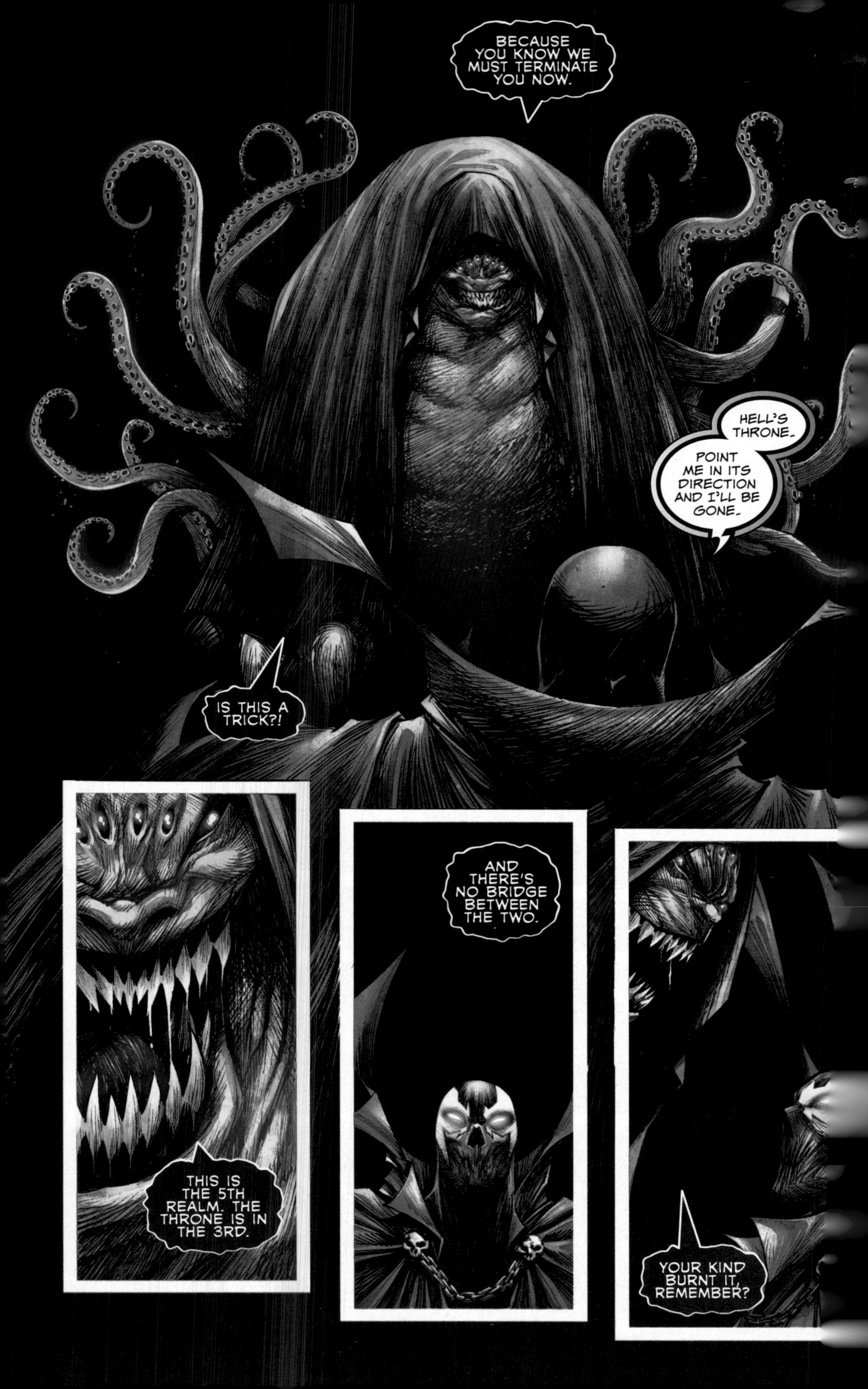
BECAUSE YOU KNOW WE MUST TERMINATE YOU NOW.
HELL'S THRONE.
POINT ME IN ITS DIRECTION AND I'LL BE GONE.
IS THIS A TRICK?!
THIS IS THE 5TH REALM. THE THRONE IS IN THE 3RD.
AND THERE'S NO BRIDGE BETWEEN THE TWO.
YOUR KIND BURNT IT, REMEMBER?

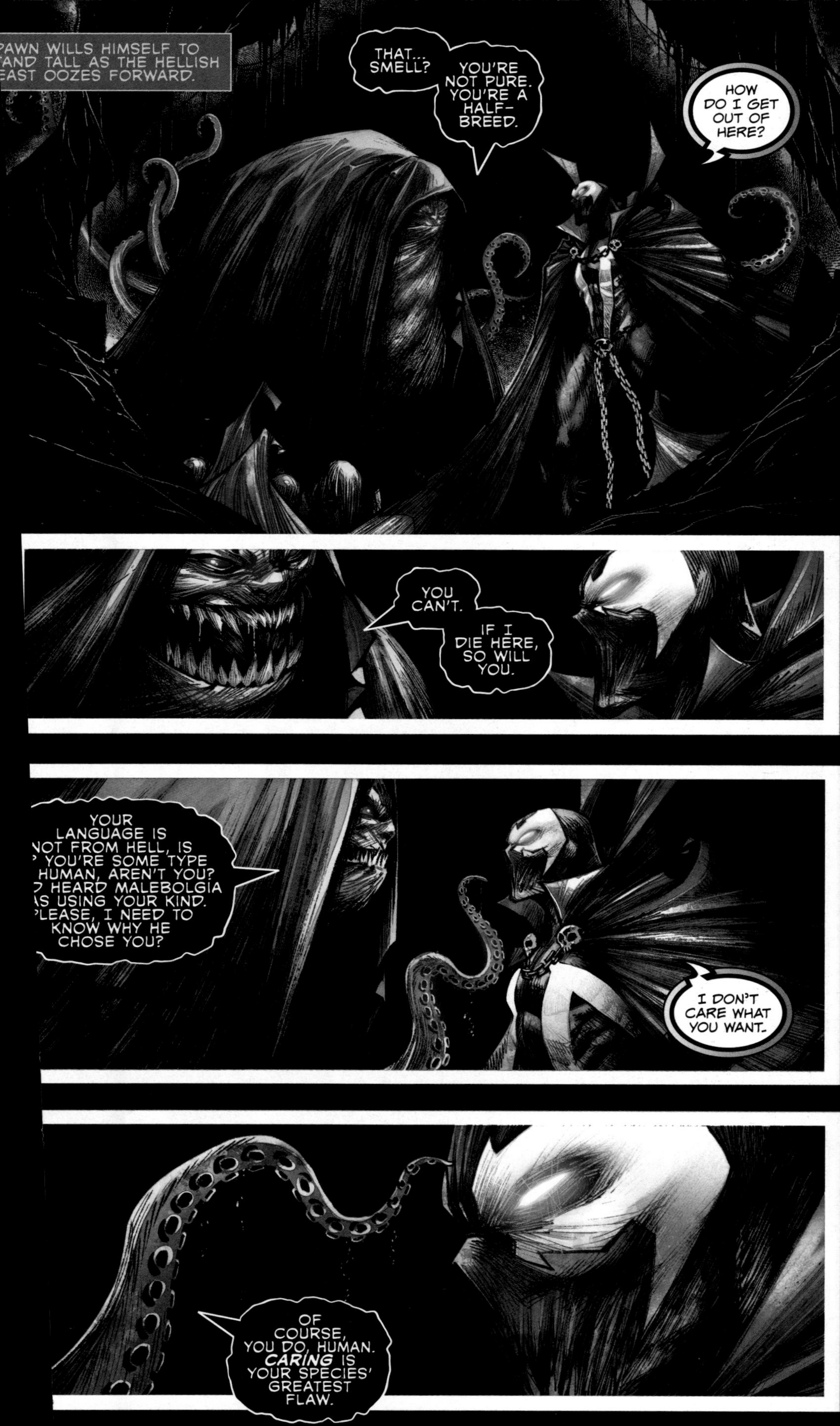
PAWN WILLS HIMSELF TO TAND TALL AS THE HELLISH EAST OOZES FORWARD.
THAT... SMELL?
YOU'RE NOT PURE. YOU'RE A HALF-BREED.
HOW DO I GET OUT OF HERE?
YOU CAN'T.
IF I DIE HERE, SO WILL YOU.
YOUR LANGUAGE IS NOT FROM HELL, IS YOU'RE SOME TYPE HUMAN, AREN'T YOU? HEARD MALEBOLGIA AS USING YOUR KIND. LEASE, I NEED TO KNOW WHY HE CHOSE YOU?
I DON'T CARE WHAT YOU WANT.
OF COURSE, YOU DO, HUMAN. ***CARING*** IS YOUR SPECIES' GREATEST FLAW.

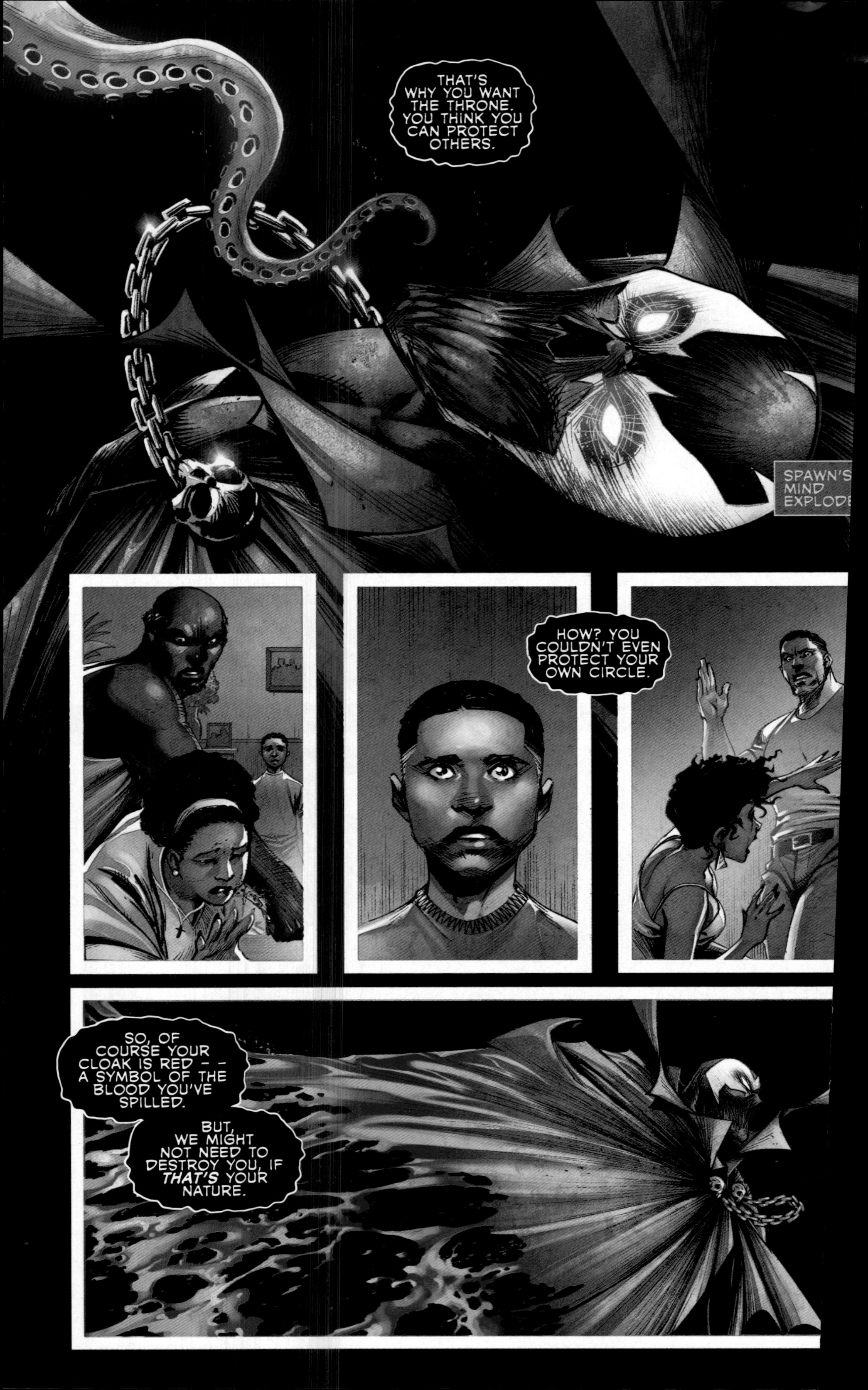
THAT'S WHY YOU WANT THE THRONE. YOU THINK YOU CAN PROTECT OTHERS.
SPAWN'S MIND EXPLODE
HOW? YOU COULDN'T EVEN PROTECT YOUR OWN CIRCLE.
SO, OF COURSE YOUR CLOAK IS RED -- A SYMBOL OF THE BLOOD YOU'VE SPILLED.
BUT, WE MIGHT NOT NEED TO DESTROY YOU, IF *THAT'S* YOUR NATURE.

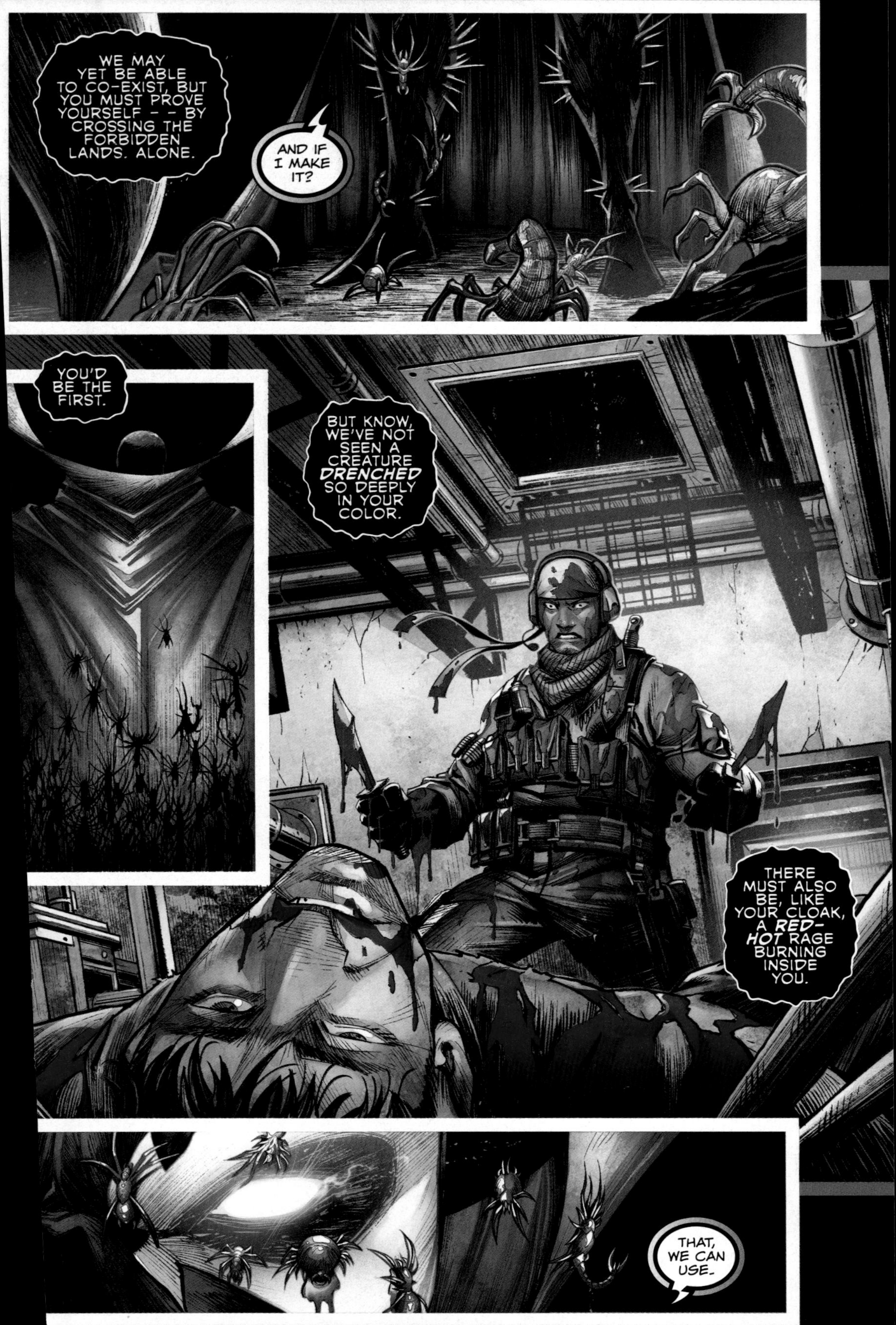
WE MAY YET BE ABLE TO CO-EXIST, BUT YOU MUST PROVE YOURSELF -- BY CROSSING THE FORBIDDEN LANDS. ALONE.
AND IF I MAKE IT?
YOU'D BE THE FIRST.
BUT KNOW, WE'VE NOT SEEN A CREATURE ***DRENCHED*** SO DEEPLY IN YOUR COLOR.
THERE MUST ALSO BE, LIKE YOUR CLOAK, A ***RED-HOT*** RAGE BURNING INSIDE YOU.
THAT, WE CAN USE.

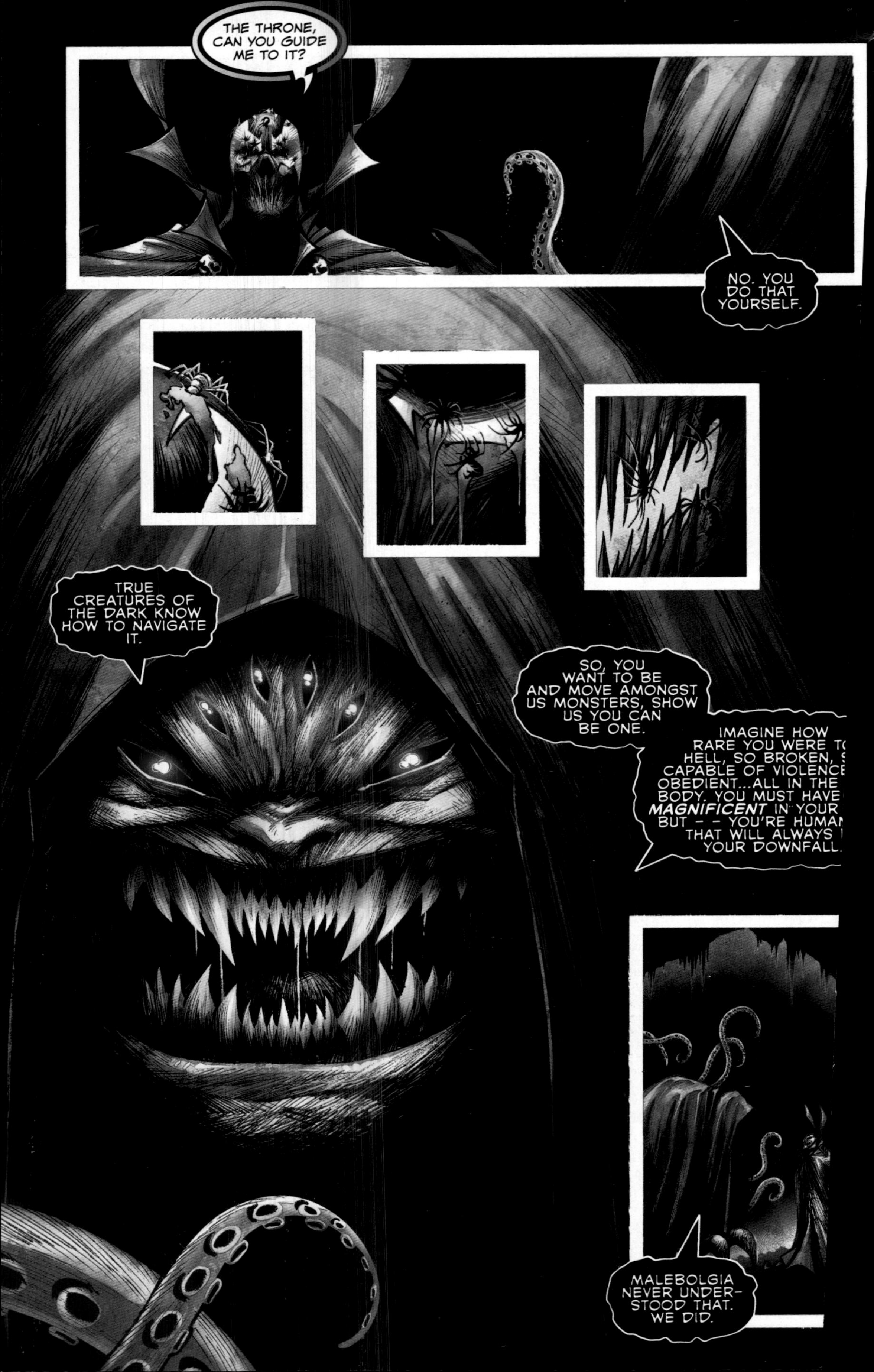
THE THRONE, CAN YOU GUIDE ME TO IT?
NO. YOU DO THAT YOURSELF.
TRUE CREATURES OF THE DARK KNOW HOW TO NAVIGATE IT.
SO, YOU WANT TO BE AND MOVE AMONGST US MONSTERS, SHOW US YOU CAN BE ONE.
IMAGINE HOW RARE YOU WERE HELL, SO BROKEN, CAPABLE OF OBEDIENT...ALL IN THE BODY. YOU MUST HAVE *MAGNIFICENT* IN YOUR BUT - - YOU'RE THAT WILL ALWAYS YOUR DOWNFALL.
MALEBOLGIA NEVER UNDER-STOOD THAT. WE DID.

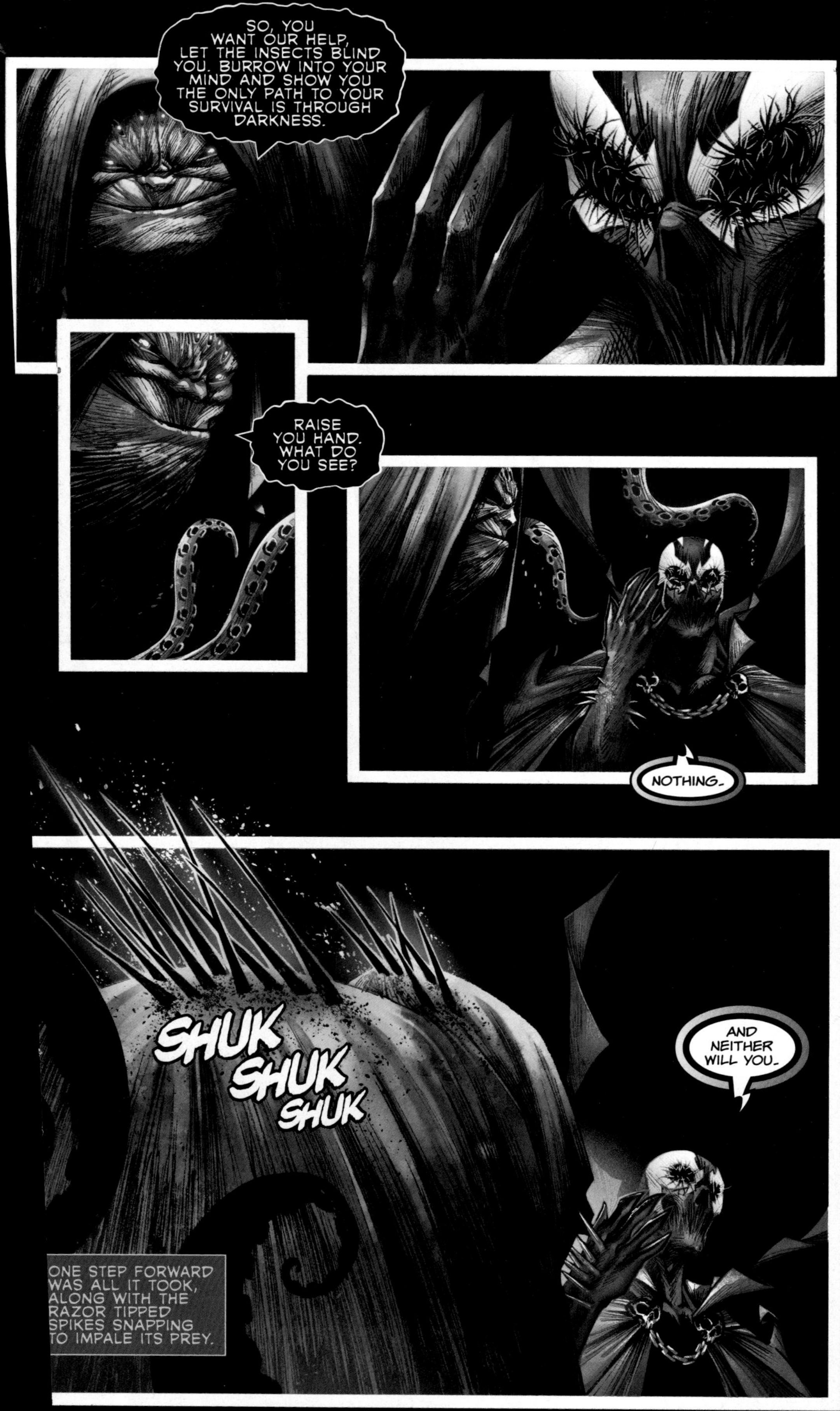
SO, YOU WANT OUR HELP, LET THE INSECTS BLIND YOU. BURROW INTO YOUR MIND AND SHOW YOU THE ONLY PATH TO YOUR SURVIVAL IS THROUGH DARKNESS.
RAISE YOU HAND. WHAT DO YOU SEE?
NOTHING.
SHUK SHUK SHUK
AND NEITHER WILL YOU.
ONE STEP FORWARD WAS ALL IT TOOK, ALONG WITH THE RAZOR TIPPED SPIKES SNAPPING TO IMPALE ITS PREY.

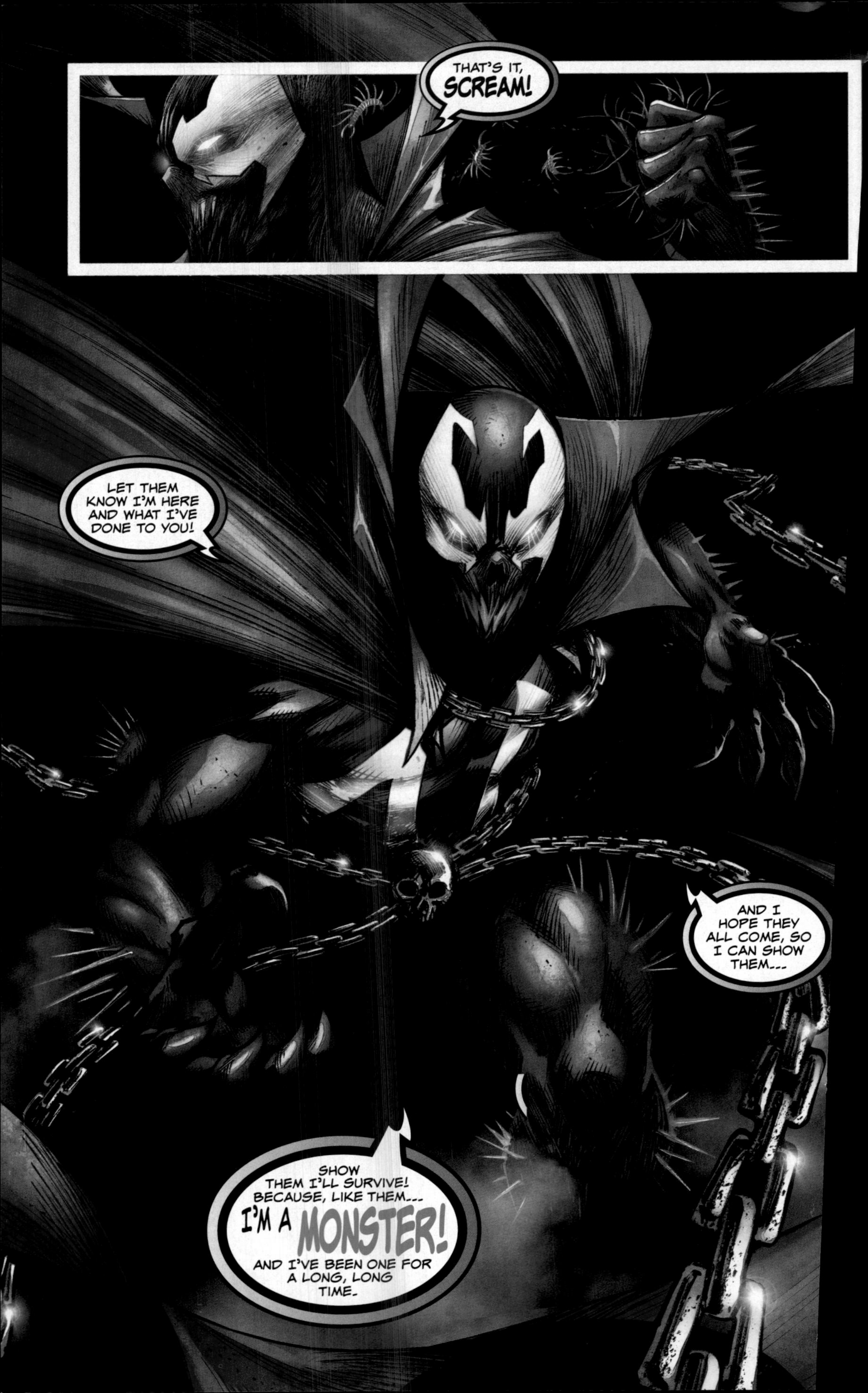

THAT'S IT, SCREAM!
LET THEM KNOW I'M HERE AND WHAT I'VE DONE TO YOU!
AND I HOPE THEY ALL COME, SO I CAN SHOW THEM...
SHOW THEM I'LL SURVIVE! BECAUSE, LIKE THEM... I'M A MONSTER! AND I'VE BEEN ONE FOR A LONG, LONG TIME.

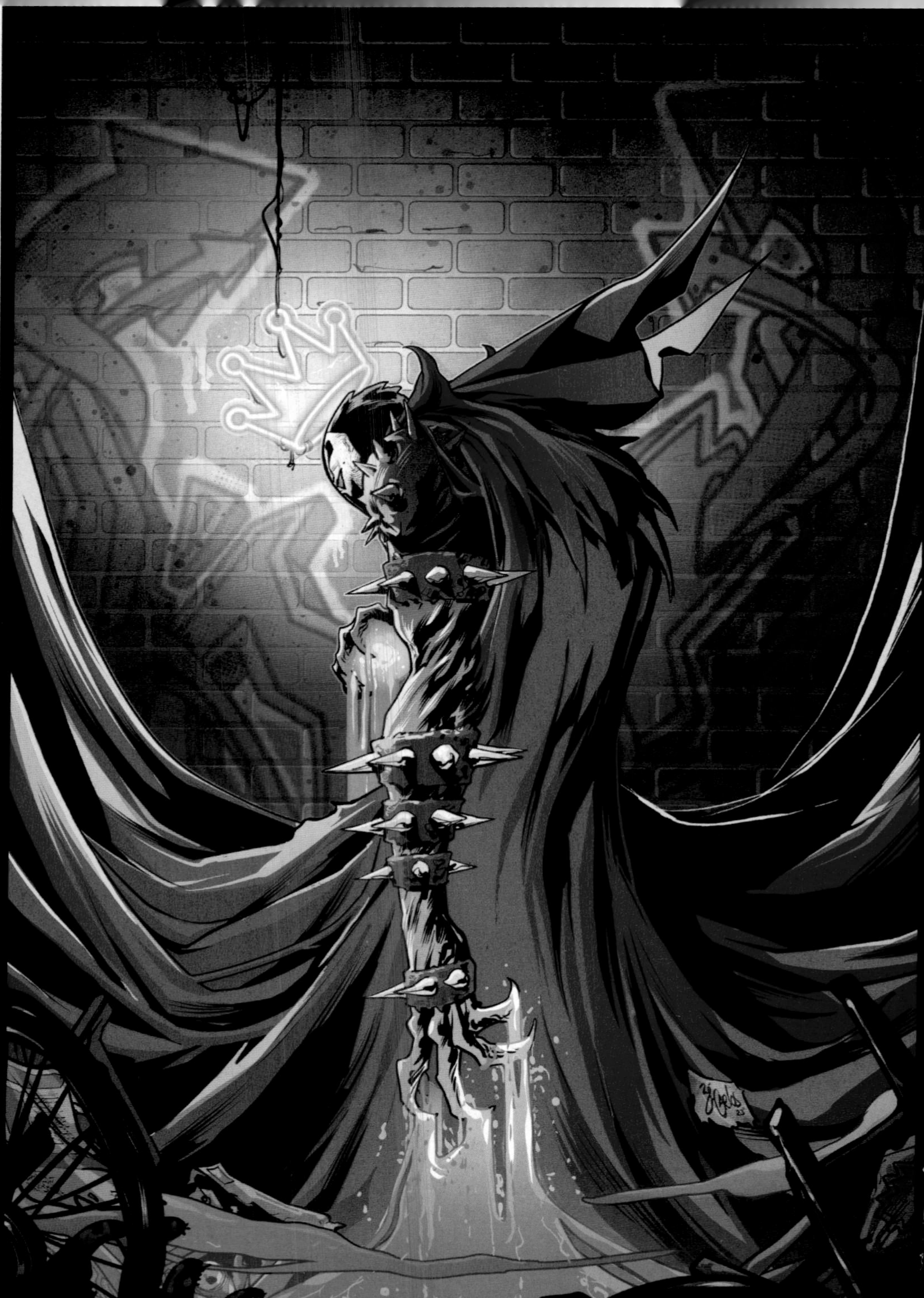

DON'T KNOW HOW LONG IT'S
BEEN, AND I **DON'T CARE.**

THOUGH, I HATE THAT IT TOOK ME SO
LONG TO DROP HIM. I SHOULD HAVE
KNOWN HE'D TRY TO GROW. THEY'RE
DESCENDANTS OF **VIOLATOR.**

BUT I GOT
WHAT I
NEEDED.

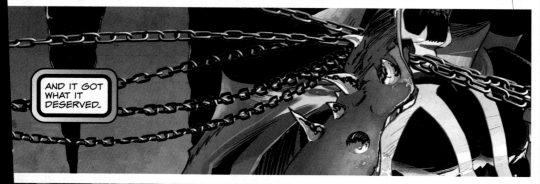

AND IT GOT
WHAT IT
DESERVED.

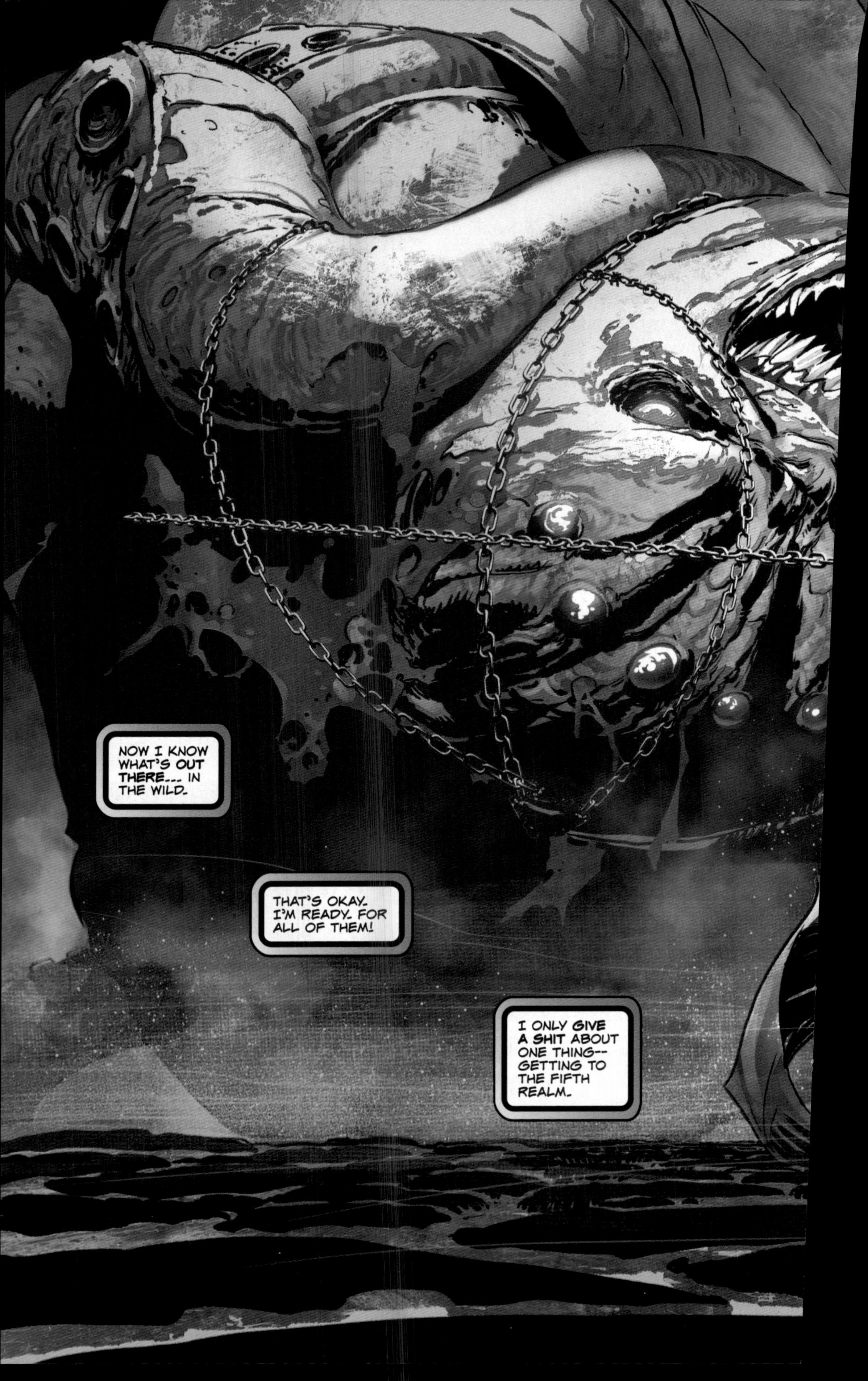
NOW I KNOW WHAT'S OUT THERE... IN THE WILD.
THAT'S OKAY. I'M READY. FOR ALL OF THEM!
I ONLY GIVE A SHIT ABOUT ONE THING-- GETTING TO THE FIFTH REALM.

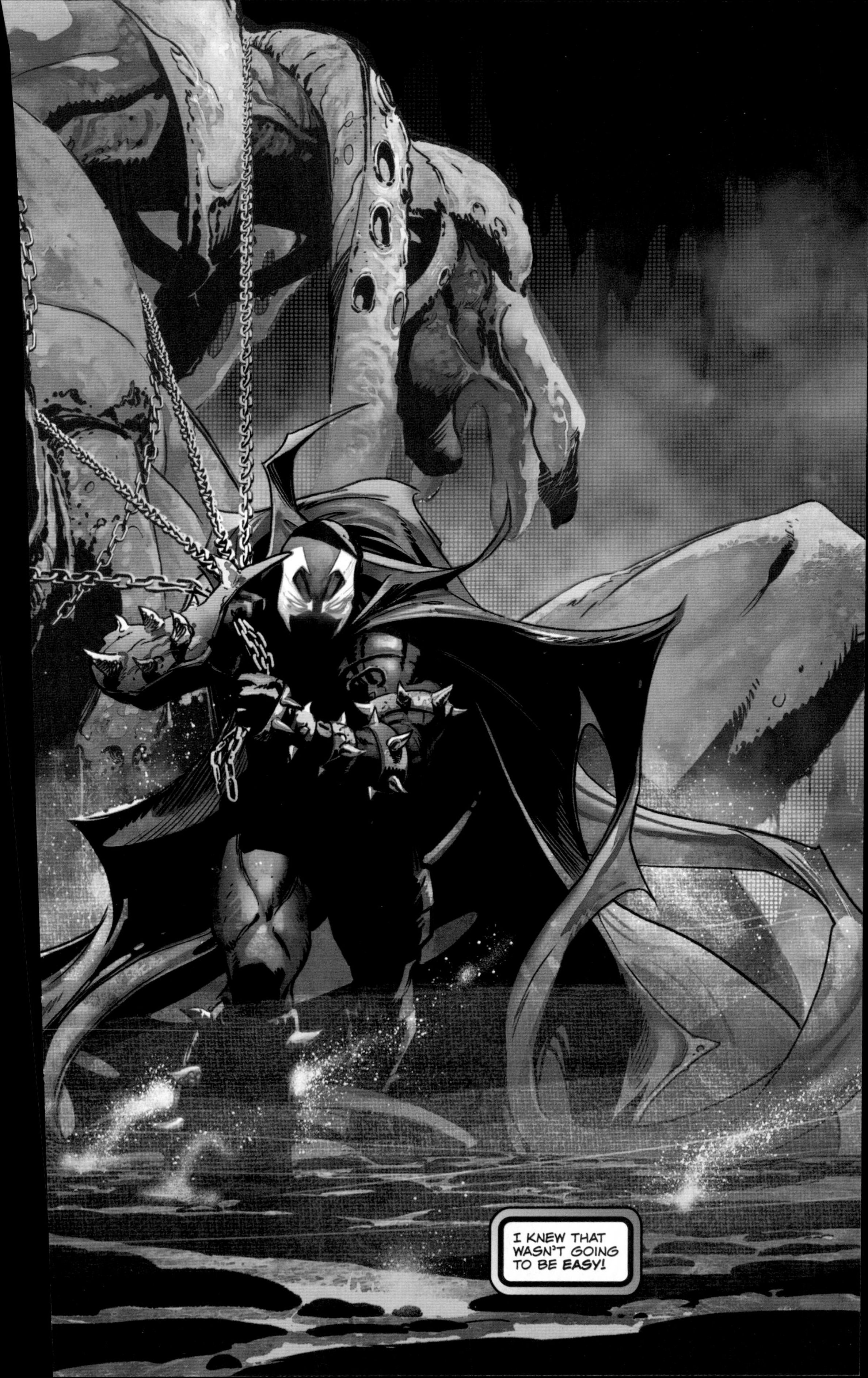
I KNEW THAT WASN'T GOING TO BE EASY!

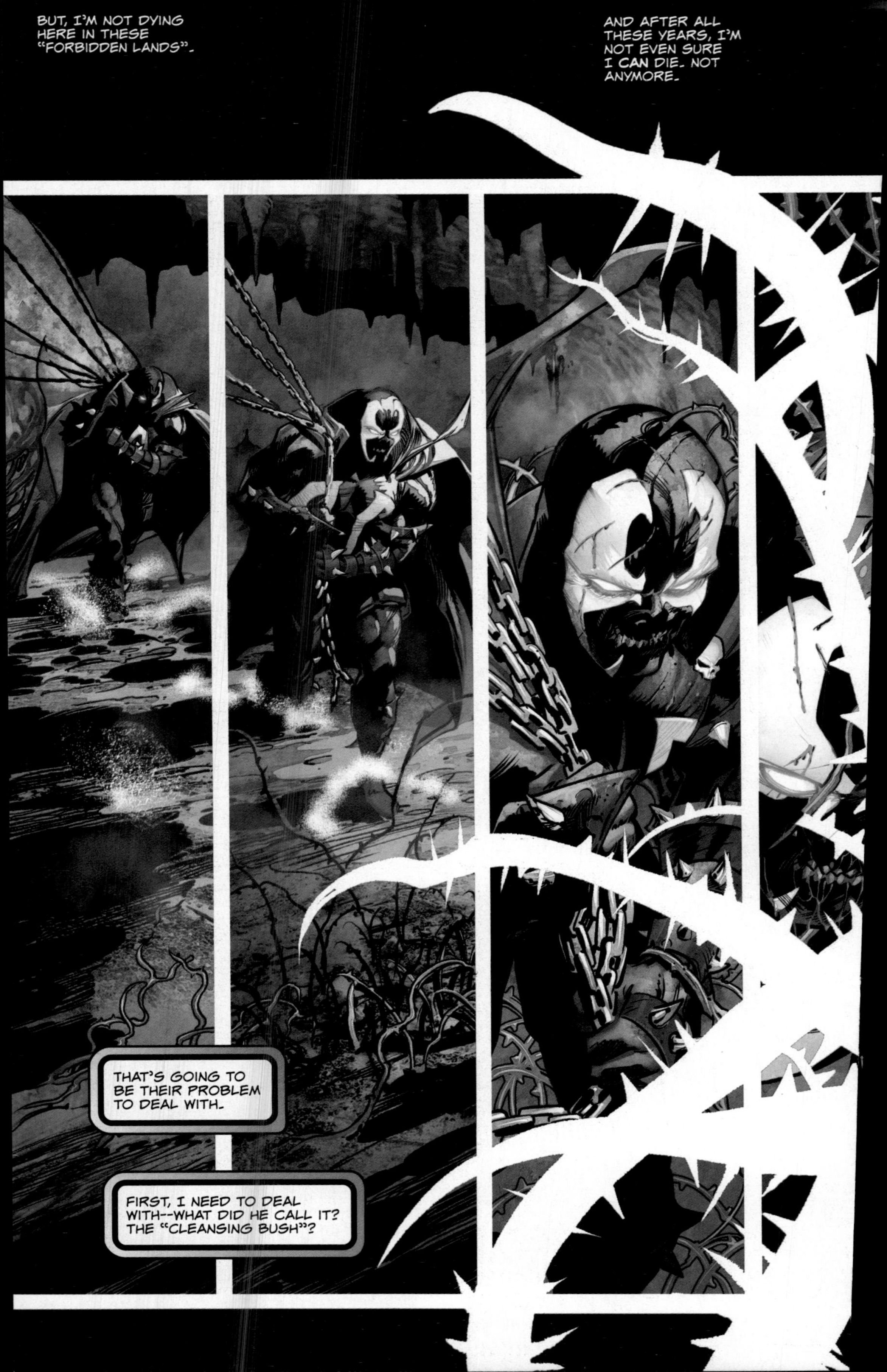
BUT, I'M NOT DYING HERE IN THESE "FORBIDDEN LANDS".
AND AFTER ALL THESE YEARS, I'M NOT EVEN SURE I CAN DIE. NOT ANYMORE.
THAT'S GOING TO BE THEIR PROBLEM TO DEAL WITH.
FIRST, I NEED TO DEAL WITH--WHAT DID HE CALL IT? THE "CLEANSING BUSH"?

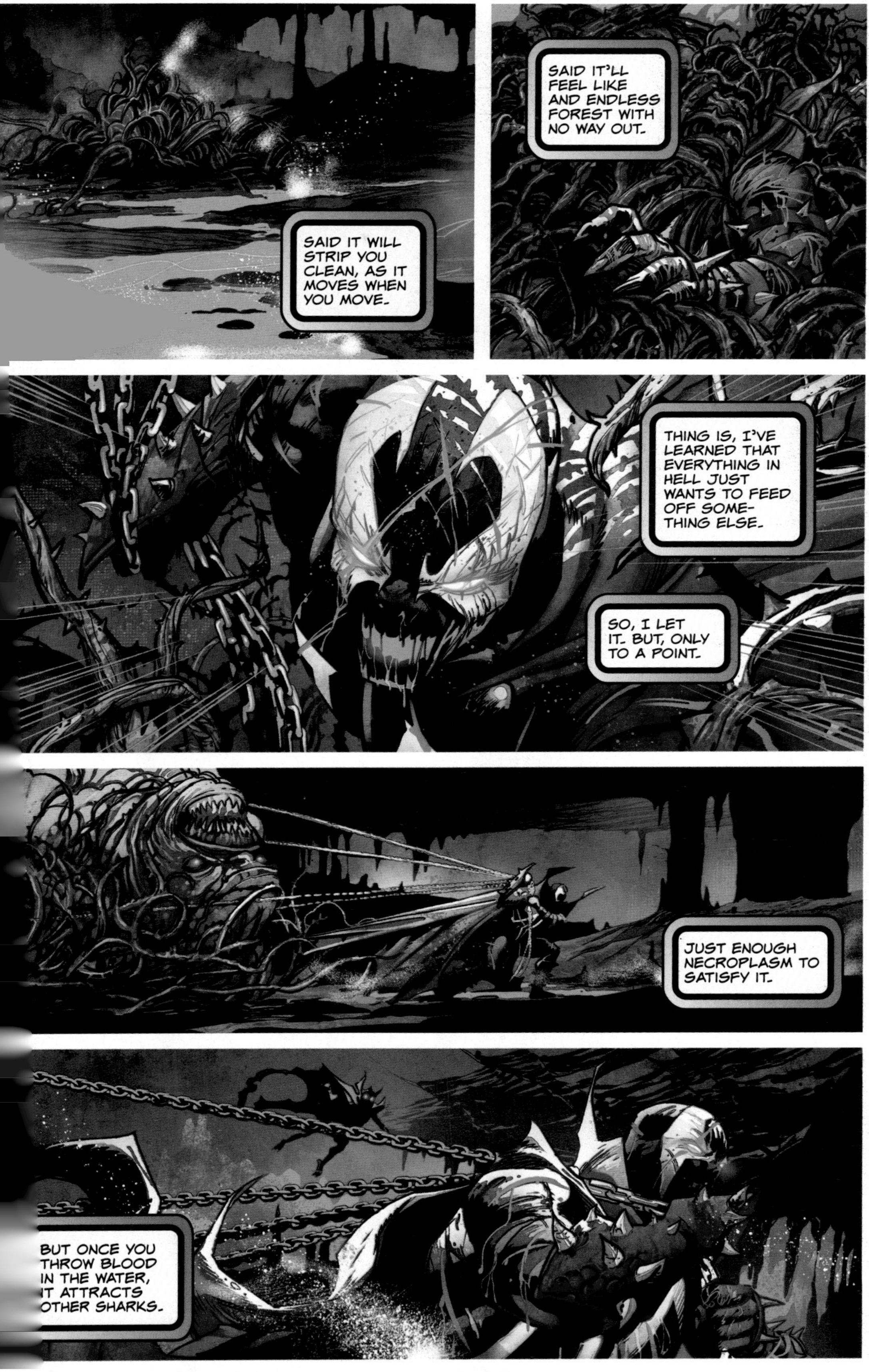
SAID IT WILL STRIP YOU CLEAN, AS IT MOVES WHEN YOU MOVE.
SAID IT'LL FEEL LIKE AND ENDLESS FOREST WITH NO WAY OUT.
THING IS, I'VE LEARNED THAT EVERYTHING IN HELL JUST WANTS TO FEED OFF SOME-THING ELSE.
SO, I LET IT. BUT, ONLY TO A POINT.
JUST ENOUGH NECROPLASM TO SATISFY IT.
BUT ONCE YOU THROW BLOOD IN THE WATER, IT ATTRACTS OTHER SHARKS.

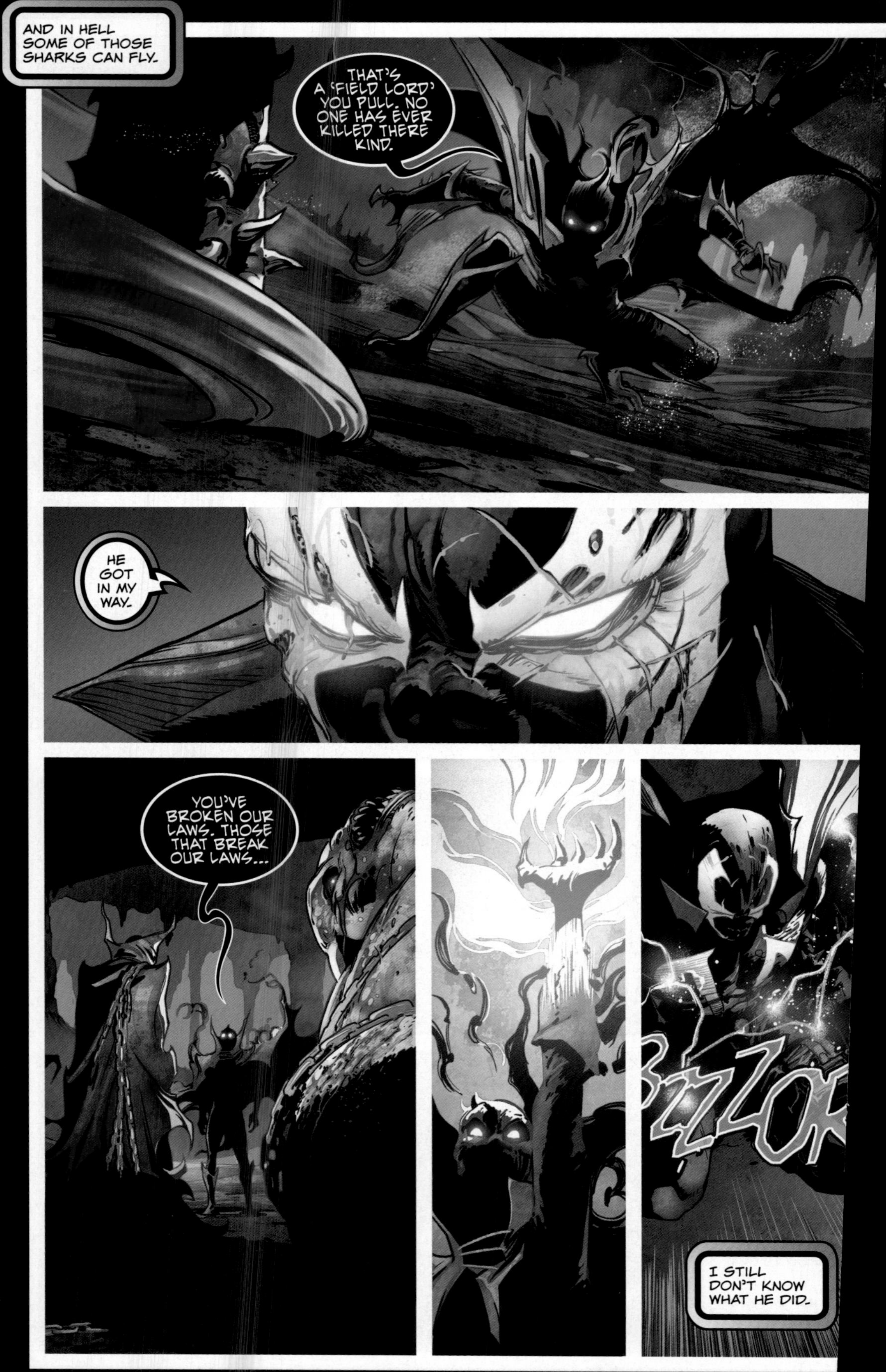
AND IN HELL SOME OF THOSE SHARKS CAN FLY.
THAT'S A 'FIELD LORD' YOU PULL. NO ONE HAS EVER KILLED THERE KIND.
HE GOT IN MY WAY.
YOU'VE BROKEN OUR LAWS. THOSE THAT BREAK OUR LAWS...
BZZZOR
I STILL DON'T KNOW WHAT HE DID.

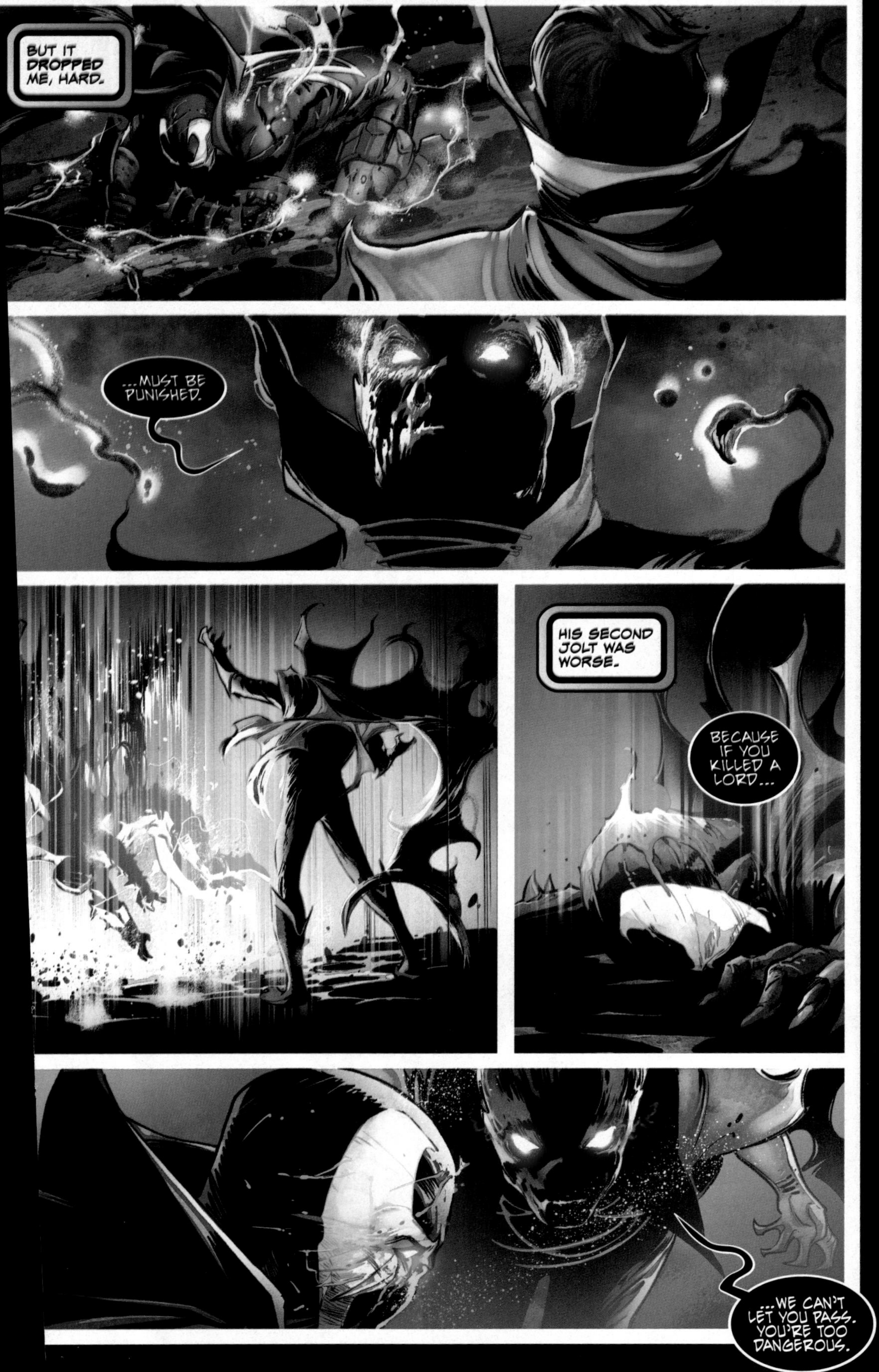
BUT IT DROPPED ME, HARD.
...MUST BE PUNISHED.
HIS SECOND JOLT WAS WORSE.
BECAUSE IF YOU KILLED A LORD...
...WE CAN'T LET YOU PASS. YOU'RE TOO DANGEROUS.

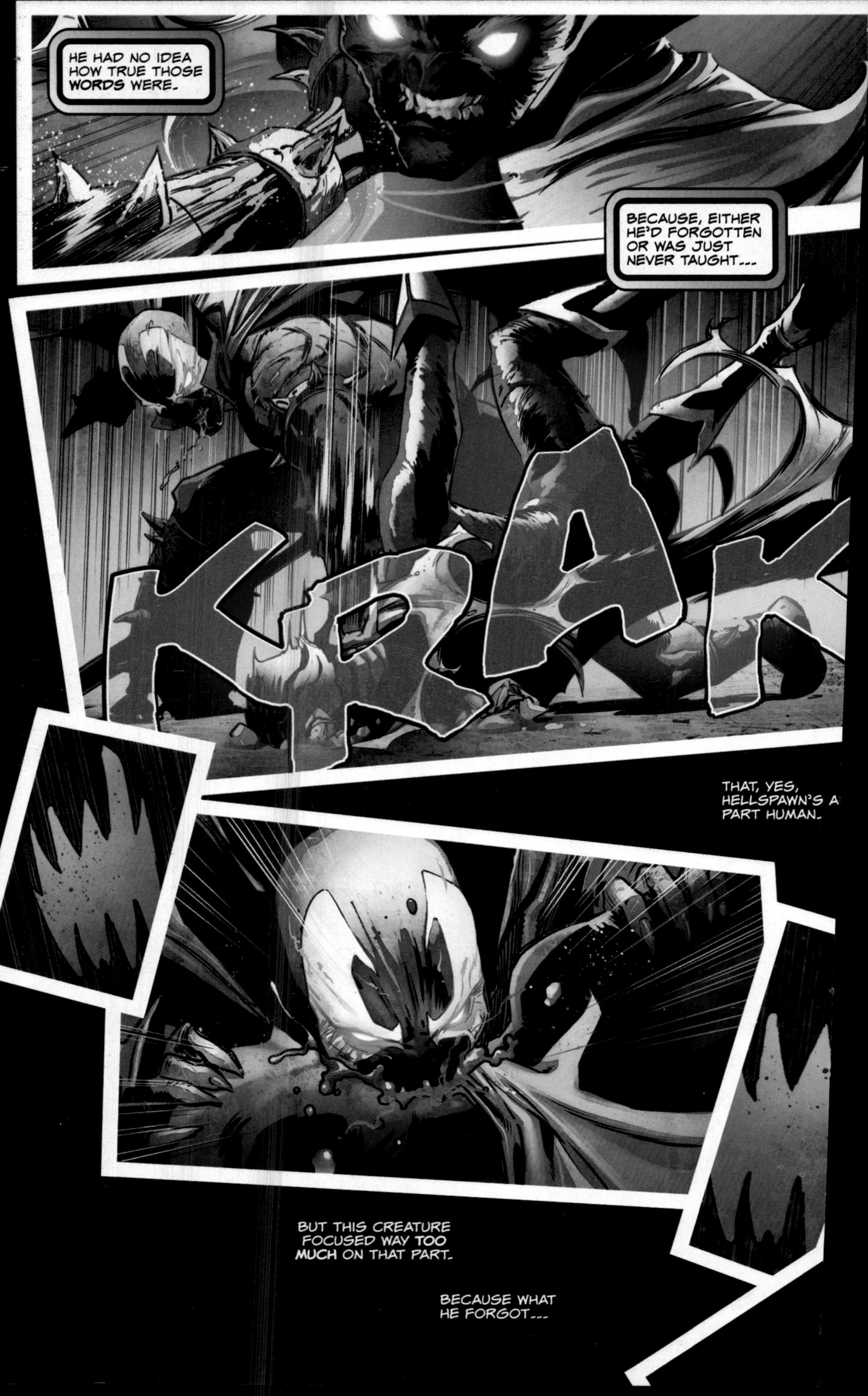
HE HAD NO IDEA HOW TRUE THOSE WORDS WERE.
BECAUSE, EITHER HE'D FORGOTTEN OR WAS JUST NEVER TAUGHT...
KRAK
THAT, YES, HELLSPAWN'S A
PART HUMAN.
BUT THIS CREATURE FOCUSED WAY TOO MUCH ON THAT PART.
BECAUSE WHAT HE FORGOT...

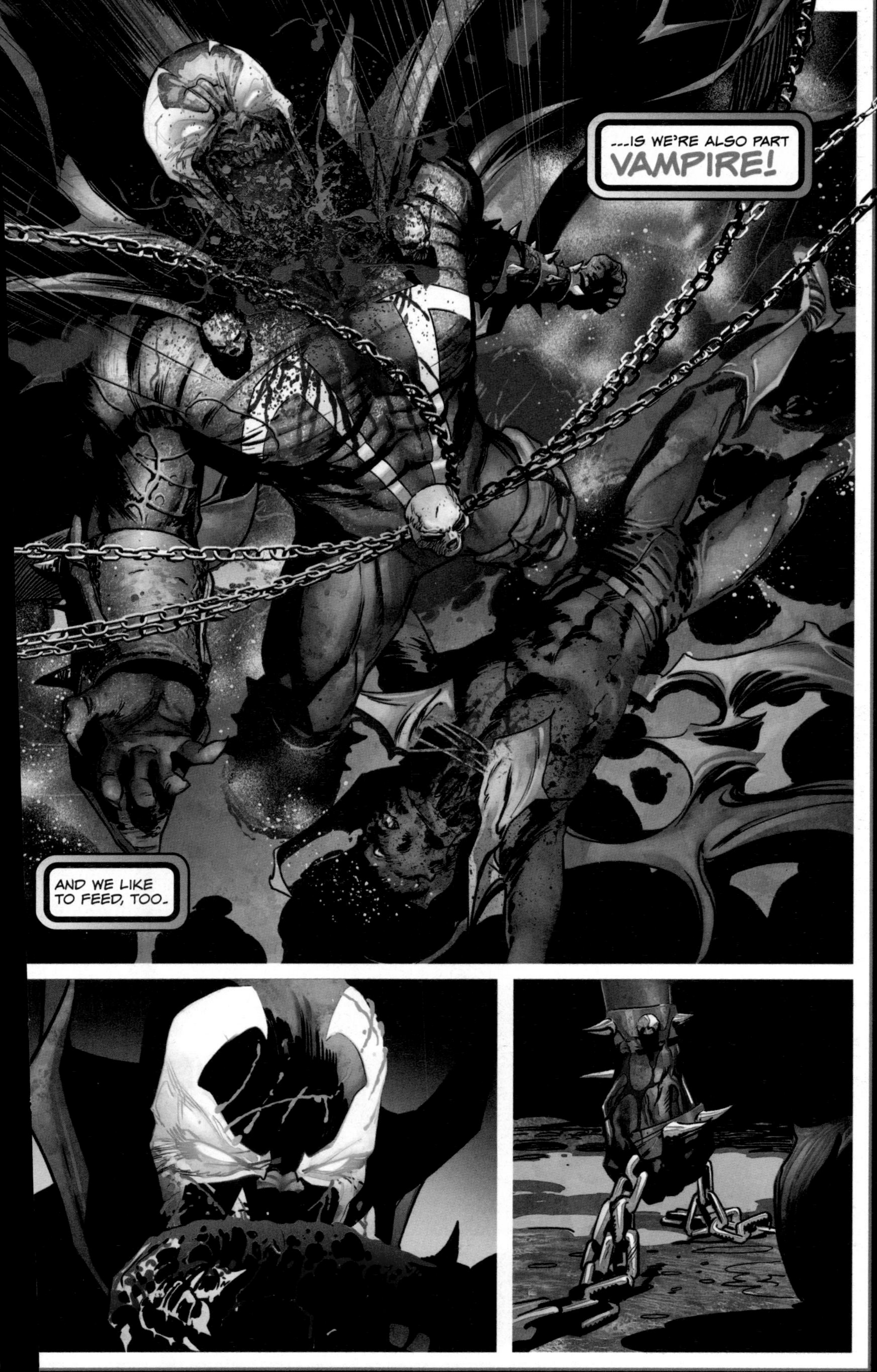

...IS WE'RE ALSO PART VAMPIRE!
AND WE LIKE TO FEED, TOO.

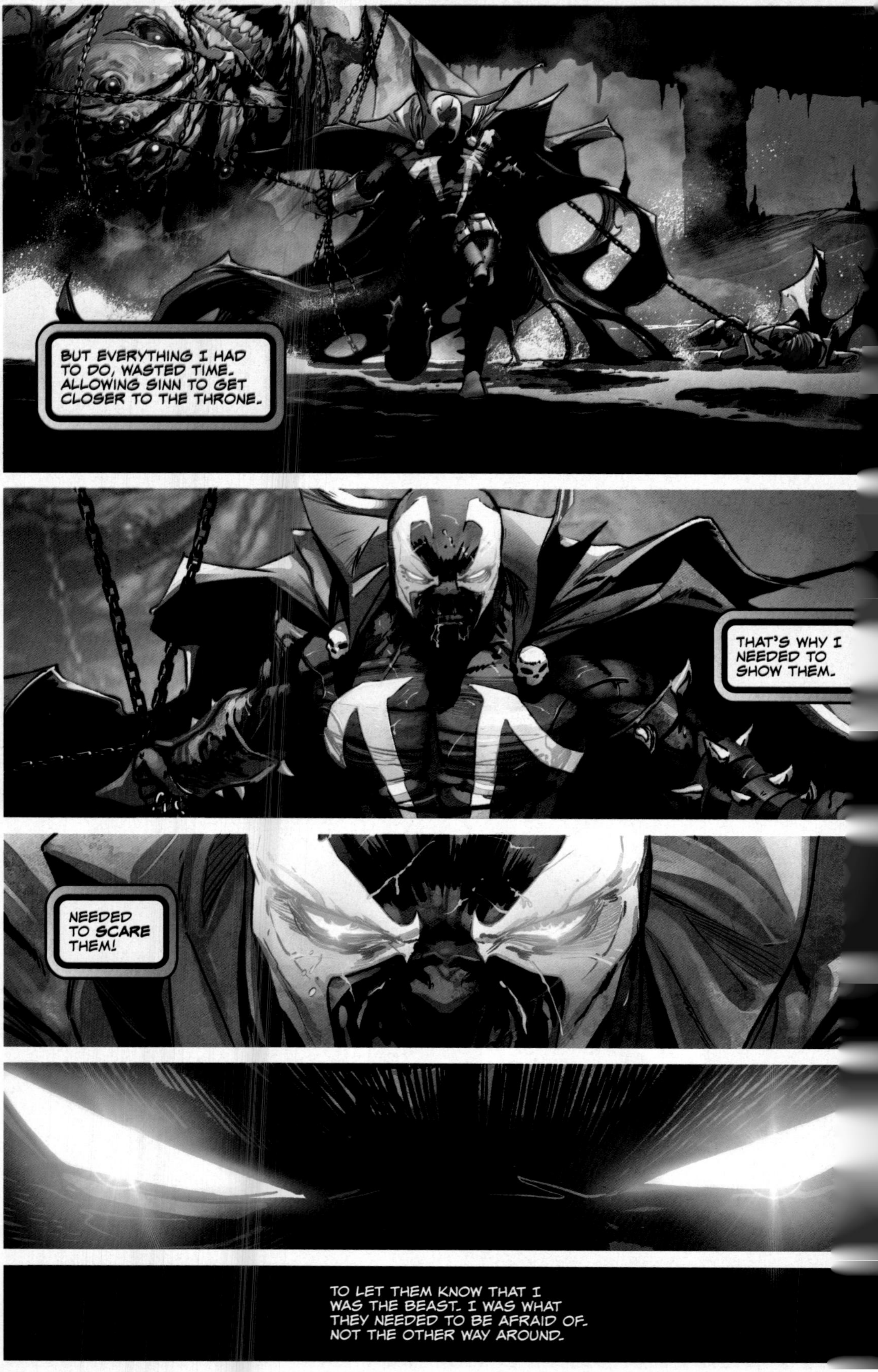

BUT EVERYTHING I HAD TO DO, WASTED TIME. ALLOWING SINN TO GET CLOSER TO THE THRONE.
THAT'S WHY I NEEDED TO SHOW THEM.
NEEDED TO SCARE THEM!
TO LET THEM KNOW THAT I WAS THE BEAST. I WAS WHAT THEY NEEDED TO BE AFRAID OF. NOT THE OTHER WAY AROUND.

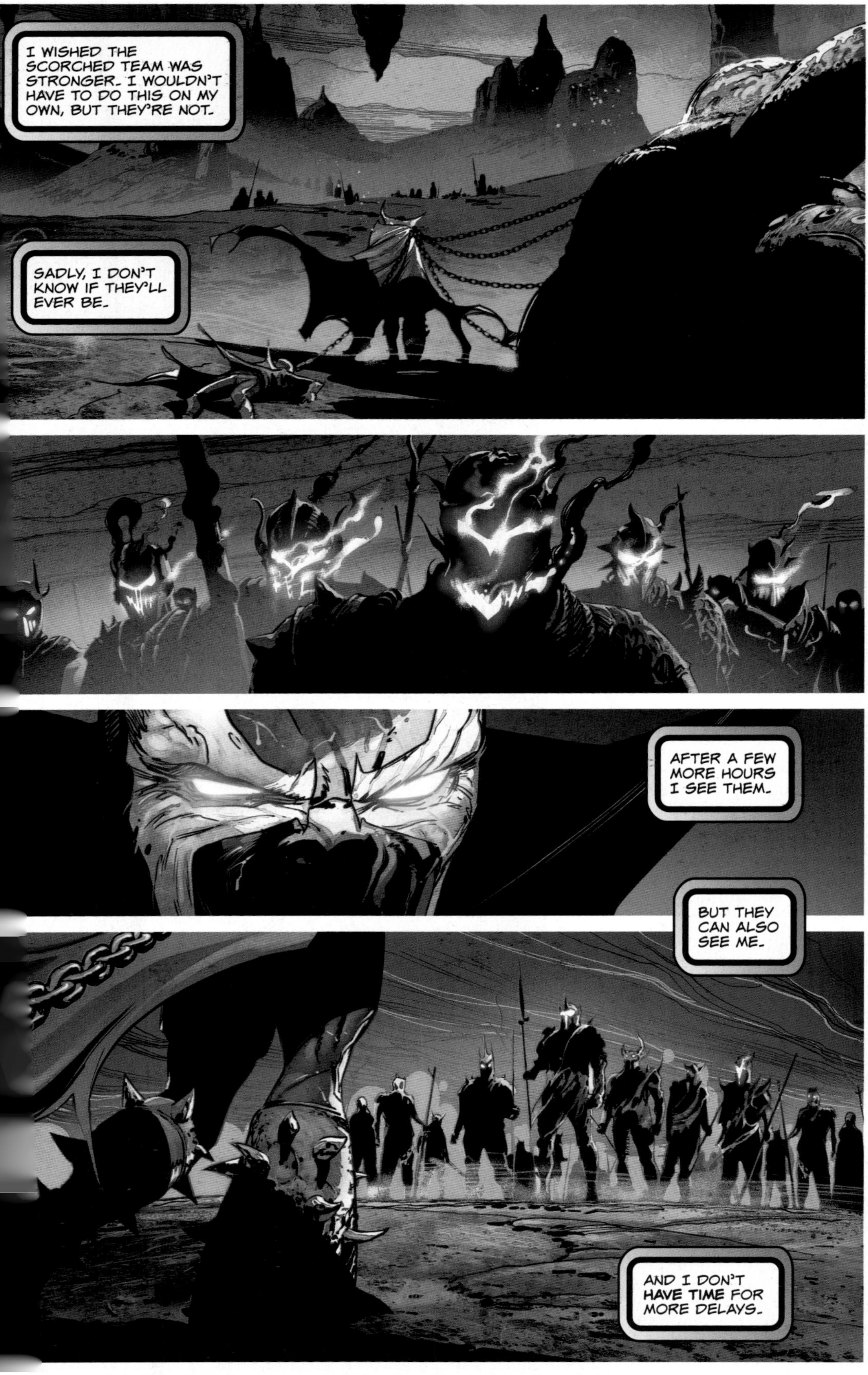
I WISHED THE SCORCHED TEAM WAS STRONGER. I WOULDN'T HAVE TO DO THIS ON MY OWN, BUT THEY'RE NOT.
SADLY, I DON'T KNOW IF THEY'LL EVER BE.
AFTER A FEW MORE HOURS I SEE THEM.
BUT THEY CAN ALSO SEE ME.
AND I DON'T HAVE TIME FOR MORE DELAYS.

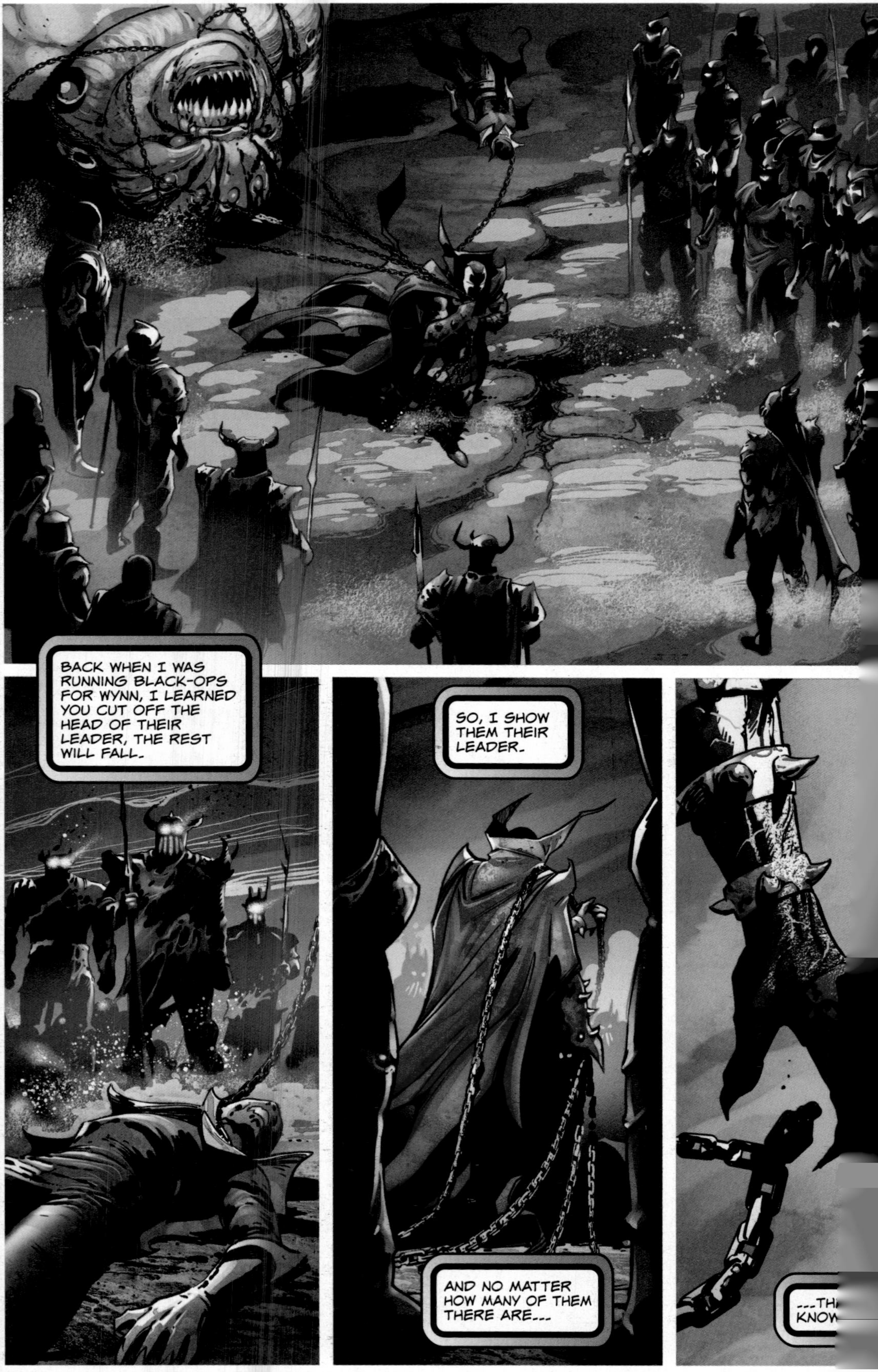
BACK WHEN I WAS RUNNING BLACK-OPS FOR WYNN, I LEARNED YOU CUT OFF THE HEAD OF THEIR LEADER, THE REST WILL FALL.
SO, I SHOW THEM THEIR LEADER.
AND NO MATTER HOW MANY OF THEM THERE ARE...
...TH
KNOW

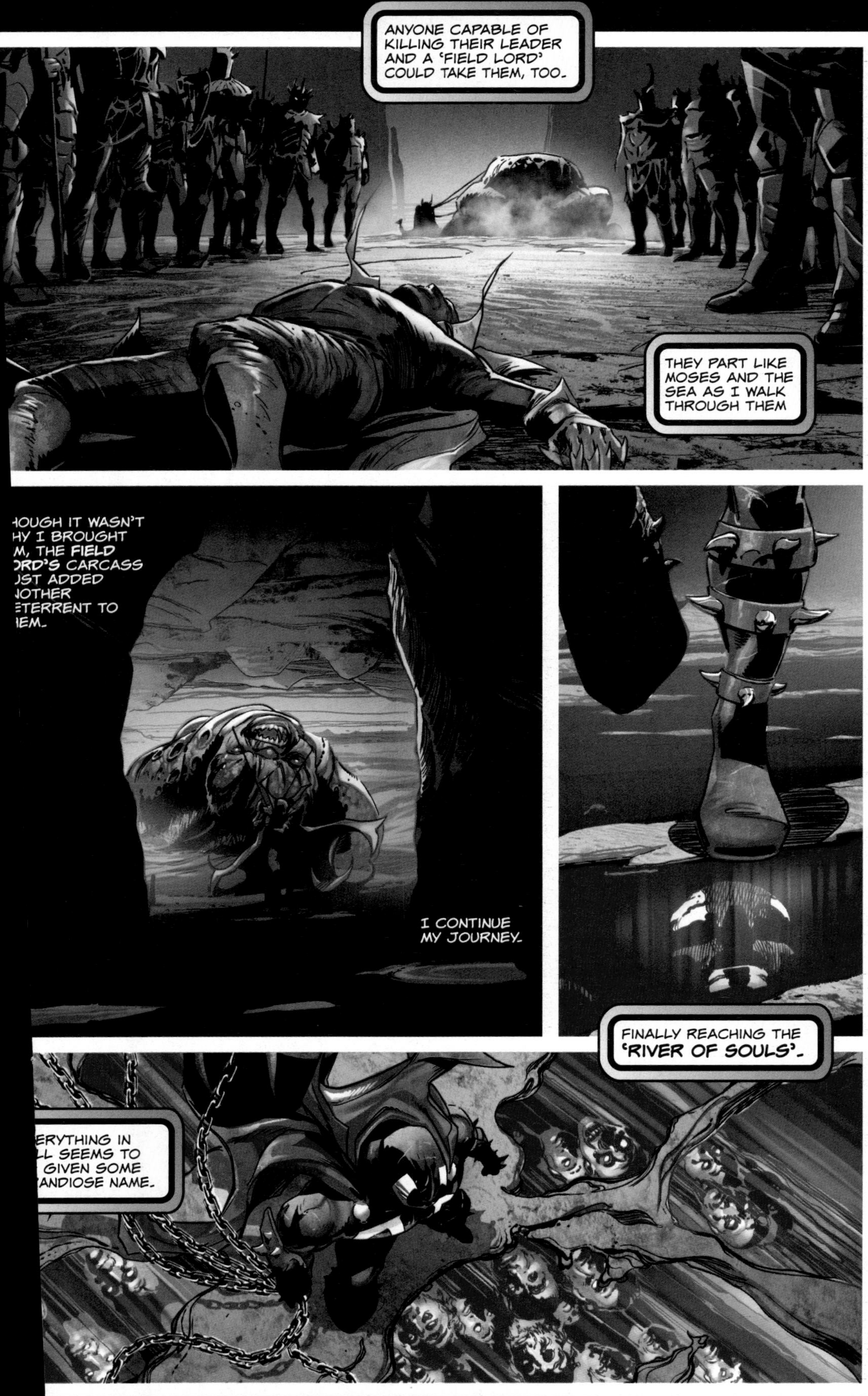

ANYONE CAPABLE OF KILLING THEIR LEADER AND A 'FIELD LORD' COULD TAKE THEM, TOO.
THEY PART LIKE MOSES AND THE SEA AS I WALK THROUGH THEM
HOUGH IT WASN'T HY I BROUGHT M, THE FIELD ORD'S CARCASS JST ADDED NOTHER ETERRENT TO IEM.
I CONTINUE MY JOURNEY.
FINALLY REACHING THE 'RIVER OF SOULS'.
ERYTHING IN LL SEEMS TO GIVEN SOME ANDIOSE NAME.

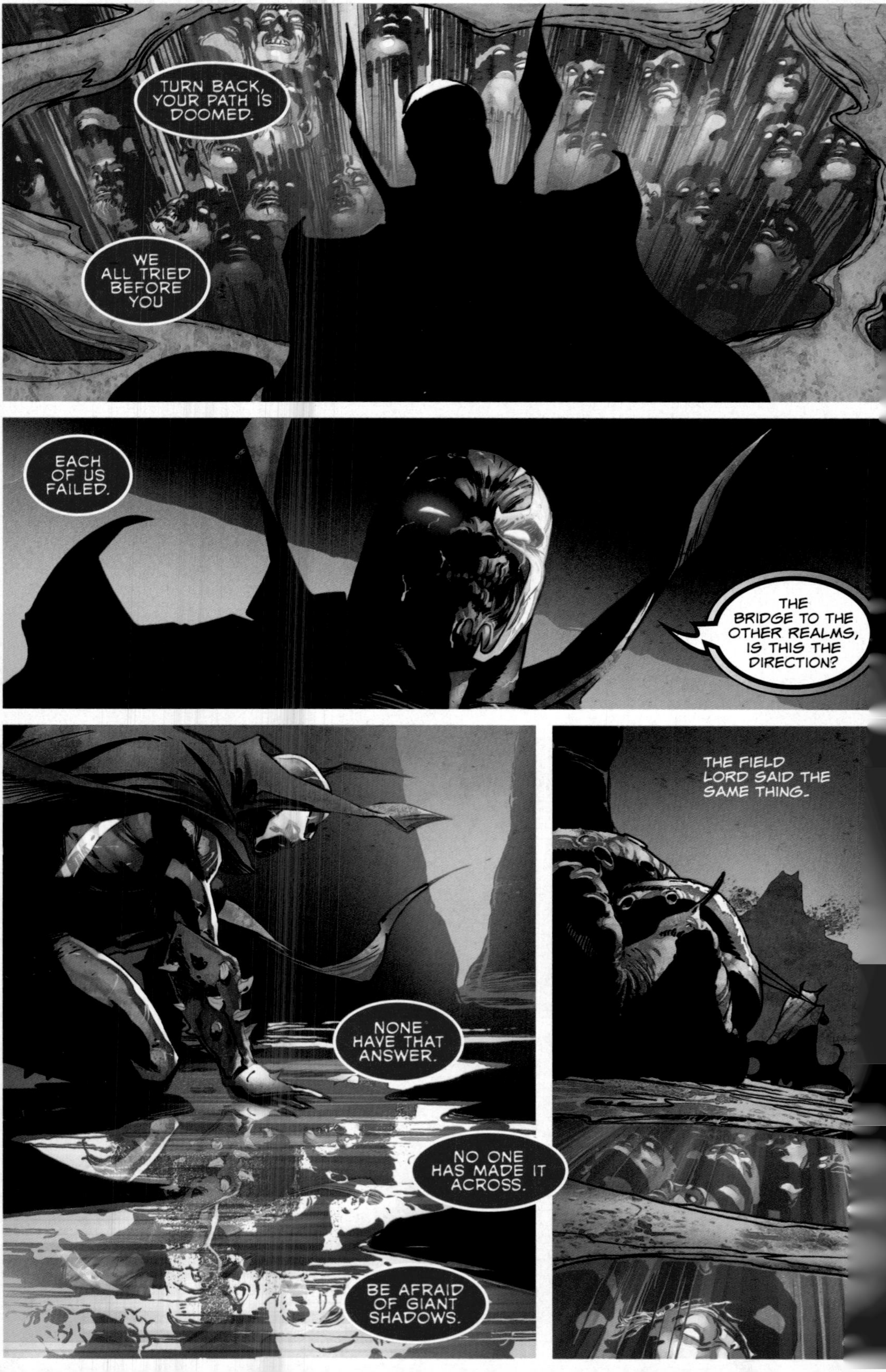
TURN BACK, YOUR PATH IS DOOMED.
WE ALL TRIED BEFORE YOU
EACH OF US FAILED.
THE BRIDGE TO THE OTHER REALMS, IS THIS THE DIRECTION?
NONE HAVE THAT ANSWER.
NO ONE HAS MADE IT ACROSS.
BE AFRAID OF GIANT SHADOWS.
THE FIELD LORD SAID THE SAME THING.

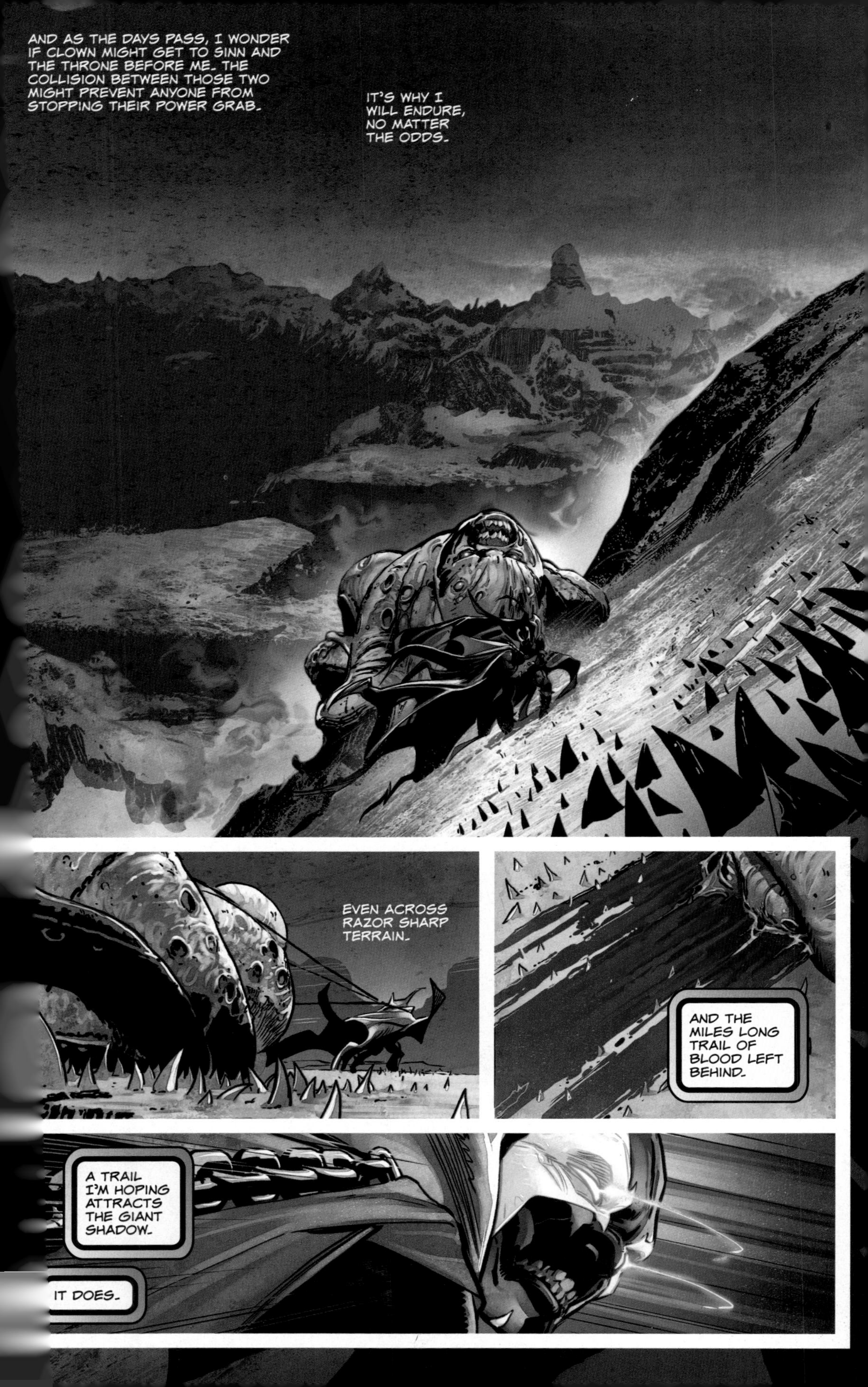
AND AS THE DAYS PASS, I WONDER IF CLOWN MIGHT GET TO SINN AND THE THRONE BEFORE ME. THE COLLISION BETWEEN THOSE TWO MIGHT PREVENT ANYONE FROM STOPPING THEIR POWER GRAB.
IT'S WHY I WILL ENDURE, NO MATTER THE ODDS.
EVEN ACROSS RAZOR SHARP TERRAIN.
AND THE MILES LONG TRAIL OF BLOOD LEFT BEHIND.
A TRAIL I'M HOPING ATTRACTS THE GIANT SHADOW.
IT DOES.

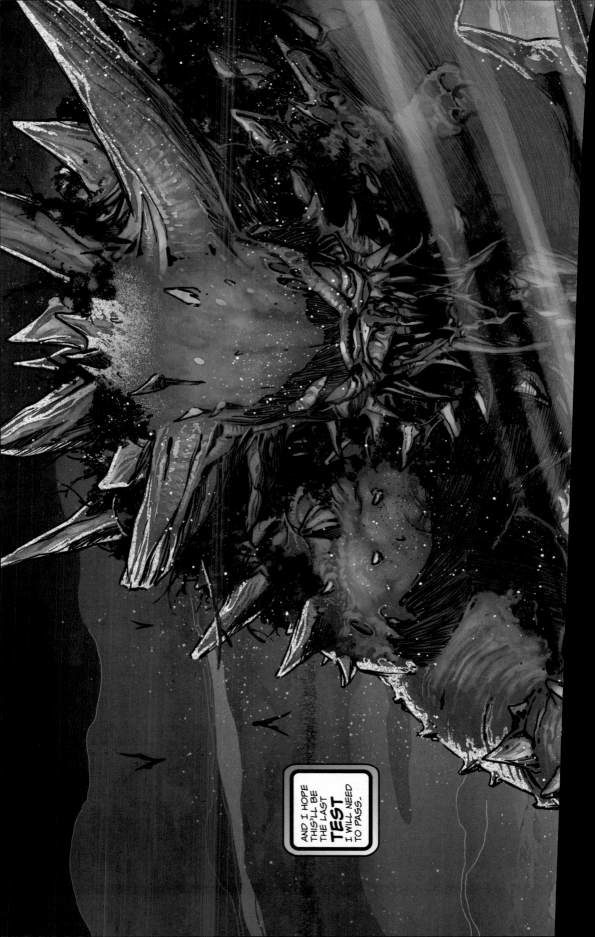

AND I HOPE THIS'LL BE THE LAST **TEST** I WILL NEED TO PASS.

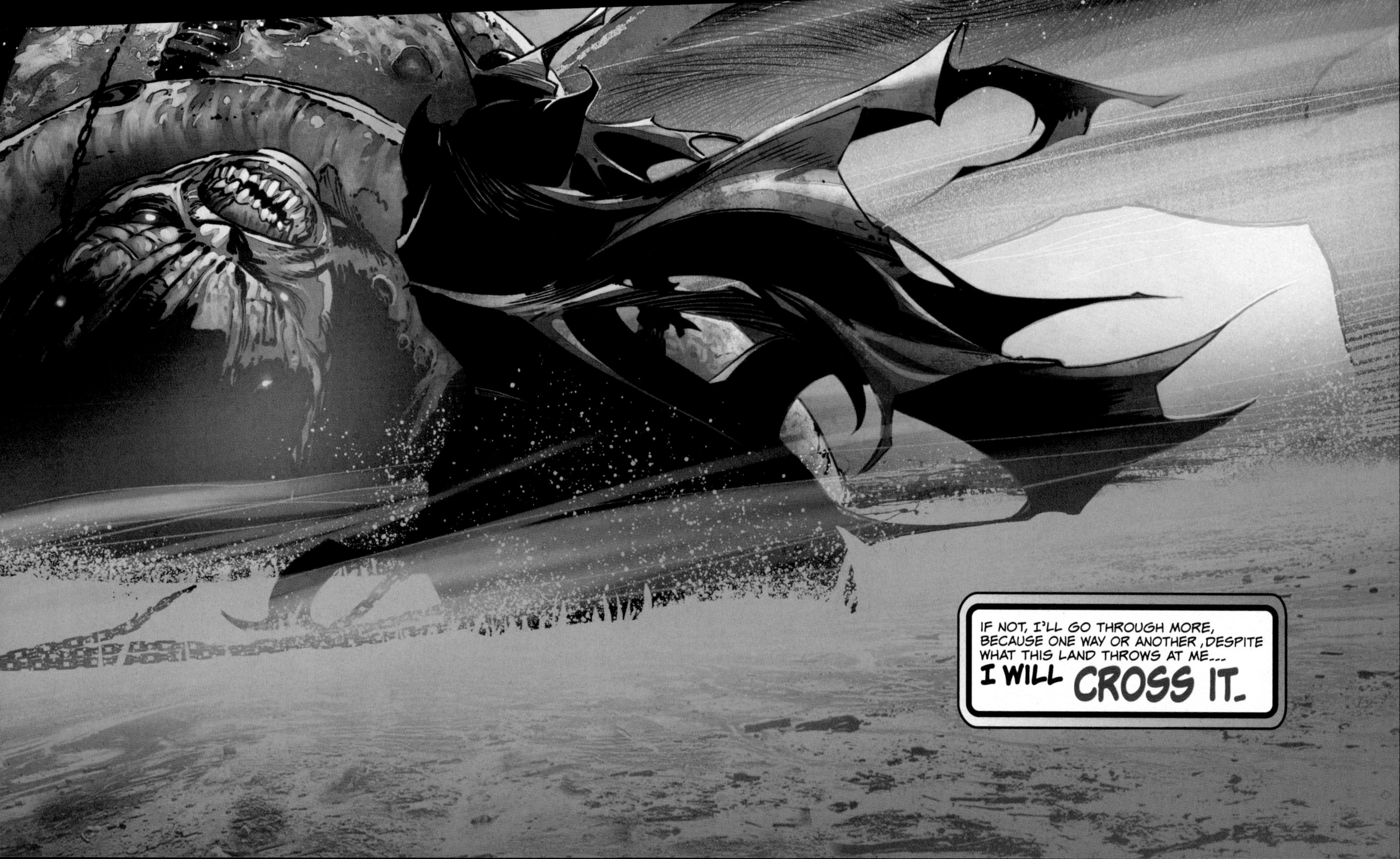
IF NOT, I'LL GO THROUGH MORE, BECAUSE ONE WAY OR ANOTHER, DESPITE WHAT THIS LAND THROWS AT ME... I WILL CROSS IT.

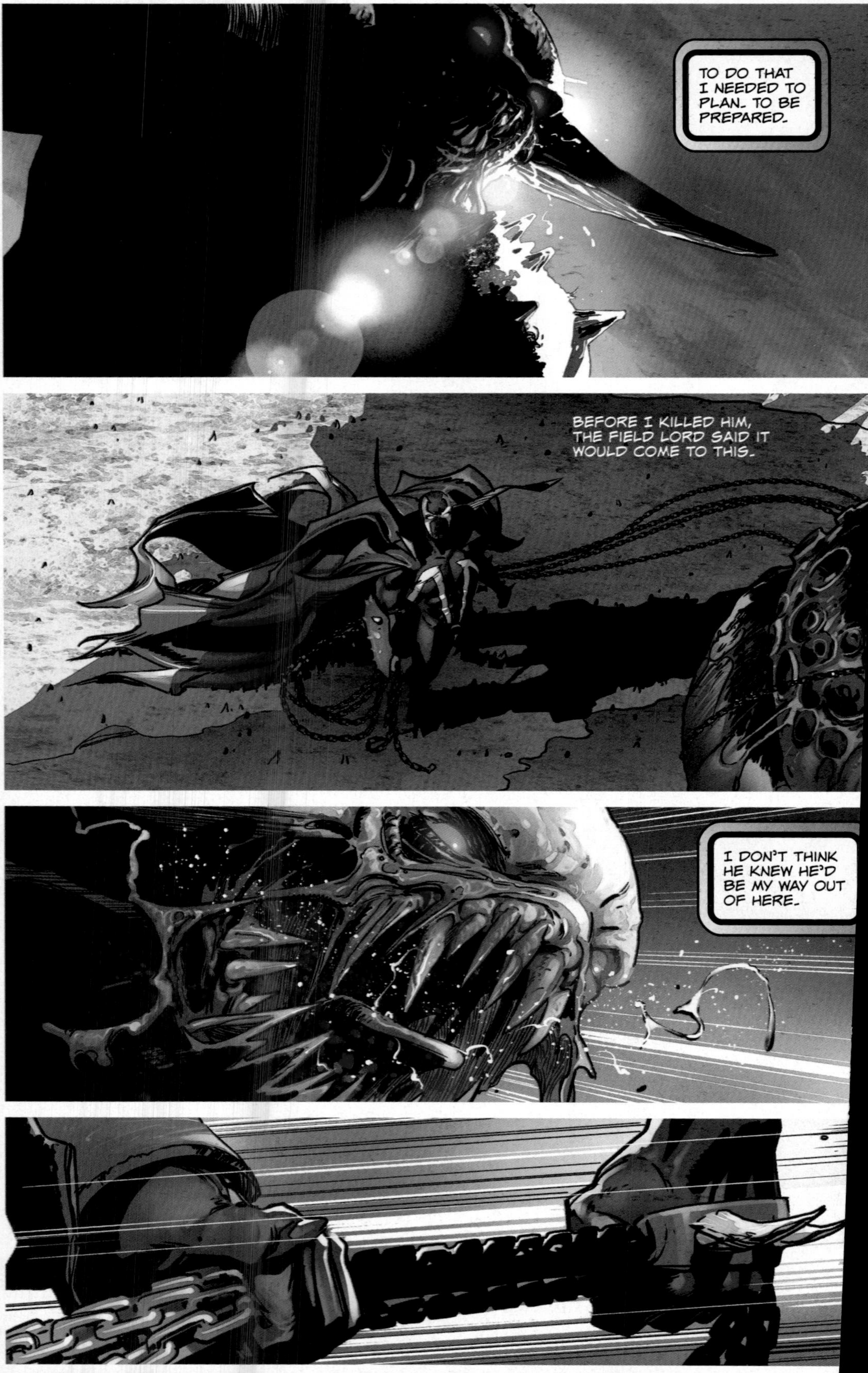
TO DO THAT I NEEDED TO PLAN. TO BE PREPARED.
BEFORE I KILLED HIM, THE FIELD LORD SAID IT WOULD COME TO THIS.
I DON'T THINK HE KNEW HE'D BE MY WAY OUT OF HERE.

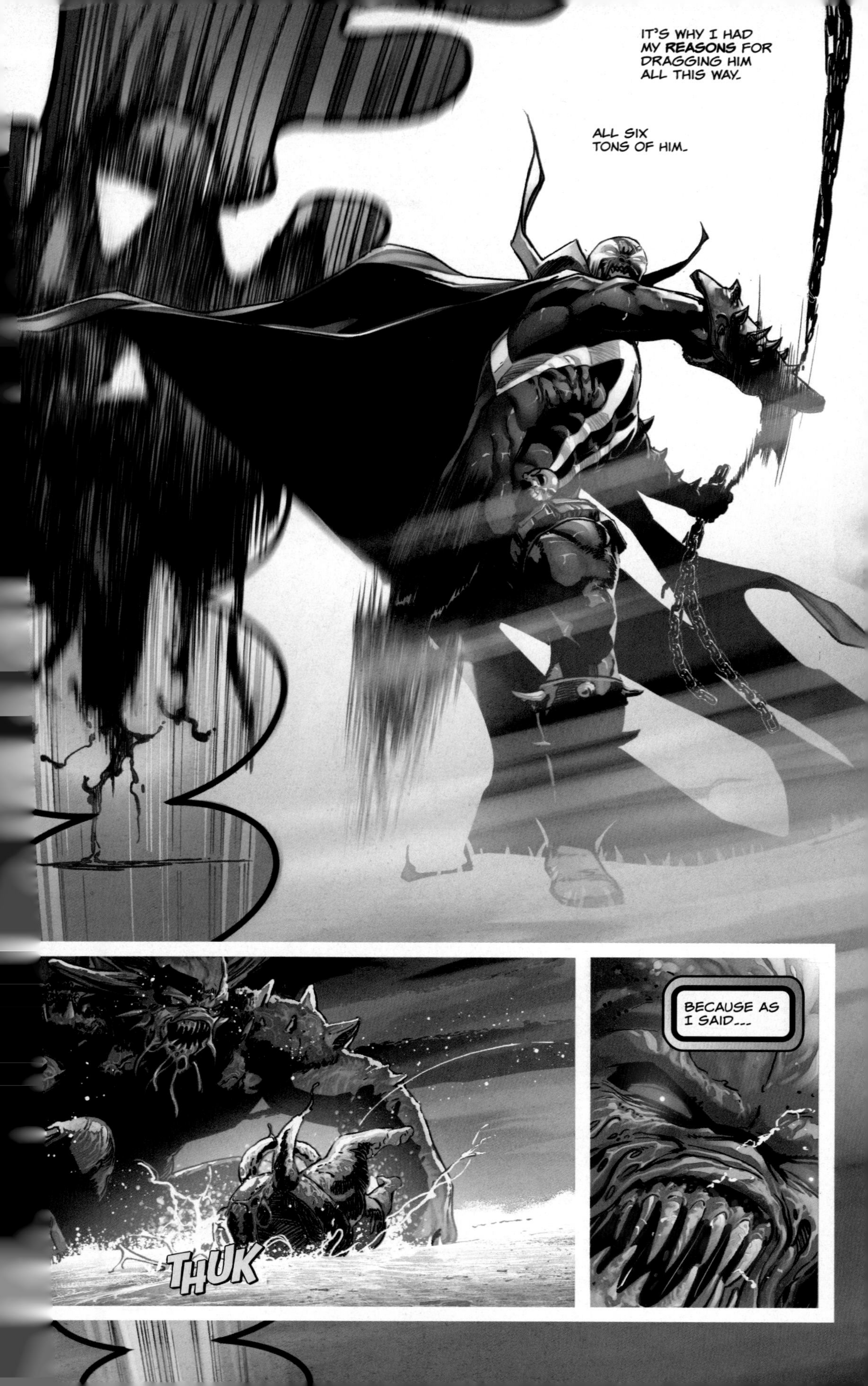
IT'S WHY I HAD MY **REASONS** FOR DRAGGING HIM ALL THIS WAY.
ALL SIX TONS OF HIM.
THUK
BECAUSE AS I SAID...

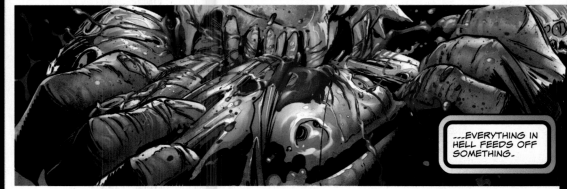

...EVERYTHING IN HELL FEEDS OFF SOMETHING.

NOW I'M FREE TO WALK ALONE.

NO MATTER HOW LONG MY WALK MIGHT BE.

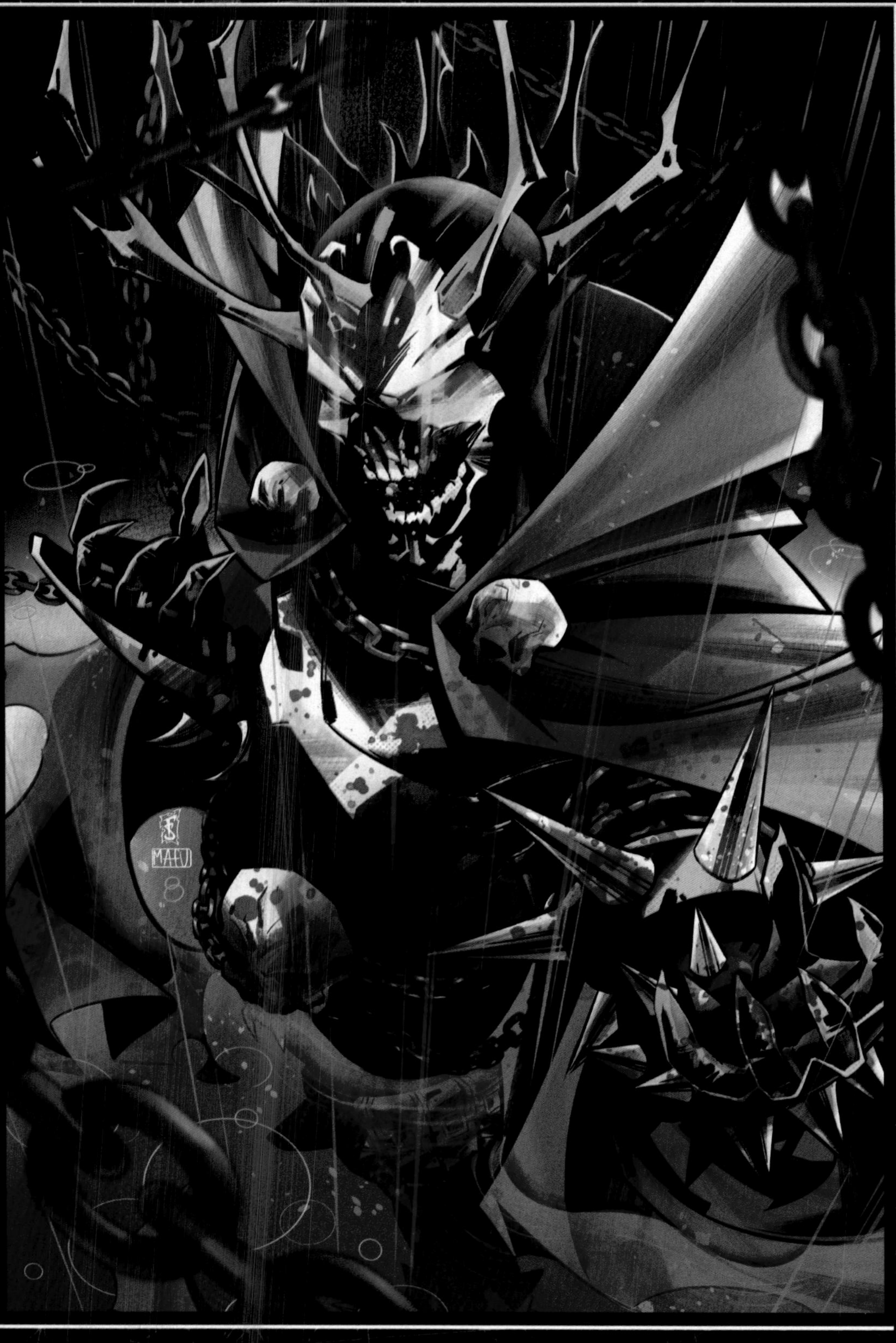

King Spawn #29 Cover by Federico Sabbatini

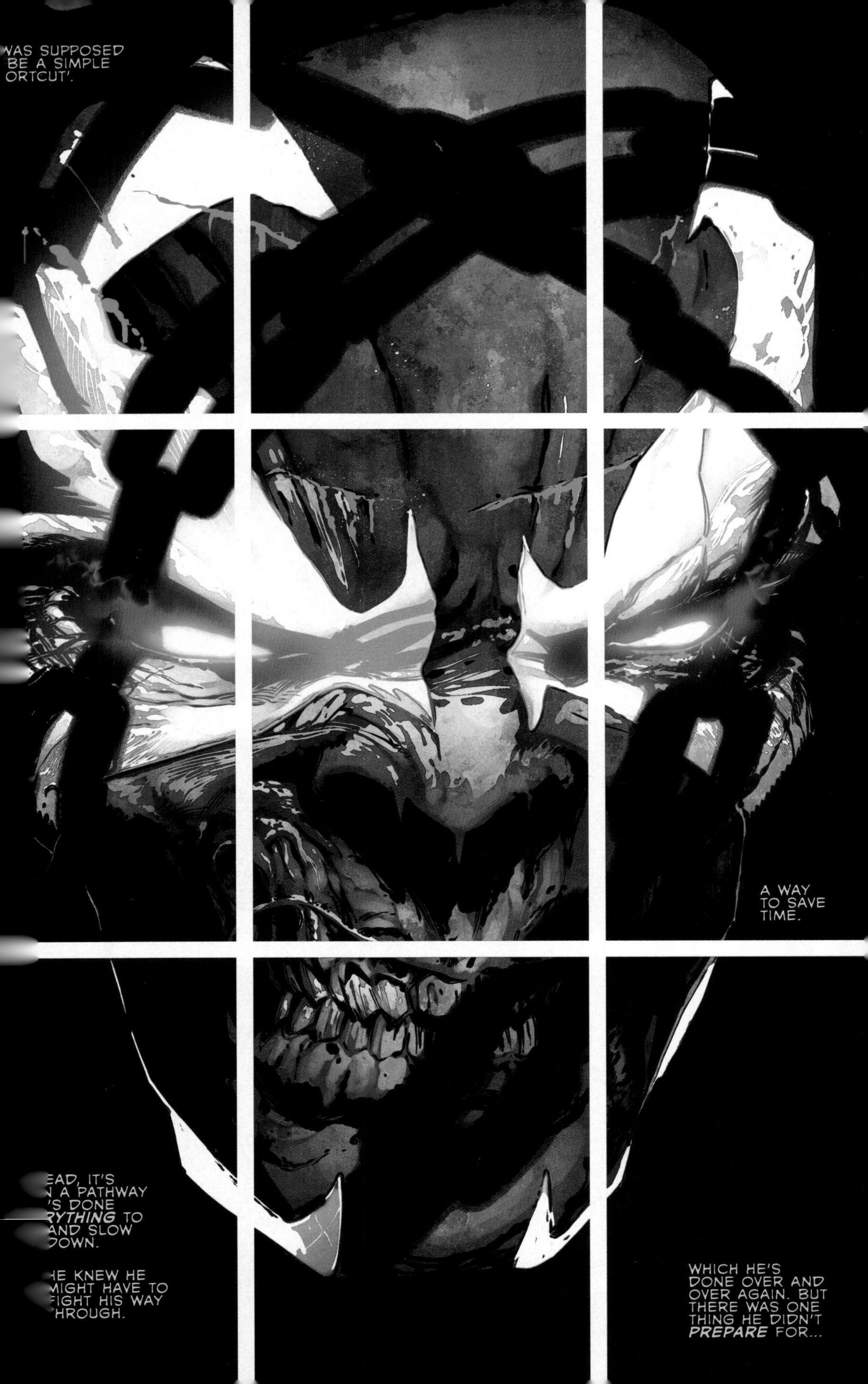

WAS SUPPOSED BE A SIMPLE ORTCUT'.
A WAY TO SAVE TIME.
EAD, IT'S N A PATHWAY 'S DONE *RYTHING* TO AND SLOW DOWN.
HE KNEW HE MIGHT HAVE TO FIGHT HIS WAY HROUGH.
WHICH HE'S DONE OVER AND OVER AGAIN. BUT THERE WAS ONE THING HE DIDN'T *PREPARE* FOR...

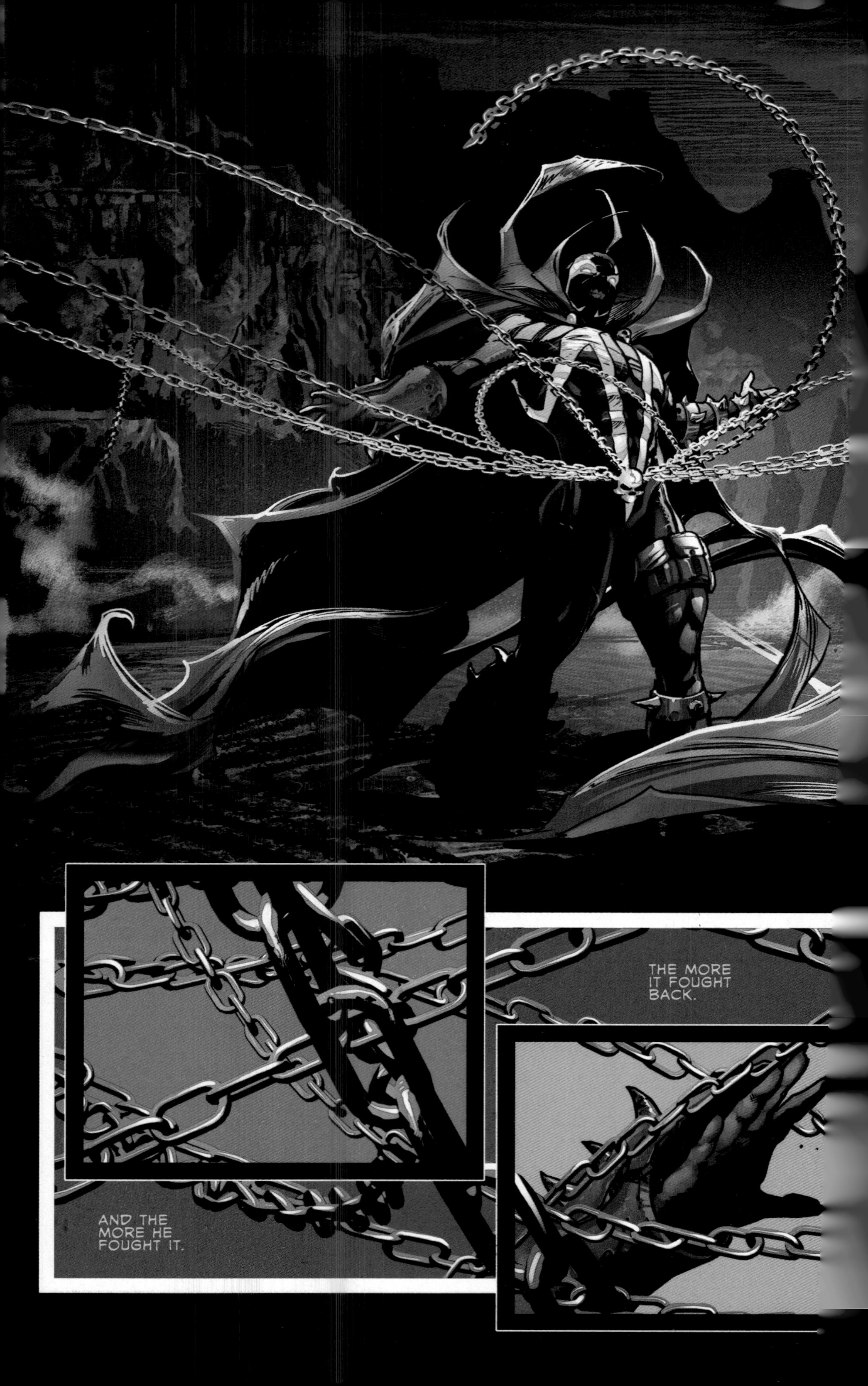
THE MORE IT FOUGHT BACK.
AND THE MORE HE FOUGHT IT.

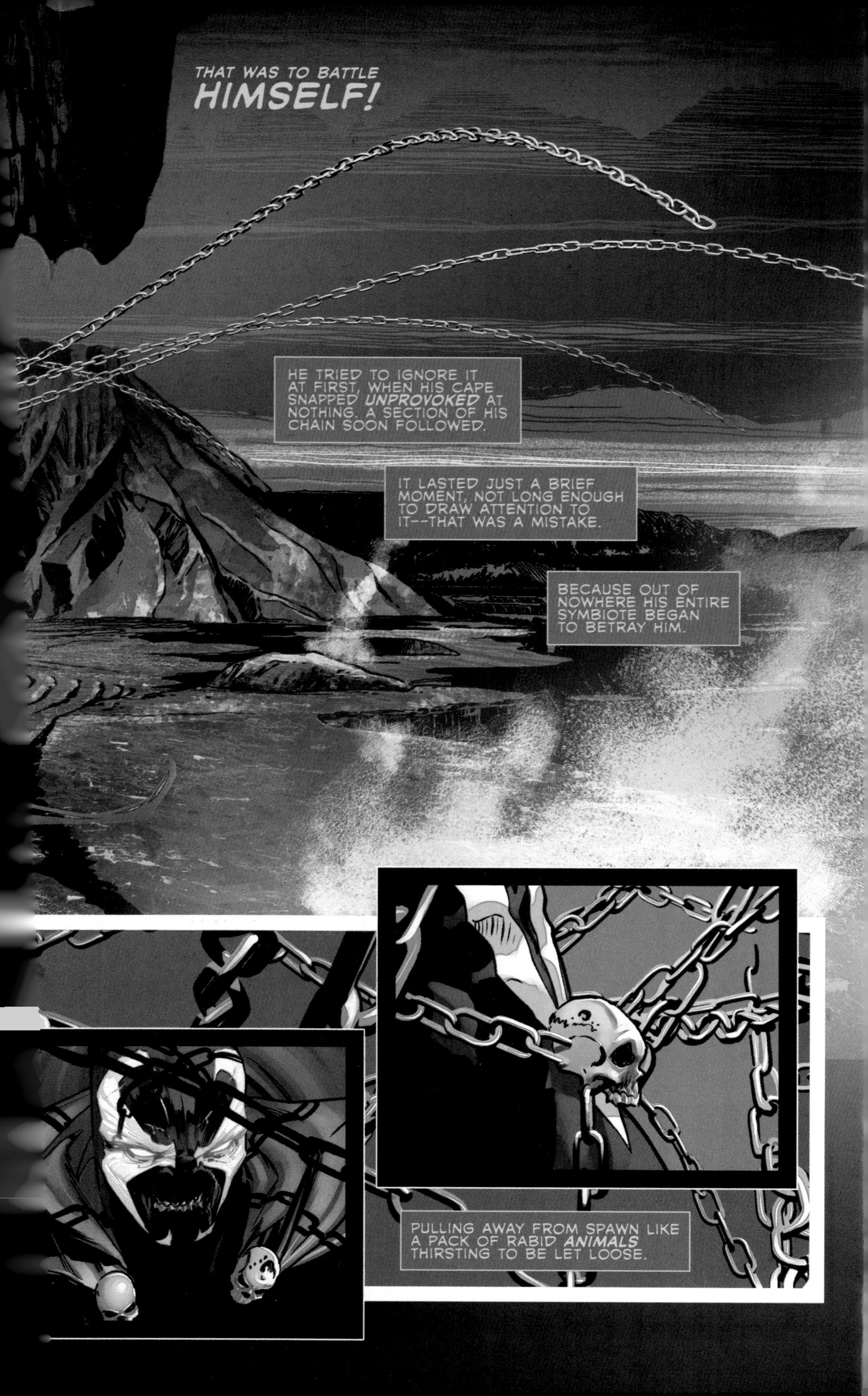
THAT WAS TO BATTLE HIMSELF!
HE TRIED TO IGNORE IT AT FIRST, WHEN HIS CAPE SNAPPED UNPROVOKED AT NOTHING. A SECTION OF HIS CHAIN SOON FOLLOWED.
IT LASTED JUST A BRIEF MOMENT, NOT LONG ENOUGH TO DRAW ATTENTION TO IT--THAT WAS A MISTAKE.
BECAUSE OUT OF NOWHERE HIS ENTIRE SYMBIOTE BEGAN TO BETRAY HIM.
PULLING AWAY FROM SPAWN LIKE A PACK OF RABID ANIMALS THIRSTING TO BE LET LOOSE.

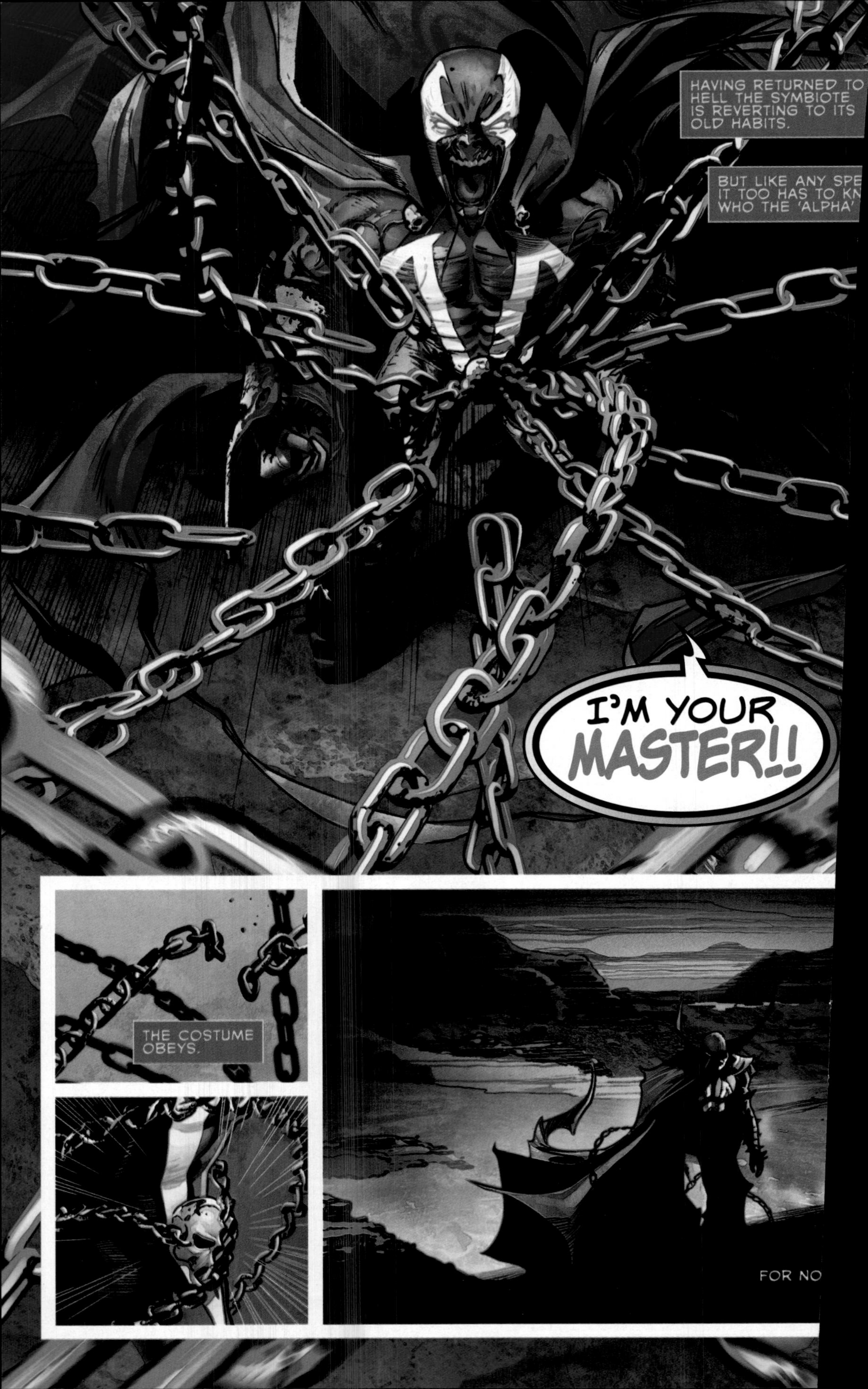
HAVING RETURNED TO HELL THE SYMBIOTE IS REVERTING TO ITS OLD HABITS.
BUT LIKE ANY SPE IT TOO HAS TO KN WHO THE 'ALPHA'
I'M YOUR MASTER!!
THE COSTUME OBEYS.
FOR NO

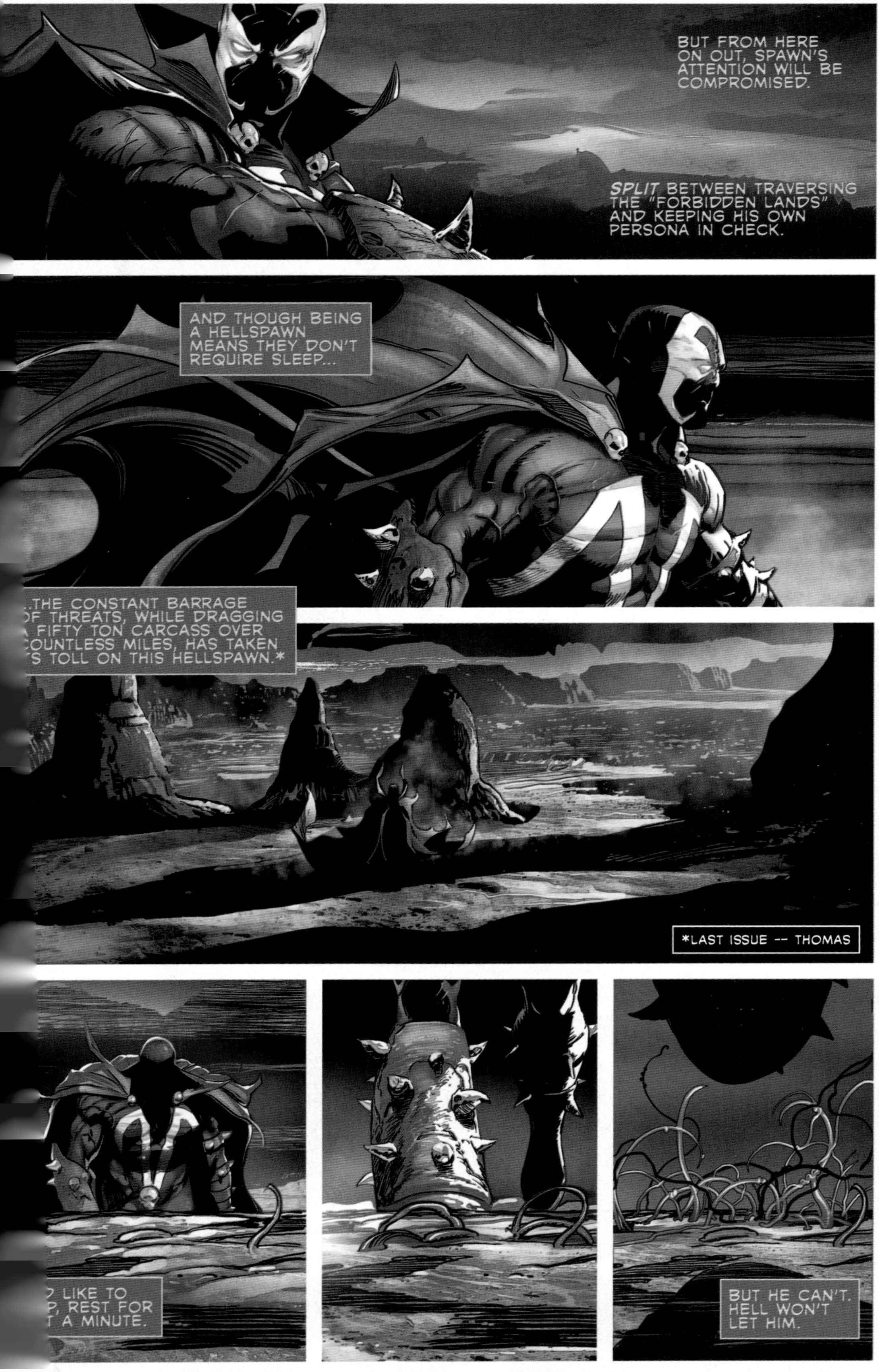
BUT FROM HERE ON OUT, SPAWN'S ATTENTION WILL BE COMPROMISED.
SPLIT BETWEEN TRAVERSING THE "FORBIDDEN LANDS" AND KEEPING HIS OWN PERSONA IN CHECK.
AND THOUGH BEING A HELLSPAWN MEANS THEY DON'T REQUIRE SLEEP...
.THE CONSTANT BARRAGE
F THREATS, WHILE DRAGGING
FIFTY TON CARCASS OVER
COUNTLESS MILES, HAS TAKEN
S TOLL ON THIS HELLSPAWN.*
*LAST ISSUE -- THOMAS
D LIKE TO
P, REST FOR
T A MINUTE.
BUT HE CAN'T. HELL WON'T LET HIM.

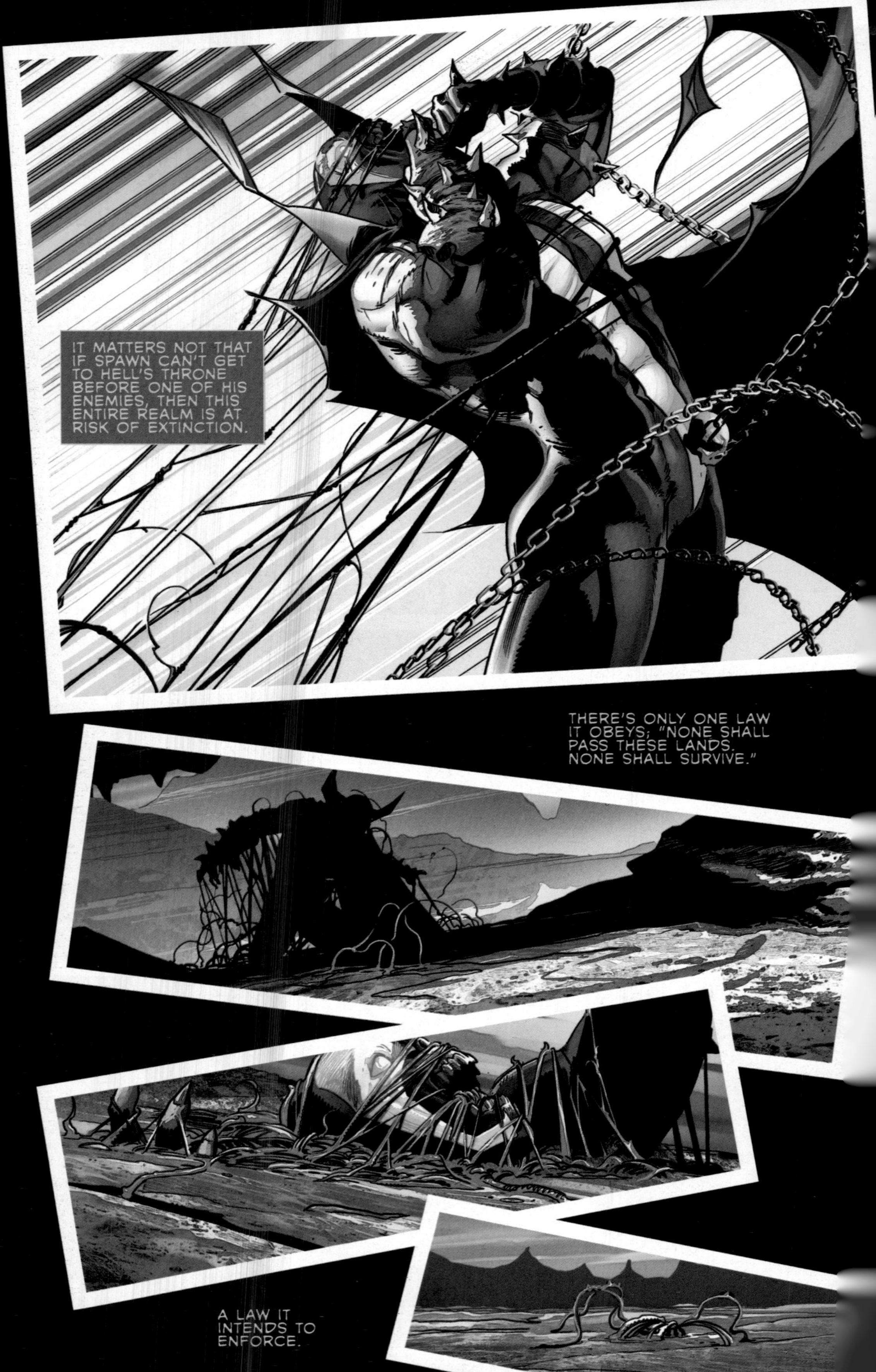
IT MATTERS NOT THAT IF SPAWN CAN'T GET TO HELL'S THRONE BEFORE ONE OF HIS ENEMIES, THEN THIS ENTIRE REALM IS AT RISK OF EXTINCTION.
THERE'S ONLY ONE LAW IT OBEYS; "NONE SHALL PASS THESE LANDS. NONE SHALL SURVIVE."
A LAW IT INTENDS TO ENFORCE.

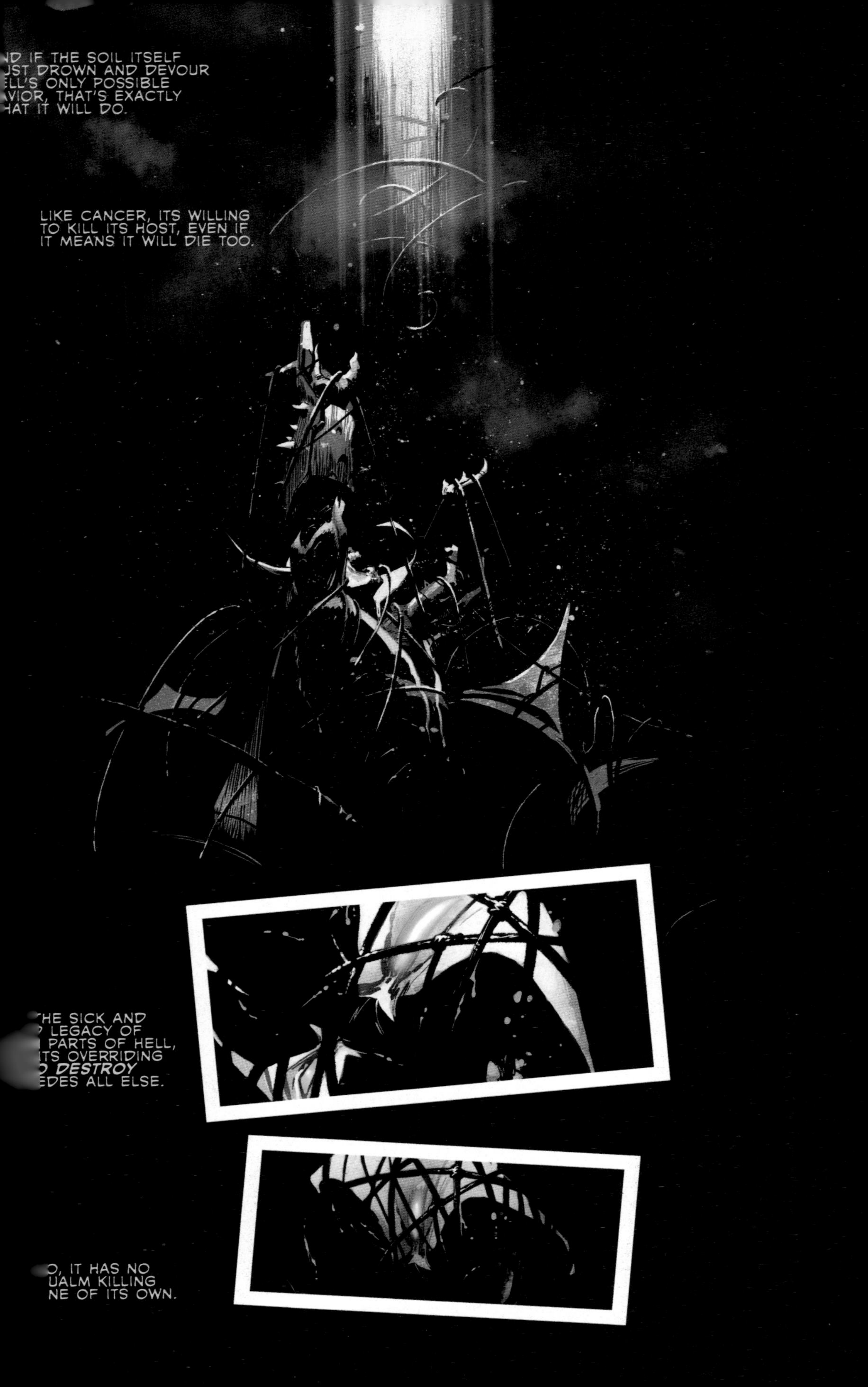
ND IF THE SOIL ITSELF JST DROWN AND DEVOUR ELL'S ONLY POSSIBLE AVIOR, THAT'S EXACTLY HAT IT WILL DO.
LIKE CANCER, ITS WILLING TO KILL ITS HOST, EVEN IF IT MEANS IT WILL DIE TOO.
HE SICK AND LEGACY OF PARTS OF HELL, ITS OVERRIDING D DESTROY EDES ALL ELSE.
O, IT HAS NO UALM KILLING NE OF ITS OWN.

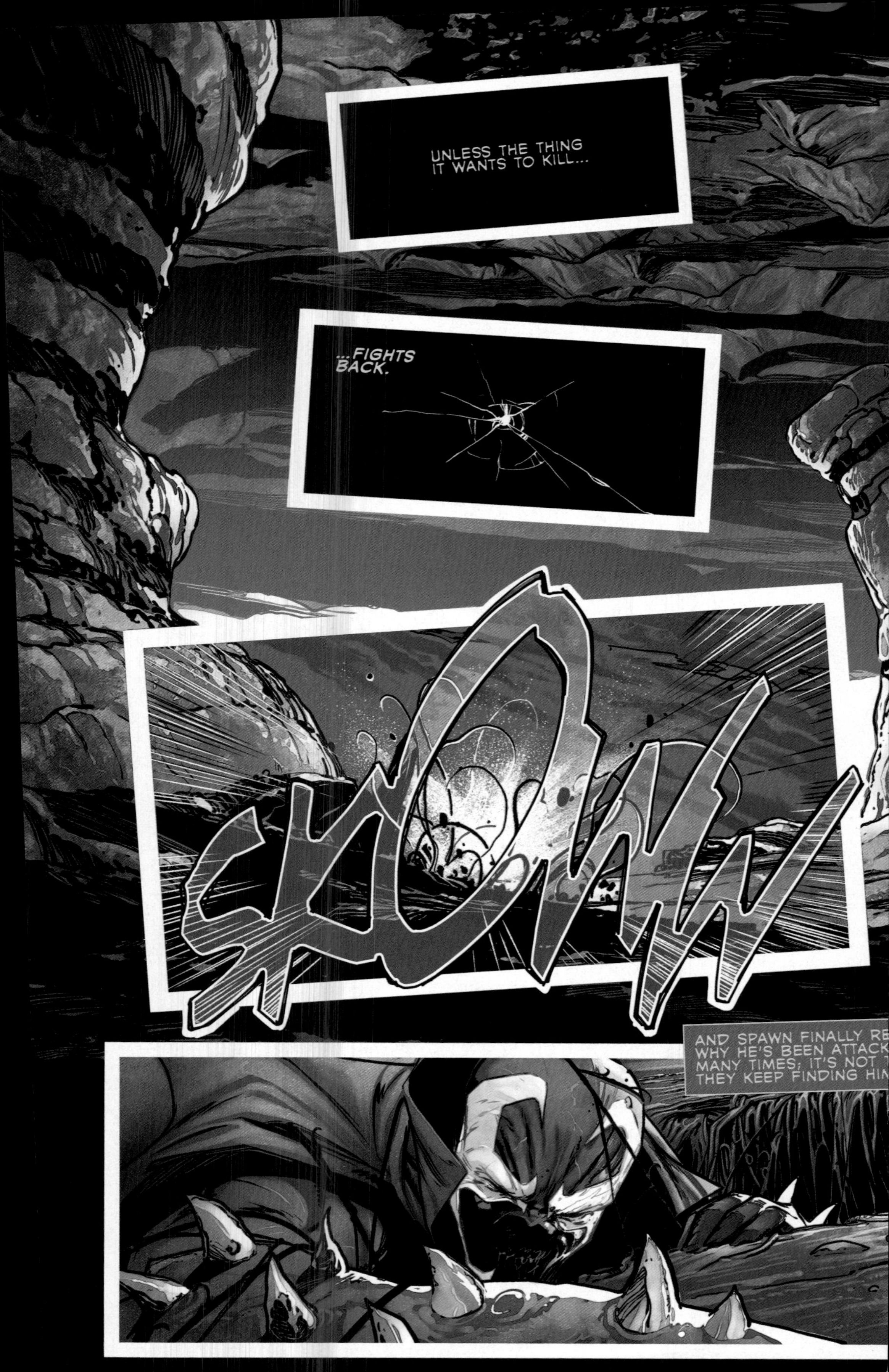

UNLESS THE THING IT WANTS TO KILL...
...FIGHTS BACK.
AND SPAWN FINALLY RE
WHY HE'S BEEN ATTACK
MANY TIMES; IT'S NOT T
THEY KEEP FINDING HIM

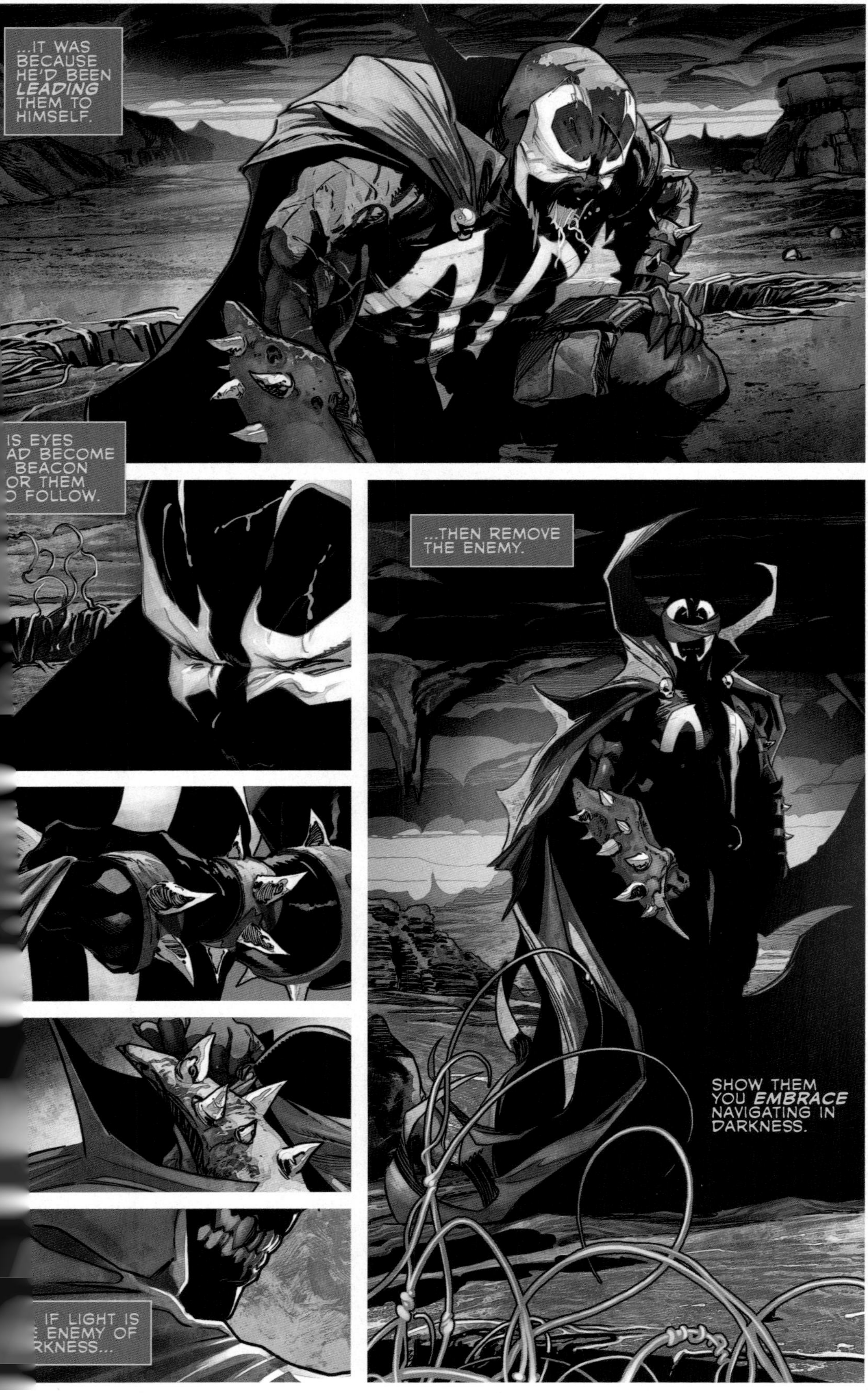

...IT WAS BECAUSE HE'D BEEN *LEADING* THEM TO HIMSELF.
IS EYES AD BECOME BEACON OR THEM O FOLLOW.
IF LIGHT IS E ENEMY OF RKNESS...
...THEN REMOVE THE ENEMY.
SHOW THEM YOU *EMBRACE* NAVIGATING IN DARKNESS.

FOR THE NEXT FEW DAYS, SPAWN'S
FRUSTRATION GROWS, AS HE BEGINS
TO DOUBT IF HE'S *ACTUALLY*
WALKING IN THE RIGHT DIRECTION.

HE SHOULD HAVE COME
TO ITS END BY NOW.

BUT IT'S THE PACE OF
HIS STRIDES THAT'S
FRUSTRATING HIM MOST.

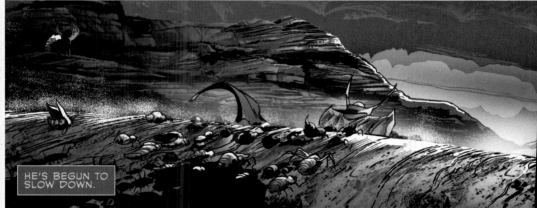

HE'S BEGUN TO
SLOW DOWN.

EVEN THOUGH
HE'S BEING
FOLLOWED
ONCE AGAIN.

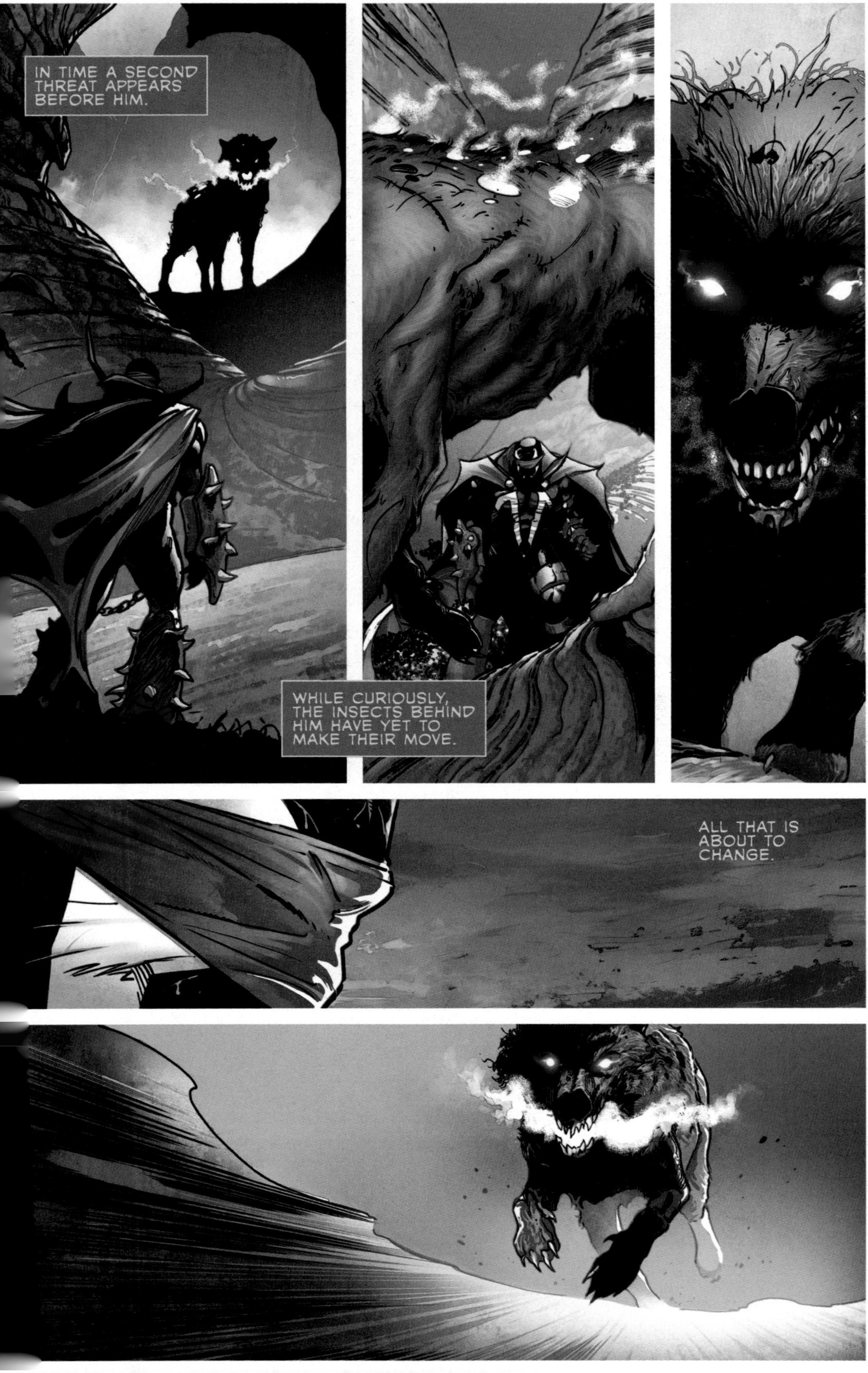
IN TIME A SECOND THREAT APPEARS BEFORE HIM.
WHILE CURIOUSLY, THE INSECTS BEHIND HIM HAVE YET TO MAKE THEIR MOVE.
ALL THAT IS ABOUT TO CHANGE.

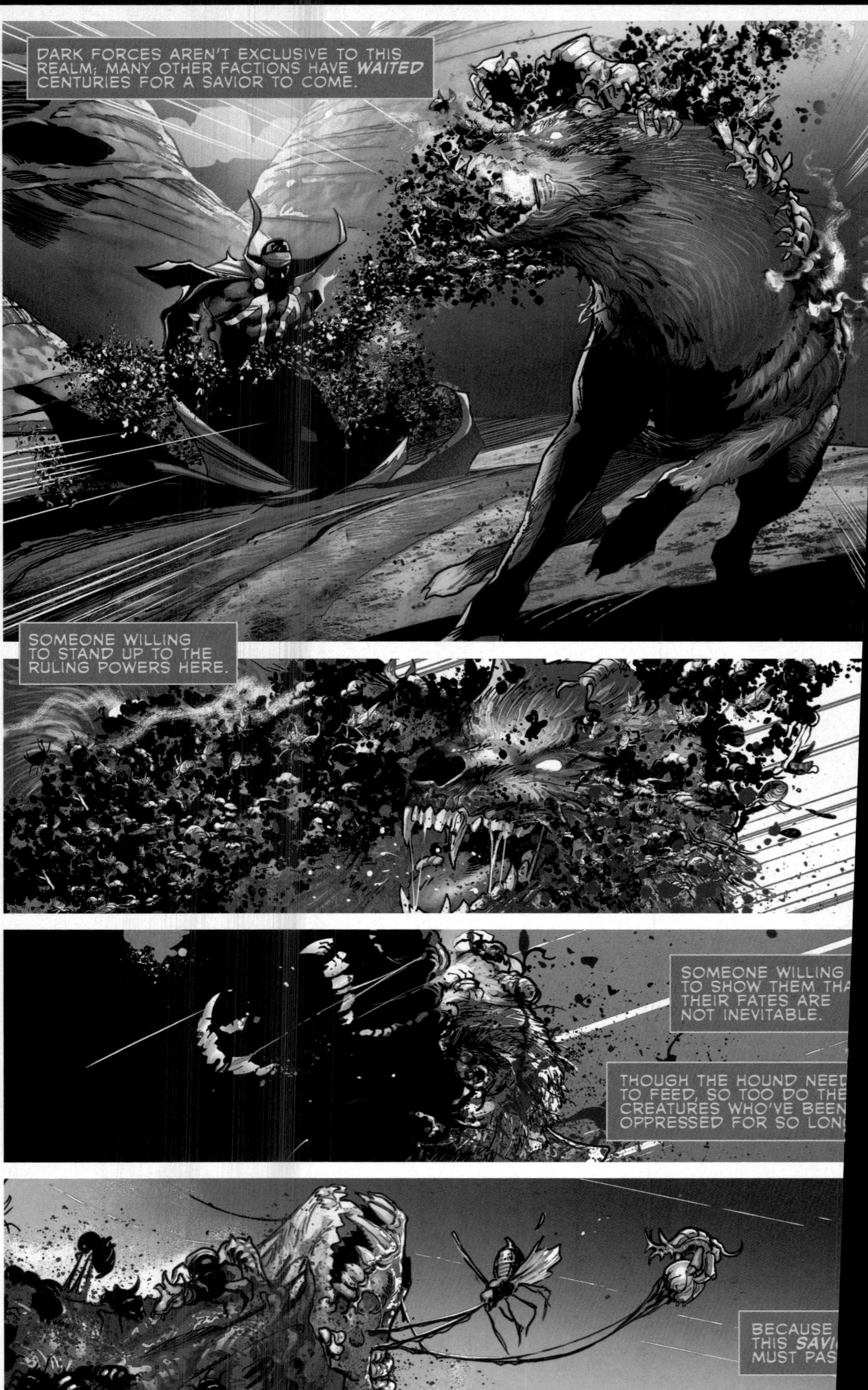
DARK FORCES AREN'T EXCLUSIVE TO THIS REALM; MANY OTHER FACTIONS HAVE *WAITED* CENTURIES FOR A SAVIOR TO COME.
SOMEONE WILLING TO STAND UP TO THE RULING POWERS HERE.
SOMEONE WILLING TO SHOW THEM THA
THEIR FATES ARE NOT INEVITABLE.
THOUGH THE HOUND NEED TO FEED, SO TOO DO THE CREATURES WHO'VE BEEN OPPRESSED FOR SO LON
BECAUSE THIS *SAVI* MUST PAS

THE QUEST OF THEIR LORD MUST CONTINUE.

HE CAN'T FAIL, NOT NOW, HE'S GONE TOO FAR.

AND THERE'S STILL TOO MUCH AT STAKE.

REGARDLESS OF WHO OR WHAT MAY WANT HIM STOPPED.

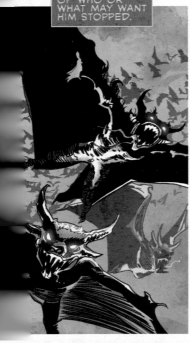

HE BRACES AS THE SOUND OF FLAPPING WINGS GROW LOUDER.

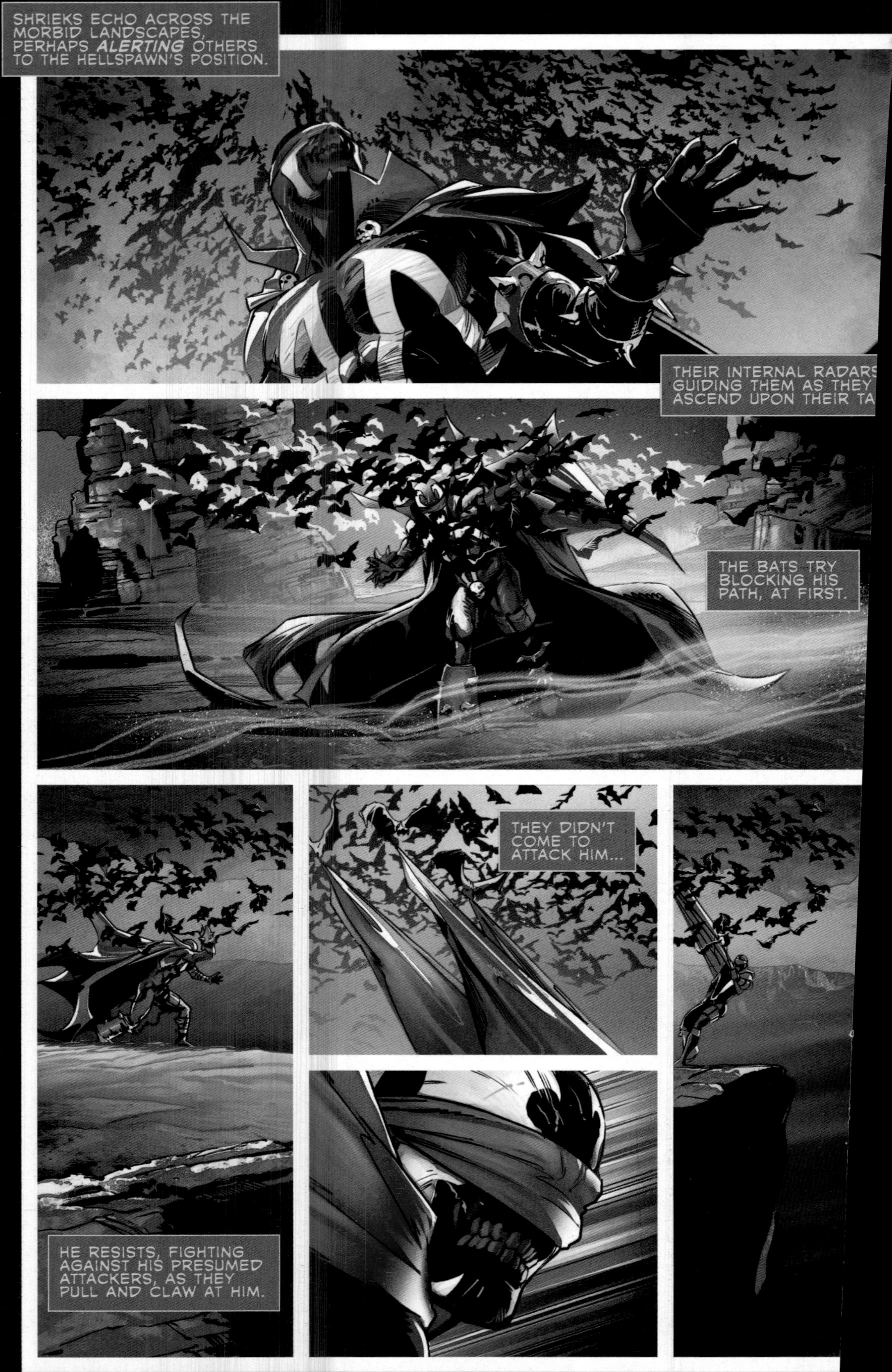
SHRIEKS ECHO ACROSS THE MORBID LANDSCAPES, PERHAPS *ALERTING* OTHERS TO THE HELLSPAWN'S POSITION.
THEIR INTERNAL RADARS GUIDING THEM AS THEY ASCEND UPON THEIR TA
THE BATS TRY BLOCKING HIS PATH, AT FIRST.
HE RESISTS, FIGHTING AGAINST HIS PRESUMED ATTACKERS, AS THEY PULL AND CLAW AT HIM.
THEY DIDN'T COME TO ATTACK HIM...

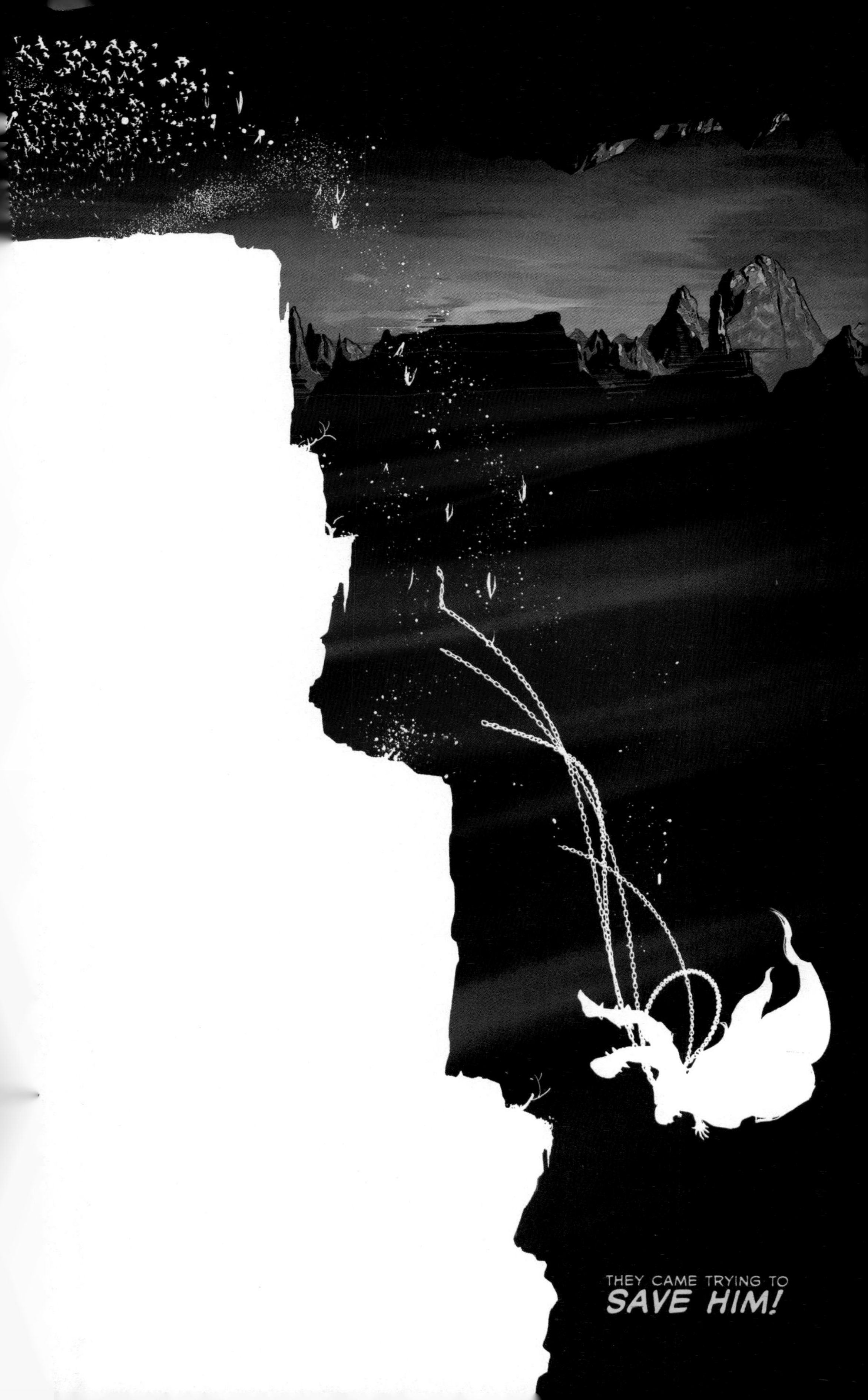
THEY CAME TRYING TO
SAVE HIM!

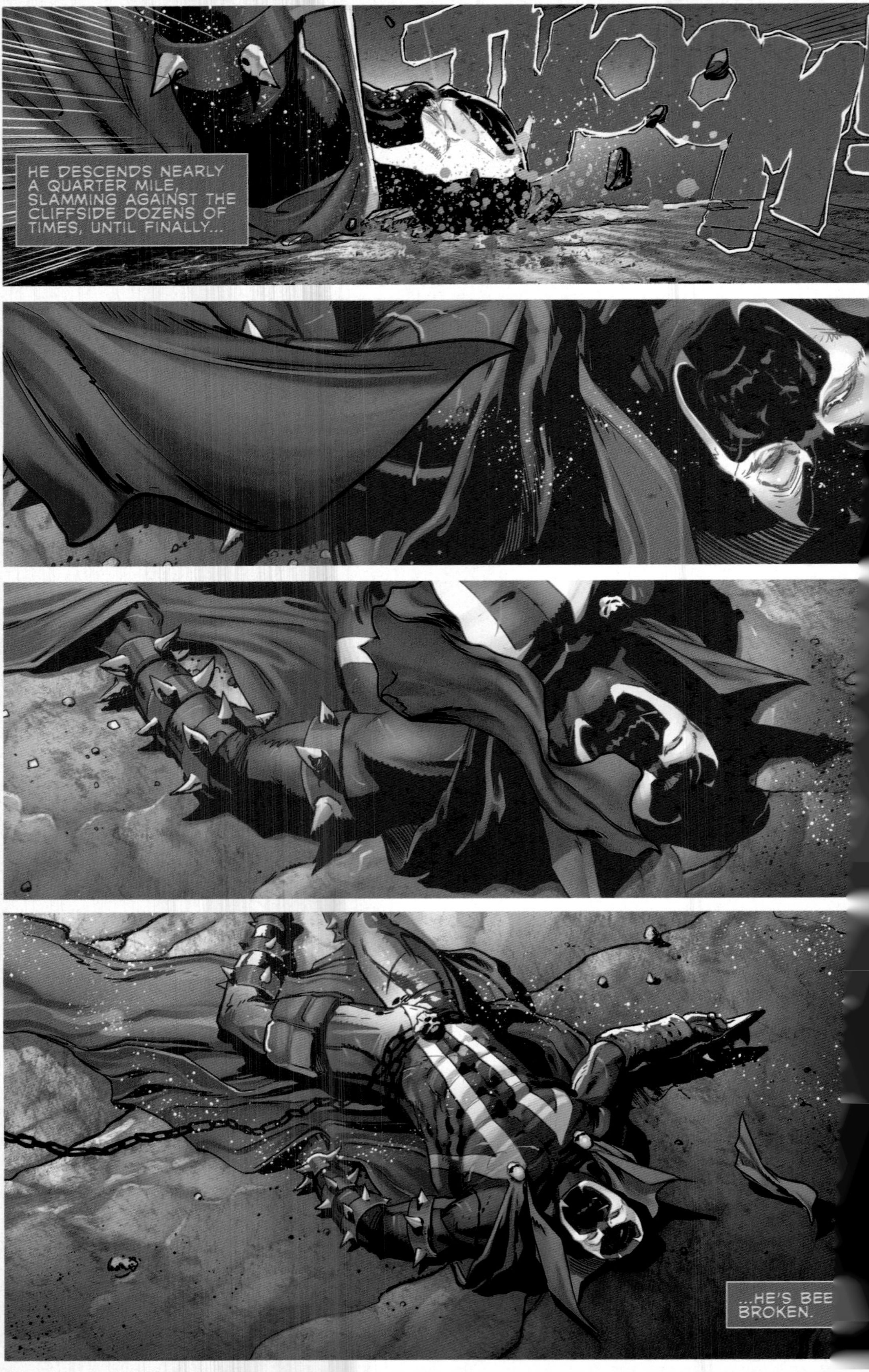
HE DESCENDS NEARLY A QUARTER MILE, SLAMMING AGAINST THE CLIFFSIDE DOZENS OF TIMES, UNTIL FINALLY...
THOOM!
...HE'S BEE
BROKEN.

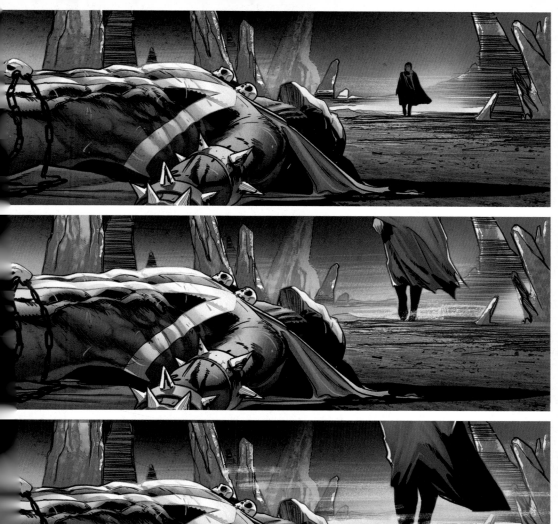
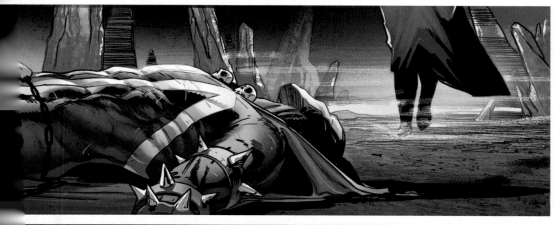

rest well.

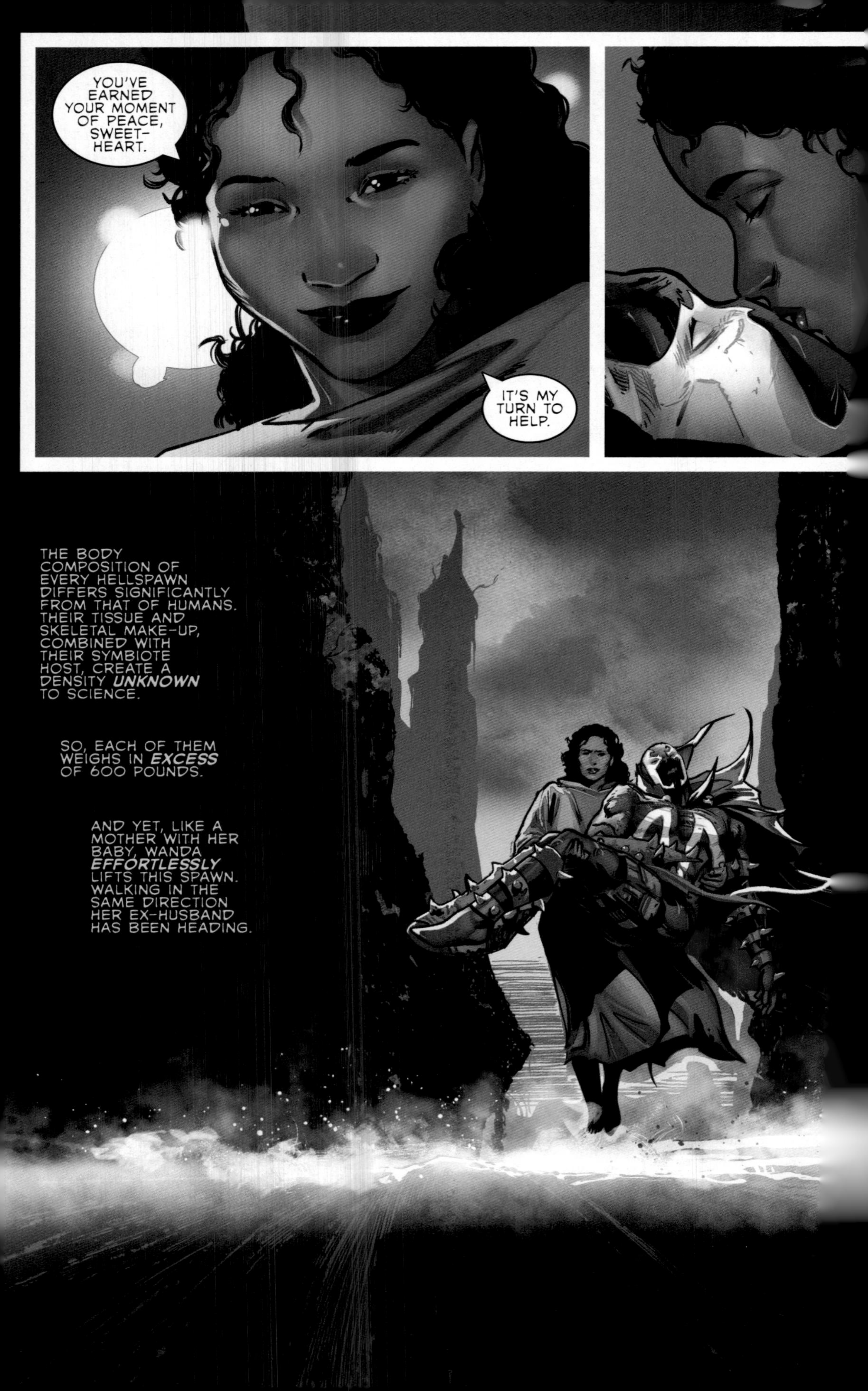
YOU'VE EARNED YOUR MOMENT OF PEACE, SWEET-HEART.
IT'S MY TURN TO HELP.
THE BODY COMPOSITION OF EVERY HELLSPAWN DIFFERS SIGNIFICANTLY FROM THAT OF HUMANS. THEIR TISSUE AND SKELETAL MAKE-UP, COMBINED WITH THEIR SYMBIOTE HOST, CREATE A DENSITY ***UNKNOWN*** TO SCIENCE.
SO, EACH OF THEM WEIGHS IN ***EXCESS*** OF 600 POUNDS.
AND YET, LIKE A MOTHER WITH HER BABY, WANDA ***EFFORTLESSLY*** LIFTS THIS SPAWN. WALKING IN THE SAME DIRECTION HER EX-HUSBAND HAS BEEN HEADING.

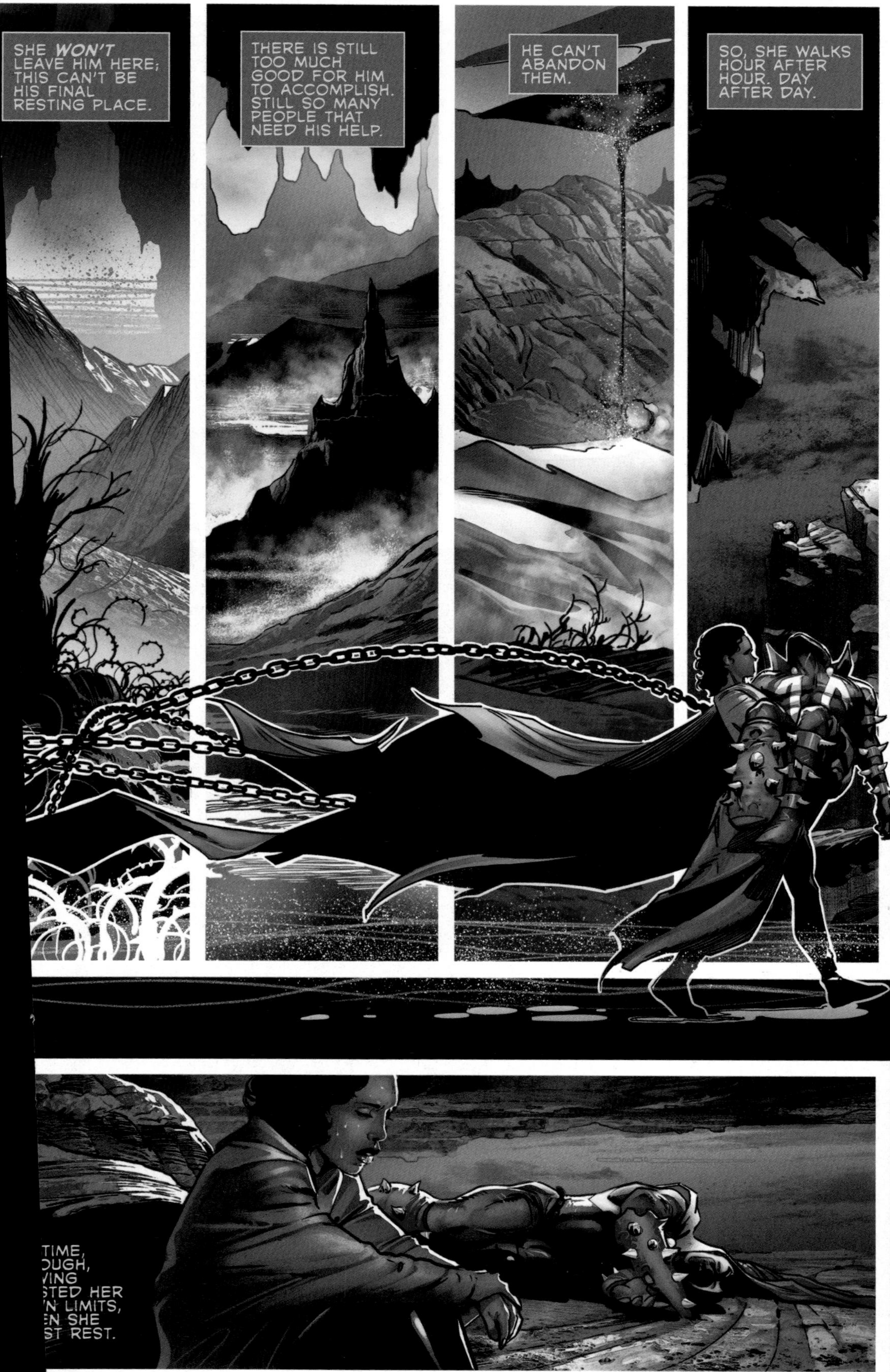

SHE *WON'T* LEAVE HIM HERE; THIS CAN'T BE HIS FINAL RESTING PLACE.
THERE IS STILL TOO MUCH GOOD FOR HIM TO ACCOMPLISH. STILL SO MANY PEOPLE THAT NEED HIS HELP.
HE CAN'T ABANDON THEM.
SO, SHE WALKS HOUR AFTER HOUR. DAY AFTER DAY.
TIME, OUGH, VING STED HER N LIMITS, EN SHE ST REST.

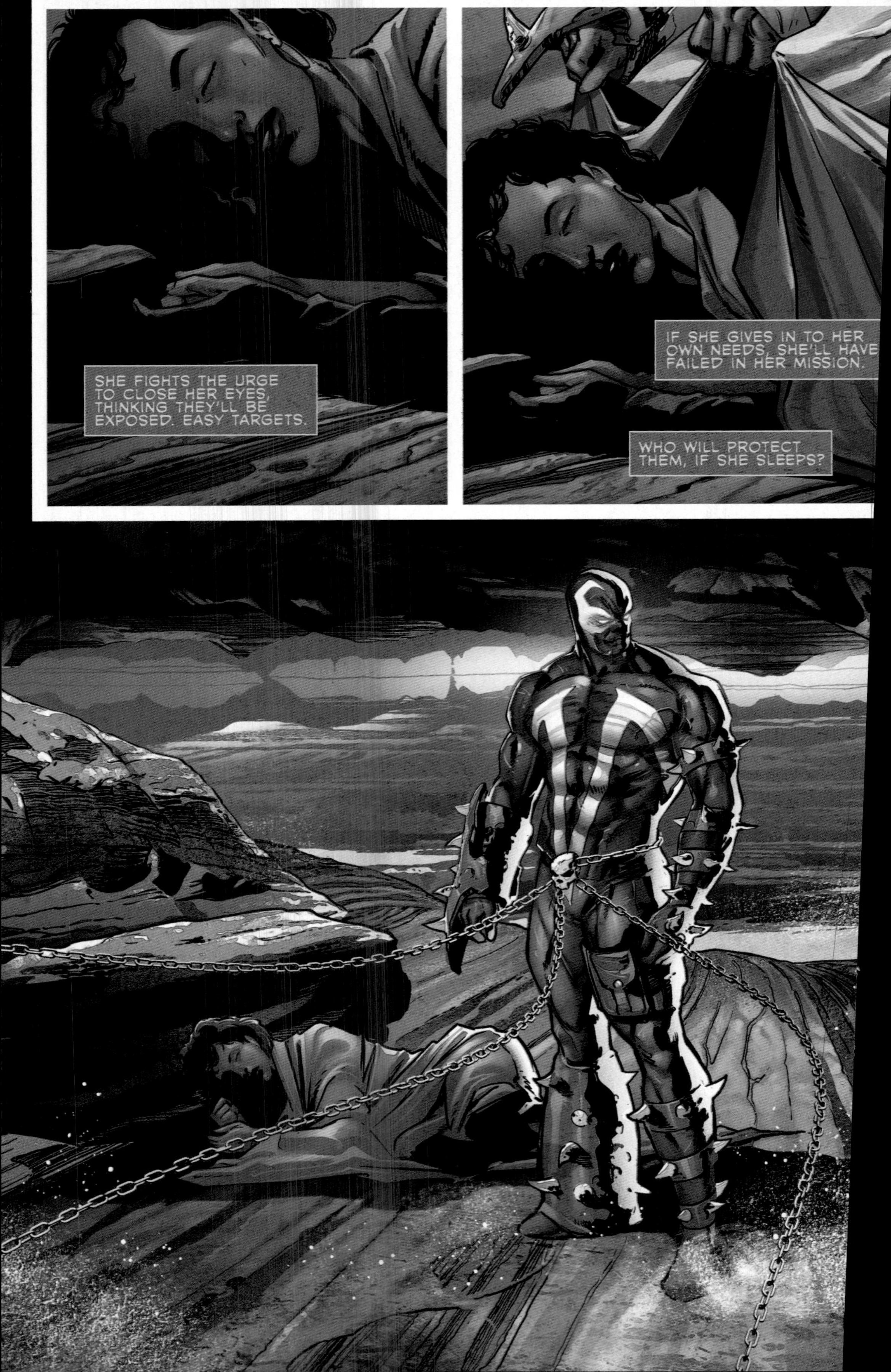
SHE FIGHTS THE URGE TO CLOSE HER EYES, THINKING THEY'LL BE EXPOSED. EASY TARGETS.
IF SHE GIVES IN TO HER OWN NEEDS, SHE'LL HAVE FAILED IN HER MISSION.
WHO WILL PROTECT THEM, IF SHE SLEEPS?

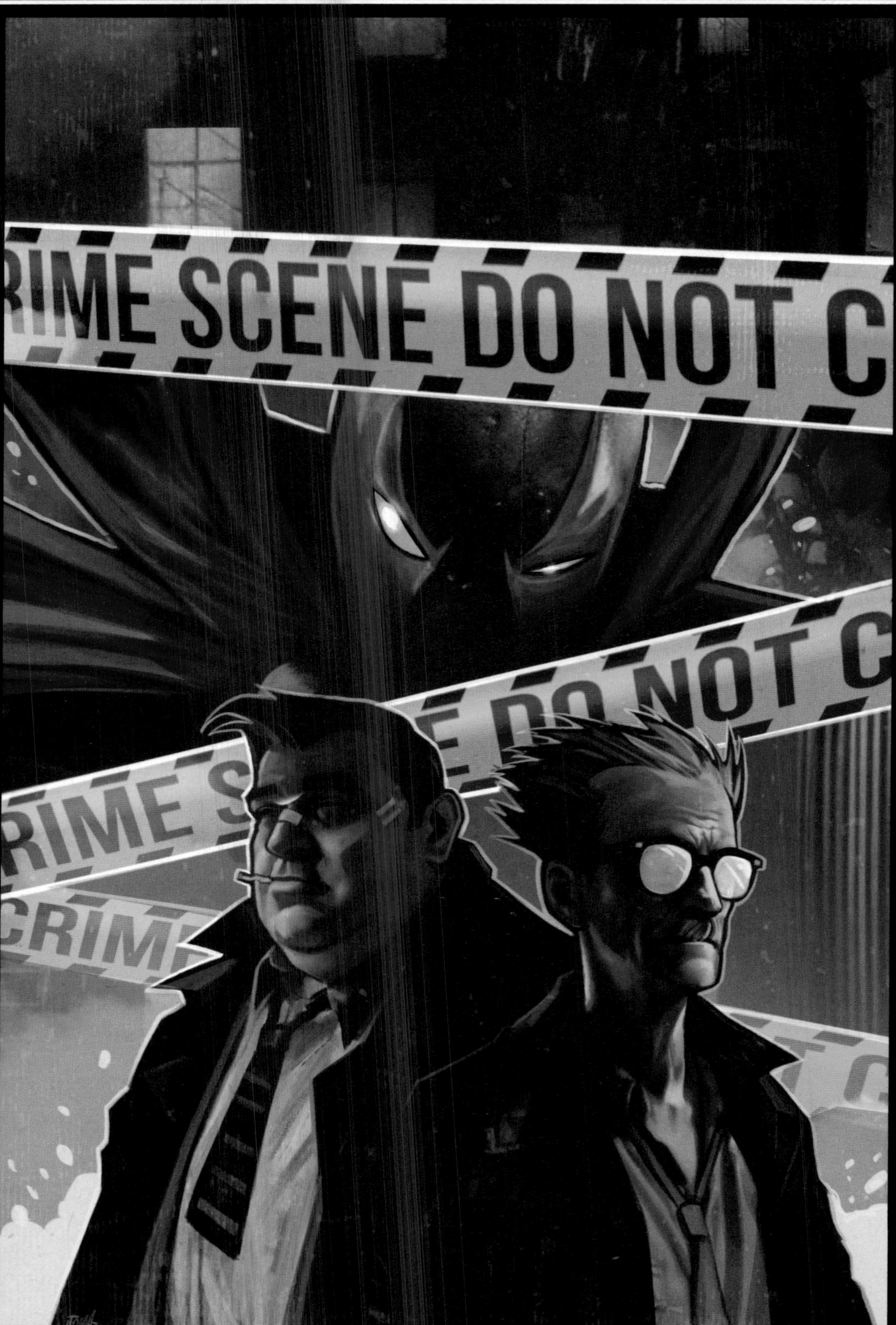
RIME SCENE DO NOT C
RIME S
E DO NOT C
CRIM
T C

King Spawn #30

Cover by Francesco Tomaselli

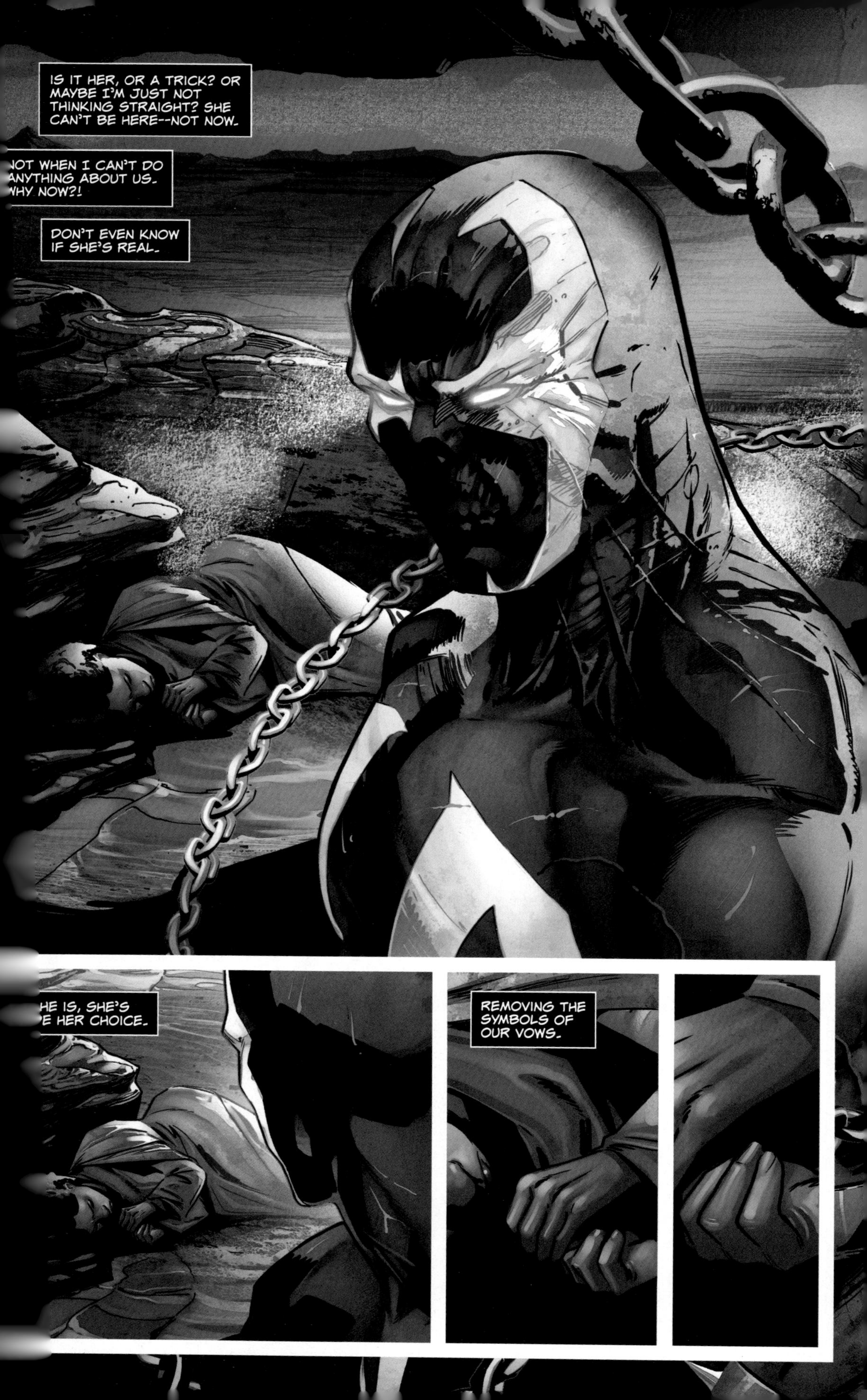
IS IT HER, OR A TRICK? OR MAYBE I'M JUST NOT THINKING STRAIGHT? SHE CAN'T BE HERE--NOT NOW.
NOT WHEN I CAN'T DO ANYTHING ABOUT US. WHY NOW?!
DON'T EVEN KNOW IF SHE'S REAL.
HE IS, SHE'S E HER CHOICE.
REMOVING THE SYMBOLS OF OUR VOWS.

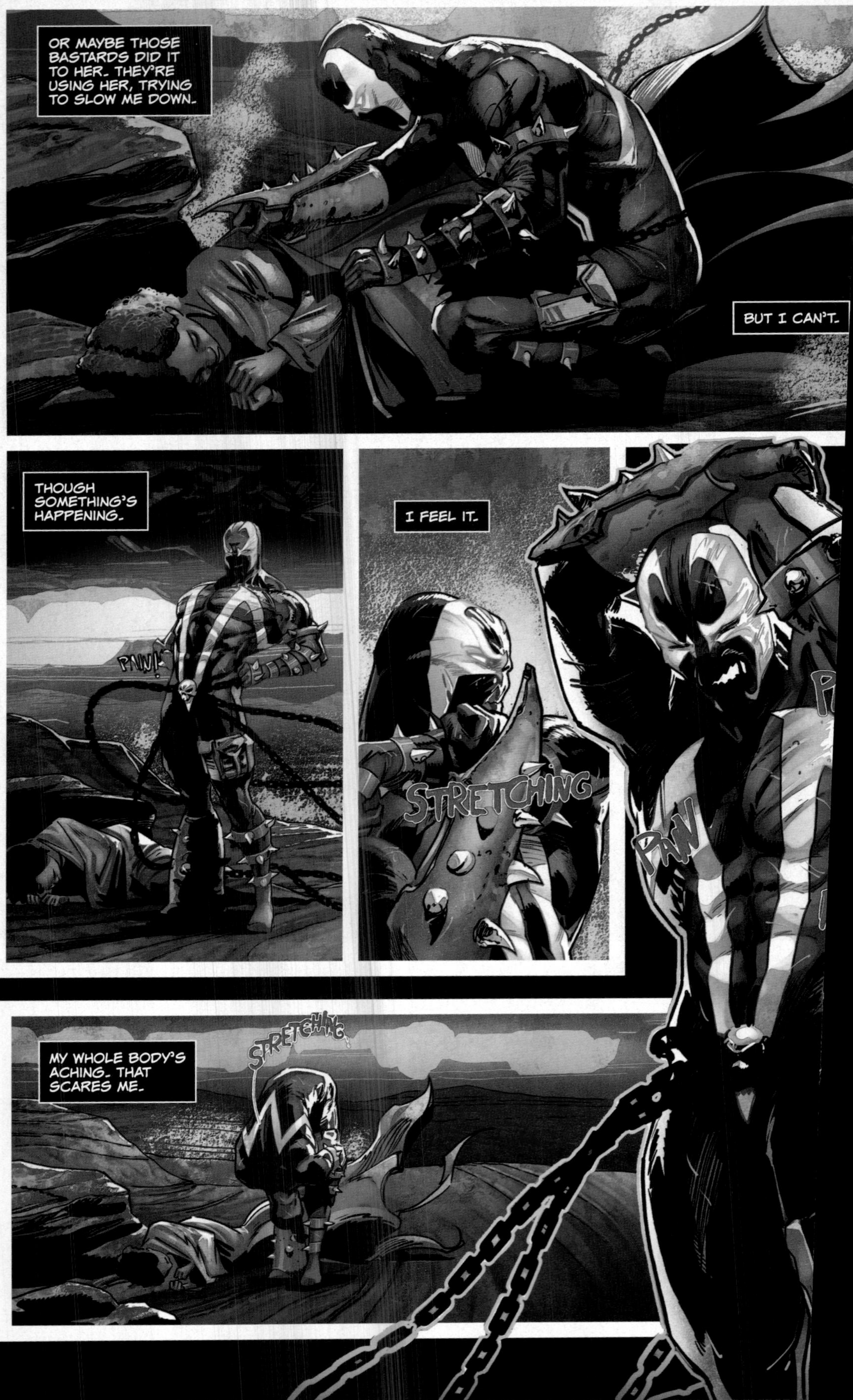

OR MAYBE THOSE BASTARDS DID IT TO HER. THEY'RE USING HER, TRYING TO SLOW ME DOWN.
BUT I CAN'T.
THOUGH SOMETHING'S HAPPENING.
PAIN!
I FEEL IT.
STRETCHING
PAIN
MY WHOLE BODY'S ACHING. THAT SCARES ME.
STRETCHING

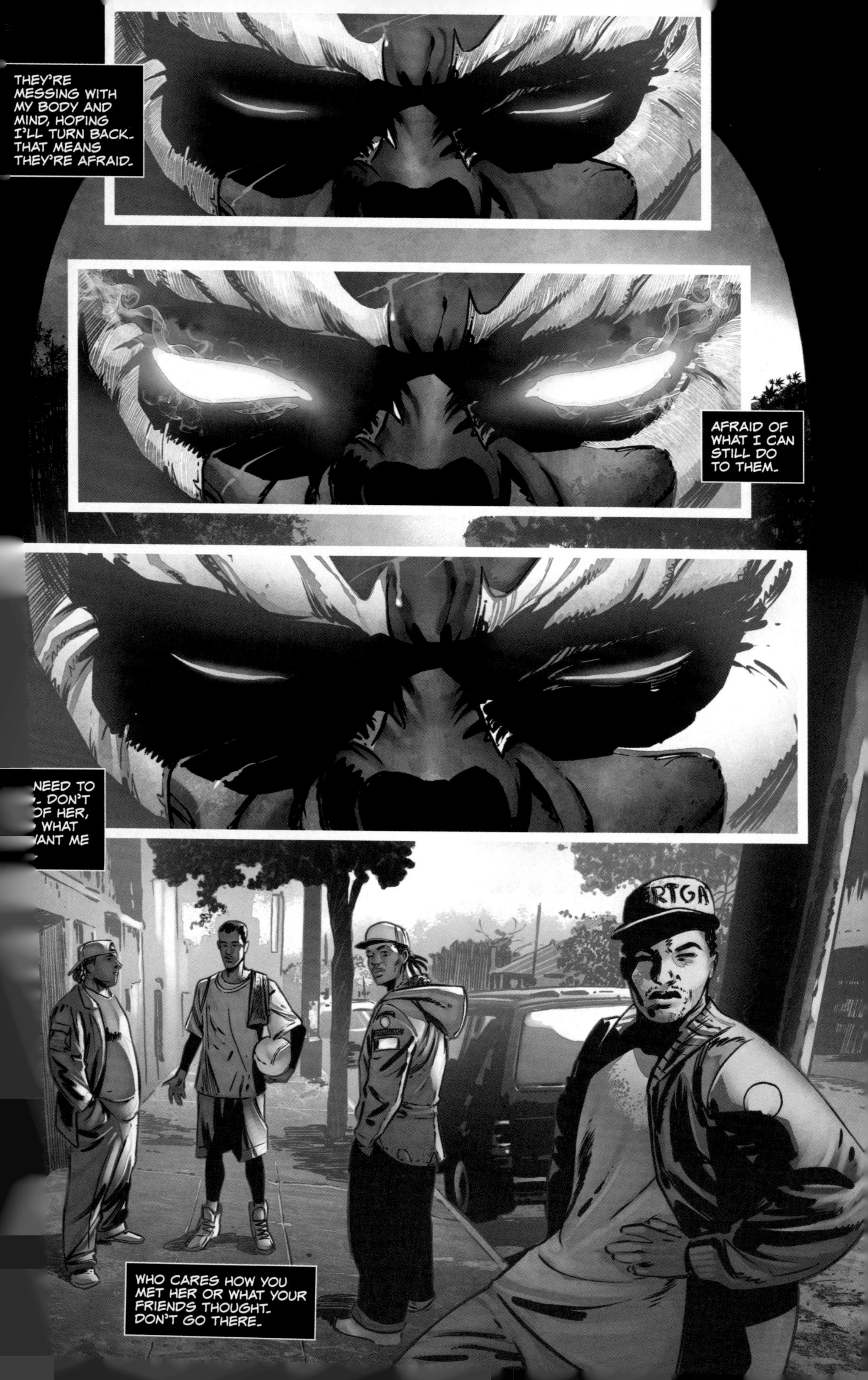
THEY'RE MESSING WITH MY BODY AND MIND, HOPING I'LL TURN BACK. THAT MEANS THEY'RE AFRAID.
AFRAID OF WHAT I CAN STILL DO TO THEM.
NEED TO . DON'T OF HER, WHAT ANT ME
RTGA
WHO CARES HOW YOU MET HER OR WHAT YOUR FRIENDS THOUGHT. DON'T GO THERE.

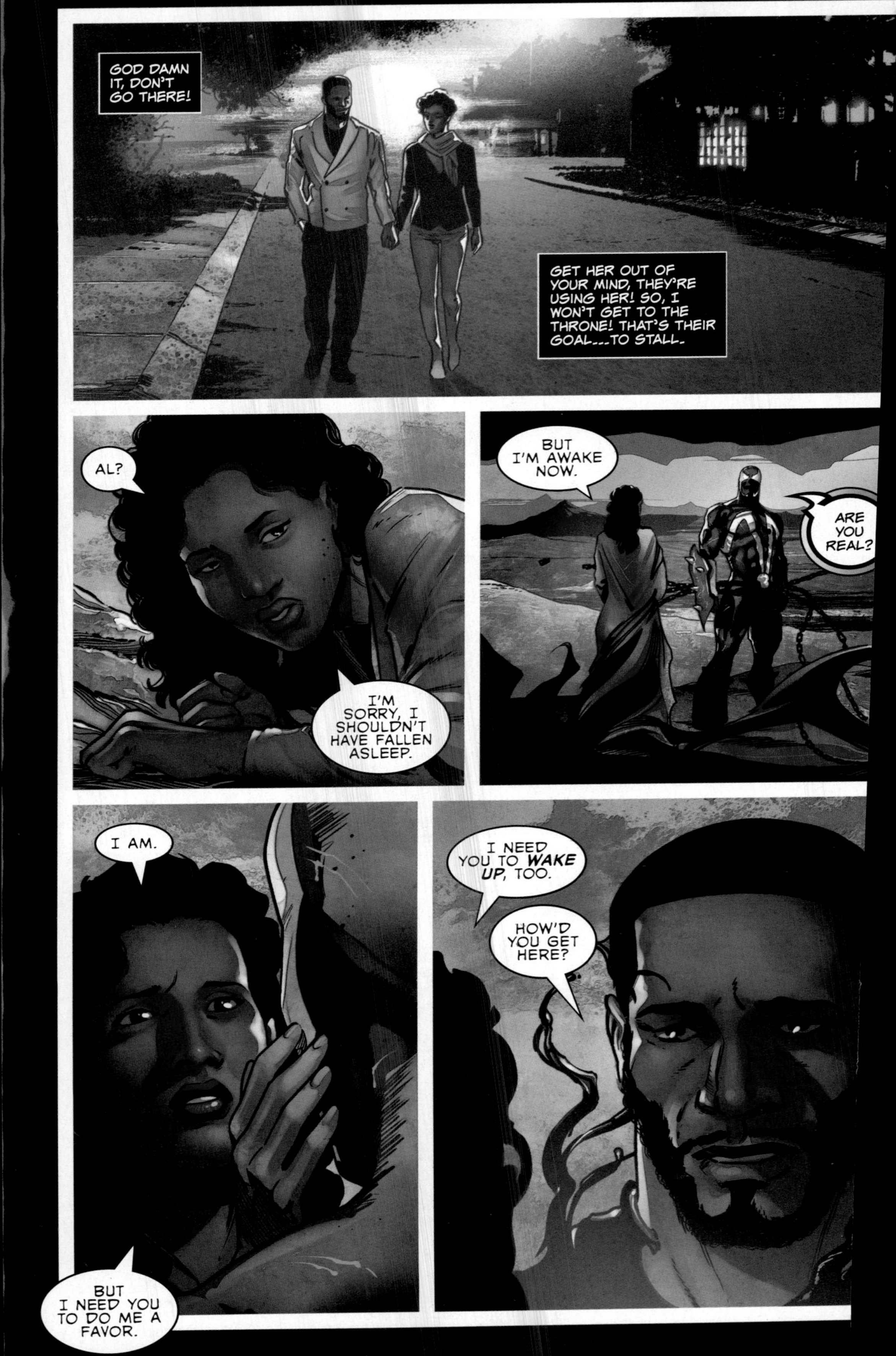
GOD DAMN IT, DON'T GO THERE!
GET HER OUT OF YOUR MIND, THEY'RE USING HER! SO, I WON'T GET TO THE THRONE! THAT'S THEIR GOAL...TO STALL.
AL?
I'M SORRY, I SHOULDN'T HAVE FALLEN ASLEEP.
BUT I'M AWAKE NOW.
ARE YOU REAL?
I AM.
BUT I NEED YOU TO DO ME A FAVOR.
I NEED YOU TO ***WAKE UP***, TOO.
HOW'D YOU GET HERE?

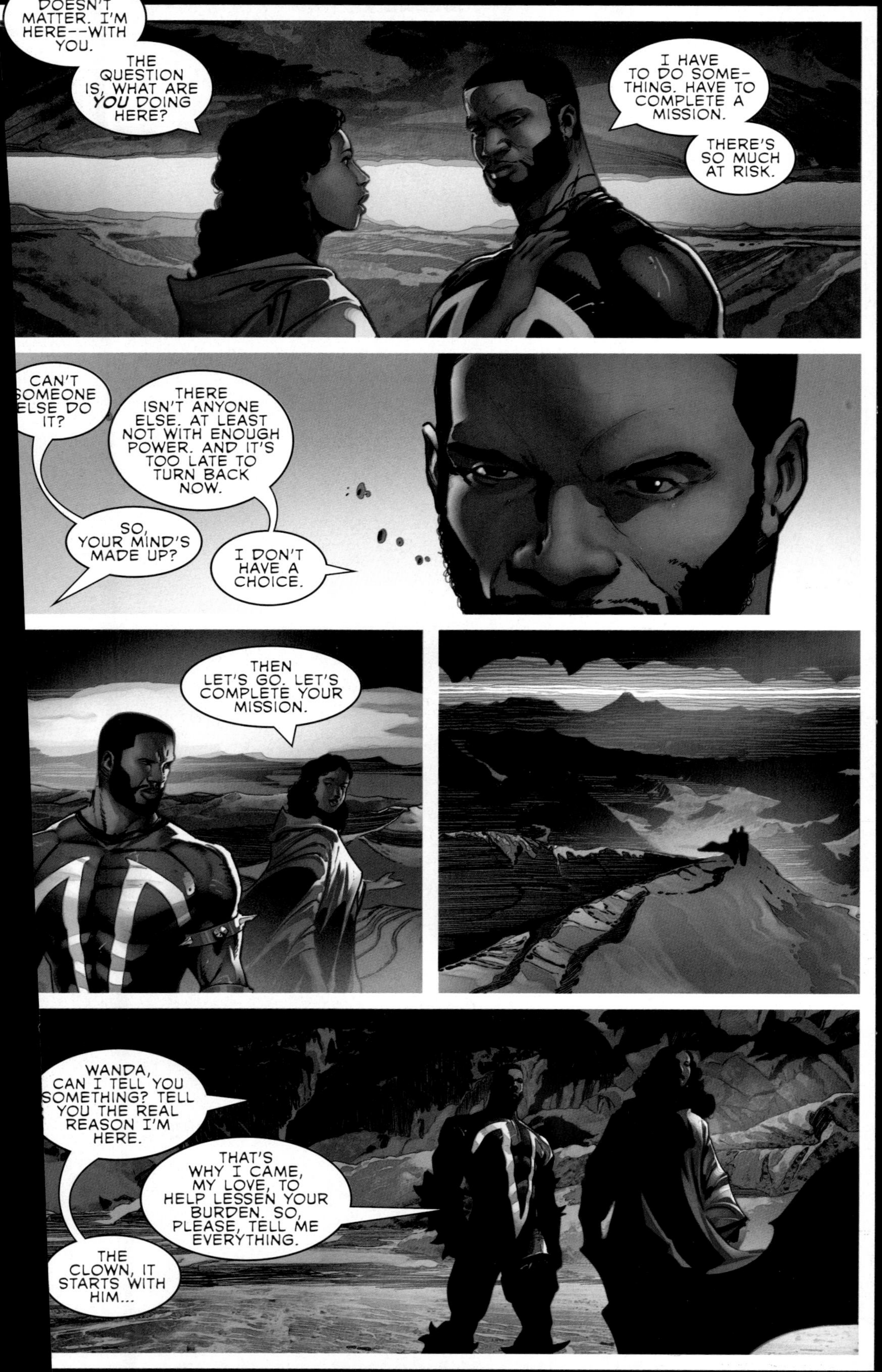
IT DOESN'T MATTER. I'M HERE--WITH YOU.
THE QUESTION IS, WHAT ARE *YOU* DOING HERE?
I HAVE TO DO SOME-THING. HAVE TO COMPLETE A MISSION.
THERE'S SO MUCH AT RISK.
CAN'T SOMEONE ELSE DO IT?
THERE ISN'T ANYONE ELSE. AT LEAST NOT WITH ENOUGH POWER. AND IT'S TOO LATE TO TURN BACK NOW.
SO, YOUR MIND'S MADE UP?
I DON'T HAVE A CHOICE.
THEN LET'S GO. LET'S COMPLETE YOUR MISSION.
WANDA, CAN I TELL YOU SOMETHING? TELL YOU THE REAL REASON I'M HERE.
THAT'S WHY I CAME, MY LOVE, TO HELP LESSEN YOUR BURDEN. SO, PLEASE, TELL ME EVERYTHING.
THE CLOWN, IT STARTS WITH HIM...

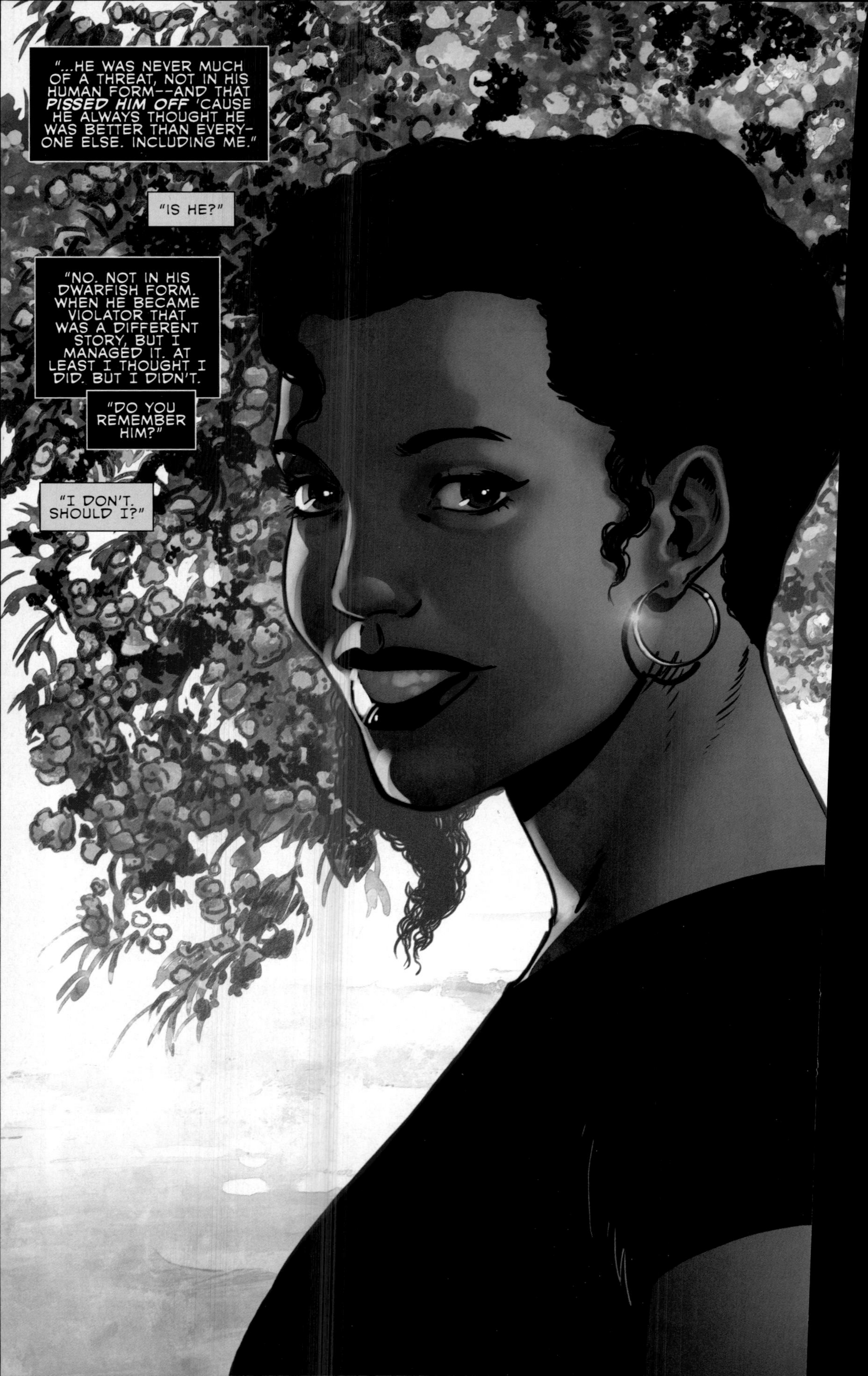
"...HE WAS NEVER MUCH OF A THREAT, NOT IN HIS HUMAN FORM--AND THAT PISSED HIM OFF 'CAUSE HE ALWAYS THOUGHT HE WAS BETTER THAN EVERY-ONE ELSE. INCLUDING ME."
"IS HE?"
"NO. NOT IN HIS DWARFISH FORM. WHEN HE BECAME VIOLATOR THAT WAS A DIFFERENT STORY, BUT I MANAGED IT. AT LEAST I THOUGHT I DID. BUT I DIDN'T.
"DO YOU REMEMBER HIM?"
"I DON'T. SHOULD I?"

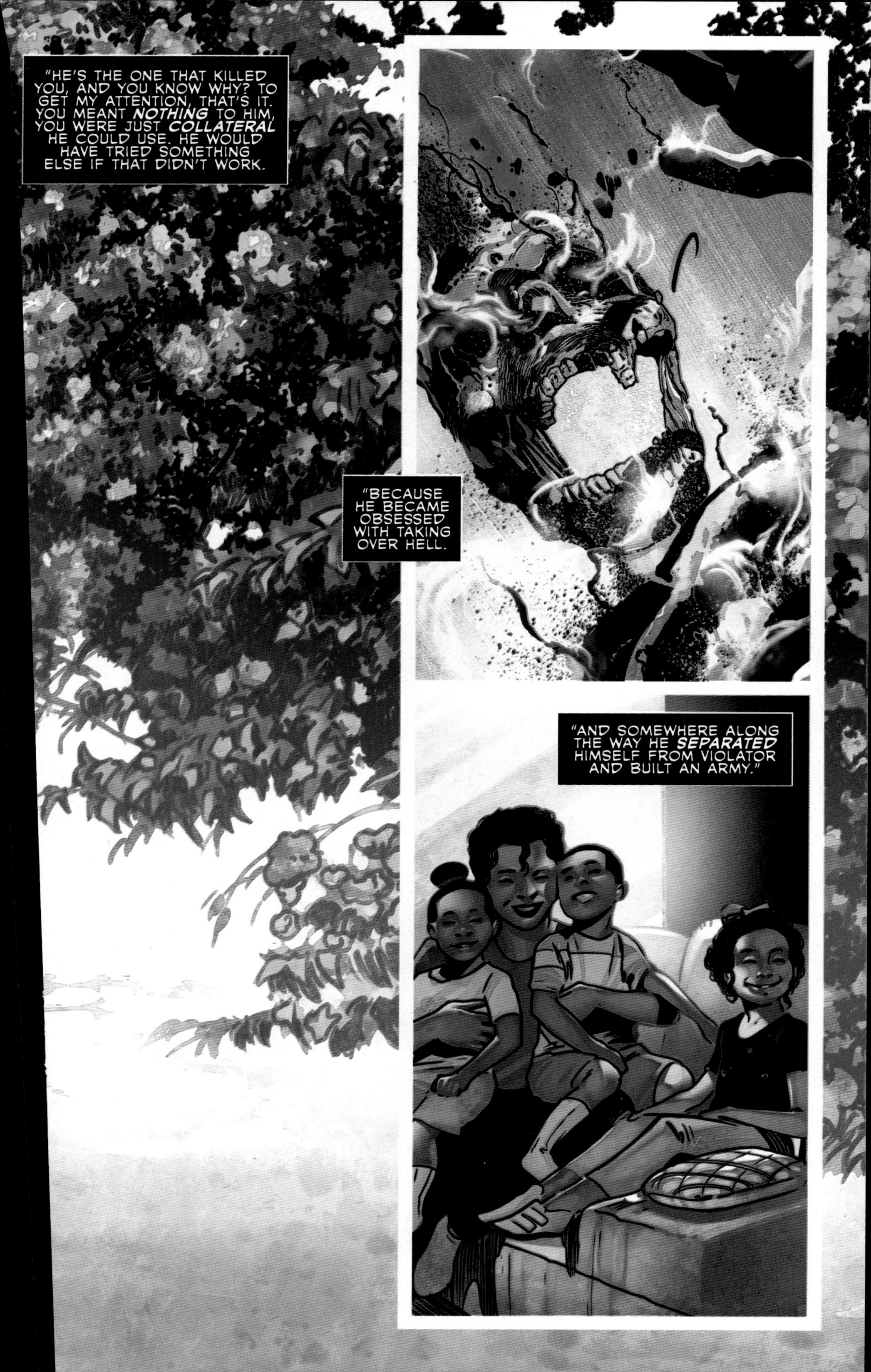
"HE'S THE ONE THAT KILLED YOU, AND YOU KNOW WHY? TO GET MY ATTENTION, THAT'S IT. YOU MEANT NOTHING TO HIM, YOU WERE JUST COLLATERAL HE COULD USE. HE WOULD HAVE TRIED SOMETHING ELSE IF THAT DIDN'T WORK.
"BECAUSE HE BECAME OBSESSED WITH TAKING OVER HELL.
"AND SOMEWHERE ALONG THE WAY HE SEPARATED HIMSELF FROM VIOLATOR AND BUILT AN ARMY."

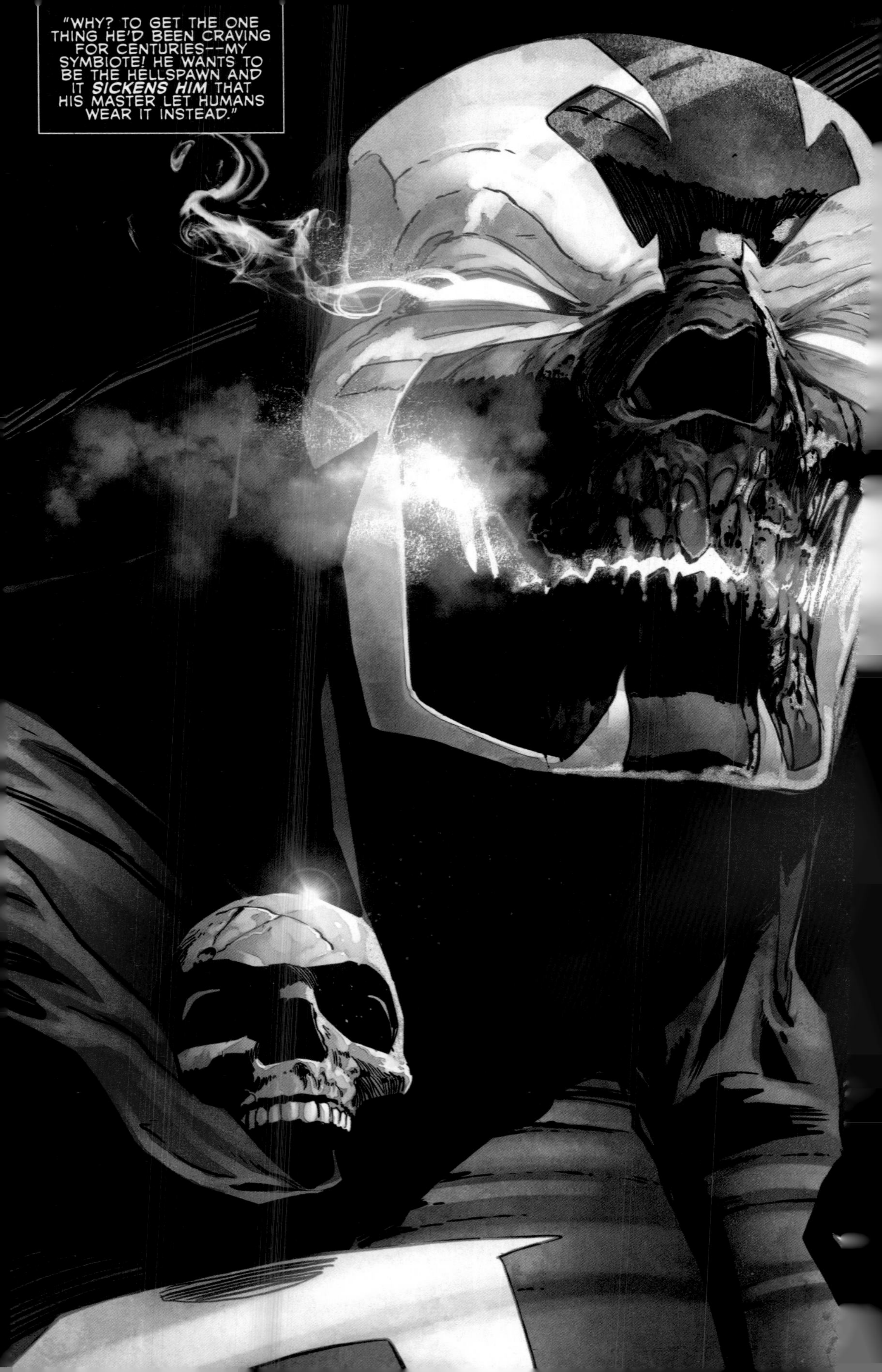
"WHY? TO GET THE ONE THING HE'D BEEN CRAVING FOR CENTURIES--MY SYMBIOTE! HE WANTS TO BE THE HELLSPAWN AND IT *SICKENS HIM* THAT HIS MASTER LET HUMANS WEAR IT INSTEAD."

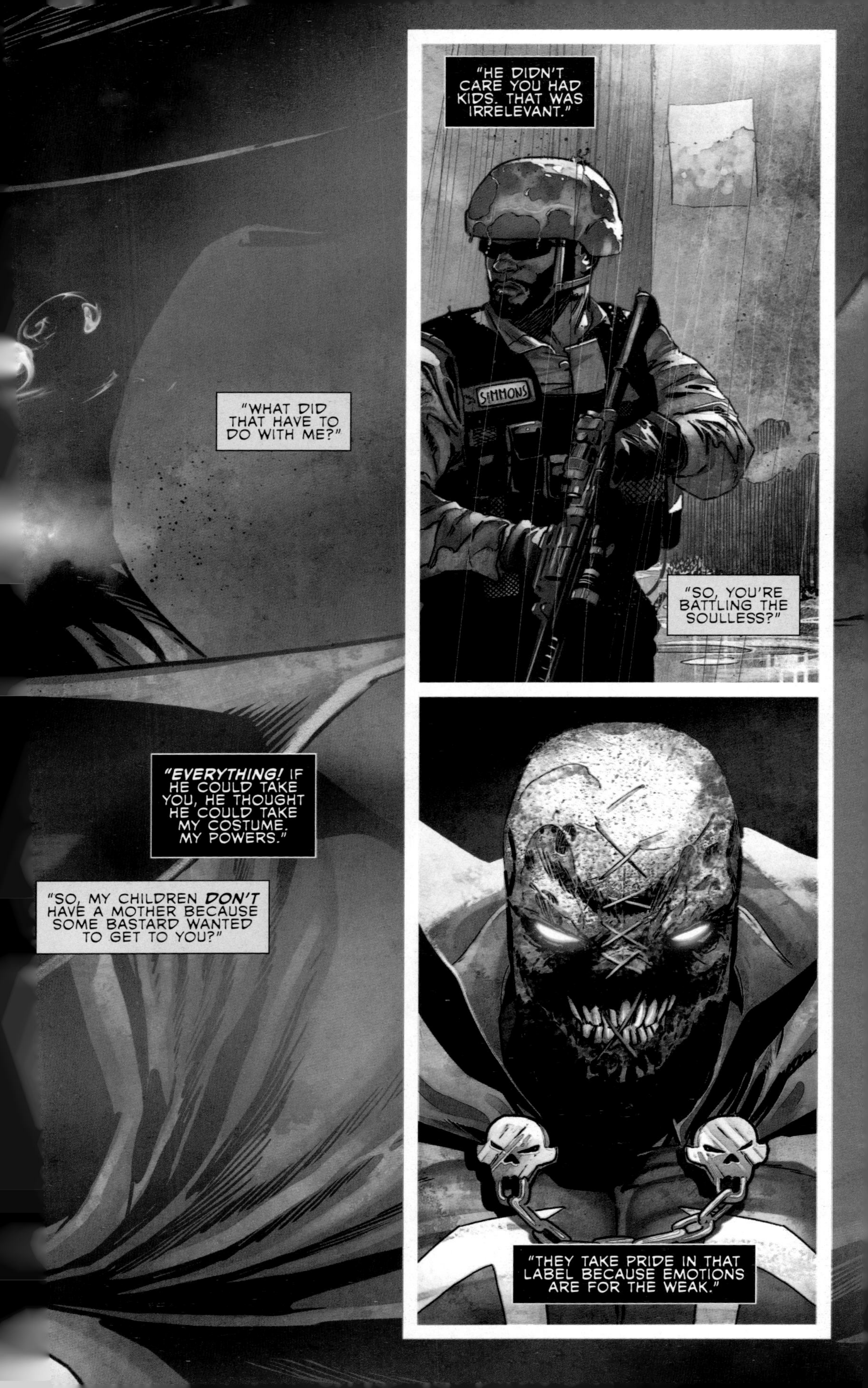
"WHAT DID THAT HAVE TO DO WITH ME?"
"HE DIDN'T CARE YOU HAD KIDS. THAT WAS IRRELEVANT."
SIMMONS
"SO, YOU'RE BATTLING THE SOULLESS?"
"EVERYTHING! IF HE COULD TAKE YOU, HE THOUGHT HE COULD TAKE MY COSTUME. MY POWERS."
"SO, MY CHILDREN DON'T HAVE A MOTHER BECAUSE SOME BASTARD WANTED TO GET TO YOU?"
"THEY TAKE PRIDE IN THAT LABEL BECAUSE EMOTIONS ARE FOR THE WEAK."

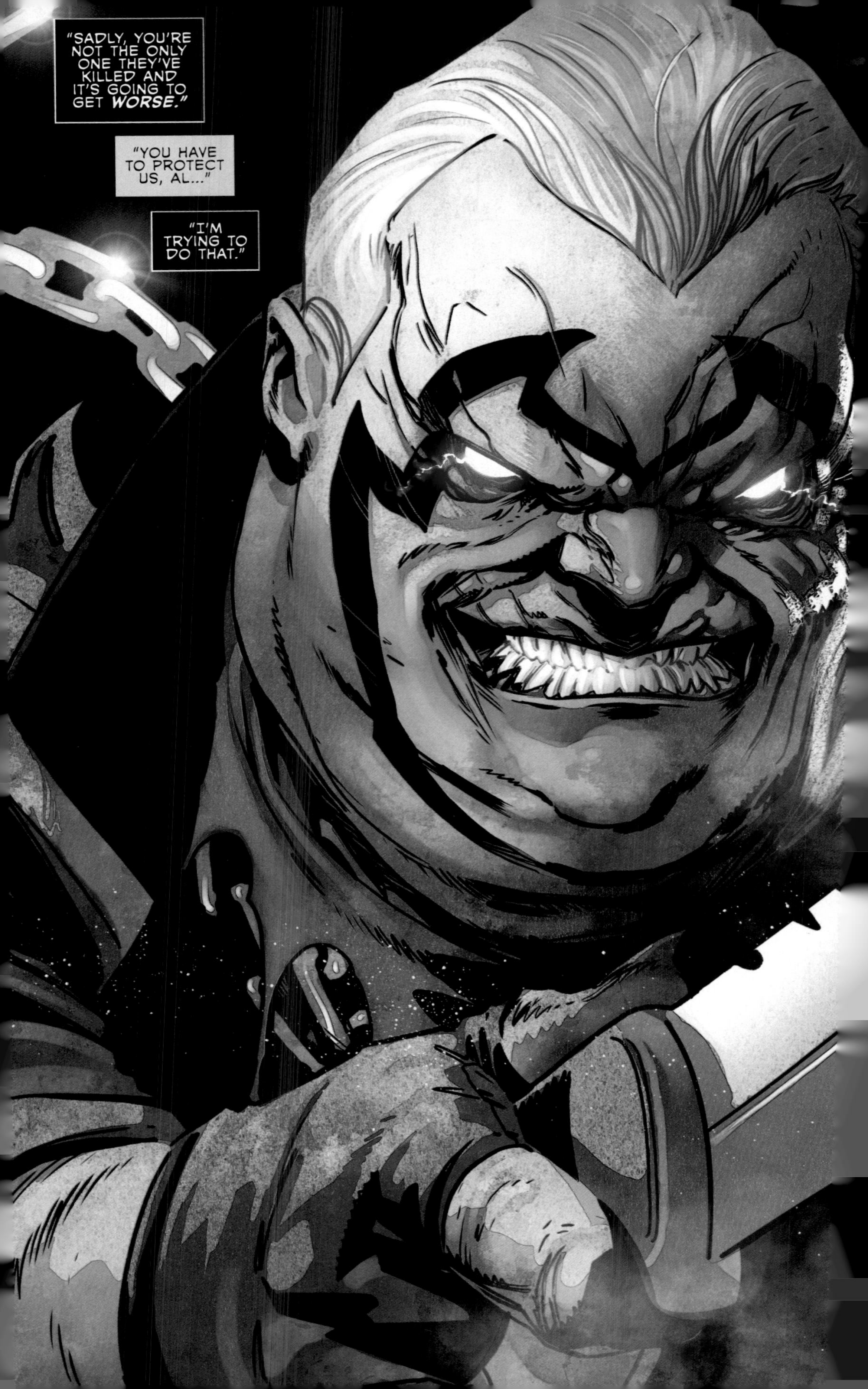
"SADLY, YOU'RE NOT THE ONLY ONE THEY'VE KILLED AND IT'S GOING TO GET *WORSE.*"
"YOU HAVE TO PROTECT US, AL..."
"I'M TRYING TO DO THAT."

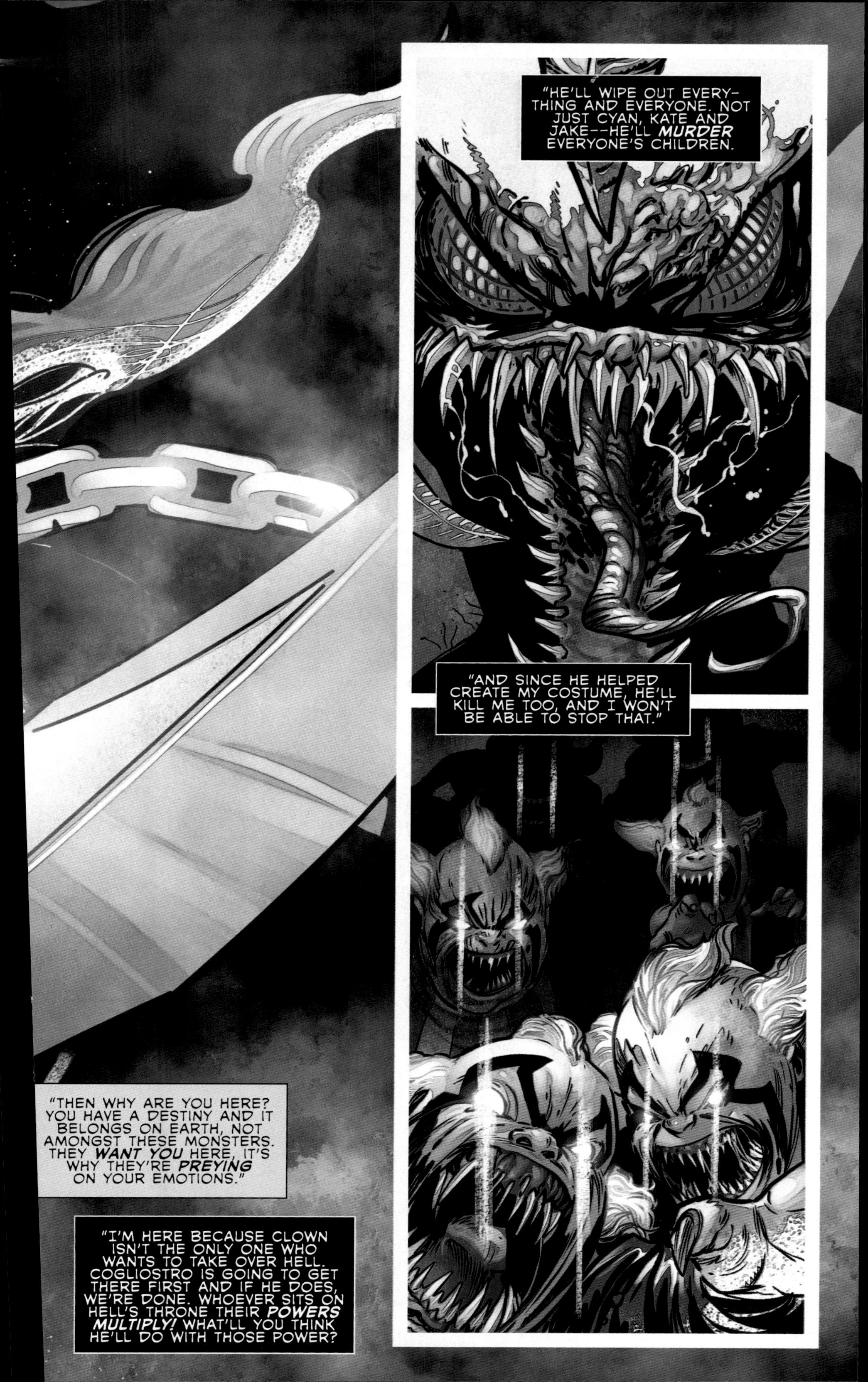
"HE'LL WIPE OUT EVERYTHING AND EVERYONE. NOT JUST CYAN, KATE AND JAKE--HE'LL MURDER EVERYONE'S CHILDREN.
"AND SINCE HE HELPED CREATE MY COSTUME, HE'LL KILL ME TOO, AND I WON'T BE ABLE TO STOP THAT."
"THEN WHY ARE YOU HERE? YOU HAVE A DESTINY AND IT BELONGS ON EARTH, NOT AMONGST THESE MONSTERS. THEY WANT YOU HERE, IT'S WHY THEY'RE PREYING ON YOUR EMOTIONS."
"I'M HERE BECAUSE CLOWN ISN'T THE ONLY ONE WHO WANTS TO TAKE OVER HELL. COGLIOSTRO IS GOING TO GET THERE FIRST AND IF HE DOES, WE'RE DONE. WHOEVER SITS ON HELL'S THRONE THEIR POWERS MULTIPLY! WHAT'LL YOU THINK HE'LL DO WITH THOSE POWER?

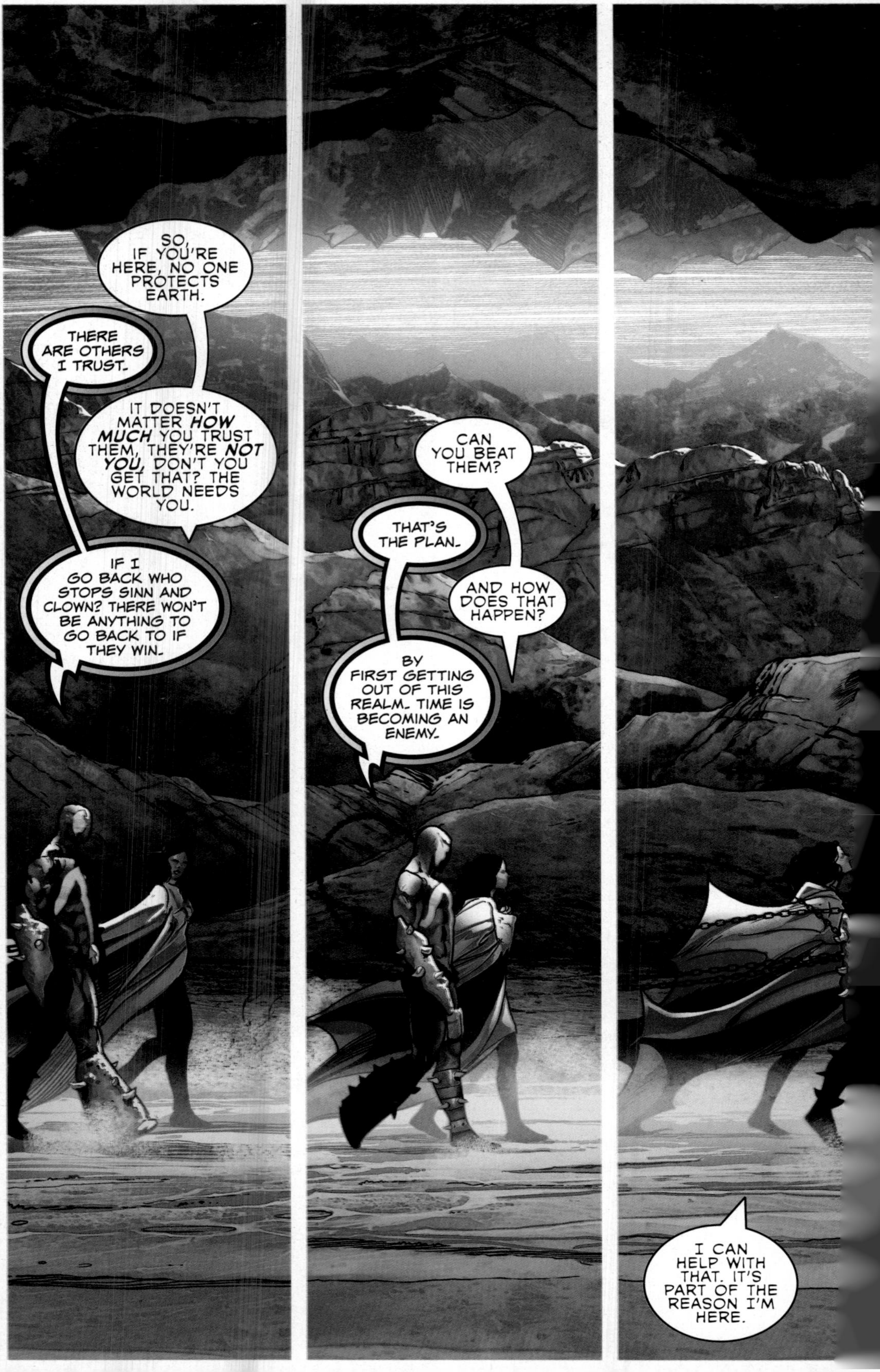

SO, IF YOU'RE HERE, NO ONE PROTECTS EARTH.
THERE ARE OTHERS I TRUST.
IT DOESN'T MATTER ***HOW MUCH*** YOU TRUST THEM, THEY'RE ***NOT YOU,*** DON'T YOU GET THAT? THE WORLD NEEDS YOU.
IF I GO BACK WHO STOPS SINN AND CLOWN? THERE WON'T BE ANYTHING TO GO BACK TO IF THEY WIN.
CAN YOU BEAT THEM?
THAT'S THE PLAN.
AND HOW DOES THAT HAPPEN?
BY FIRST GETTING OUT OF THIS REALM. TIME IS BECOMING AN ENEMY.
I CAN HELP WITH THAT. IT'S PART OF THE REASON I'M HERE.

CAN I ASK YOU SOME- THING?

SURE.

DO YOU LOVE ME?

of course.

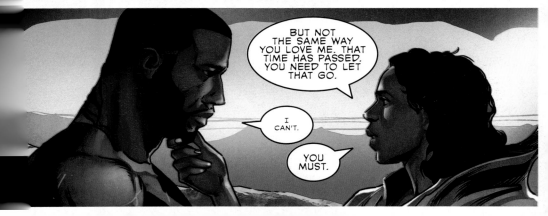

BUT NOT THE SAME WAY YOU LOVE ME. THAT TIME HAS PASSED. YOU NEED TO LET THAT GO.

I CAN'T.

YOU MUST.

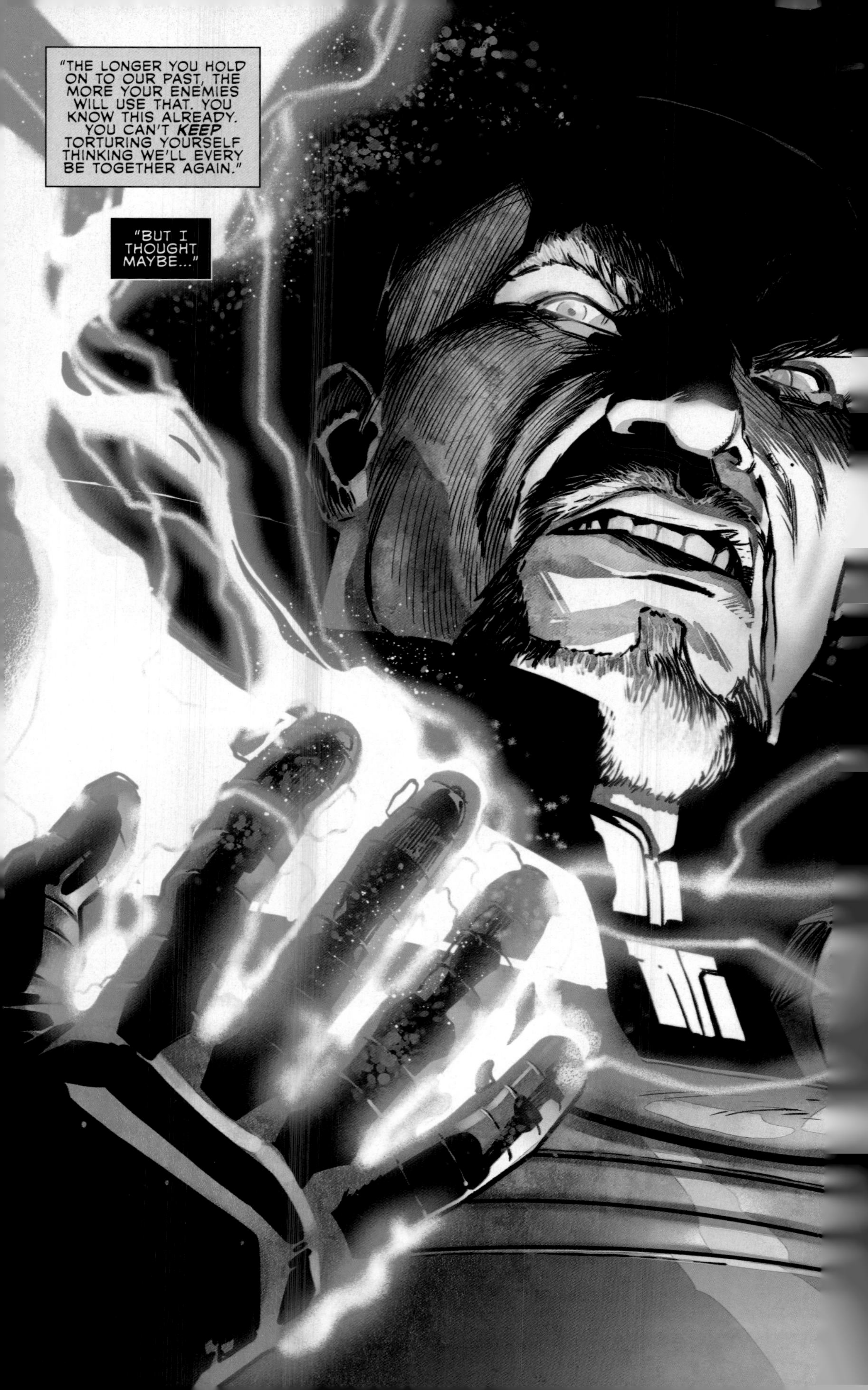
"THE LONGER YOU HOLD ON TO OUR PAST, THE MORE YOUR ENEMIES WILL USE THAT. YOU KNOW THIS ALREADY. YOU CAN'T *KEEP* TORTURING YOURSELF THINKING WE'LL EVERY BE TOGETHER AGAIN."
"BUT I THOUGHT MAYBE..."

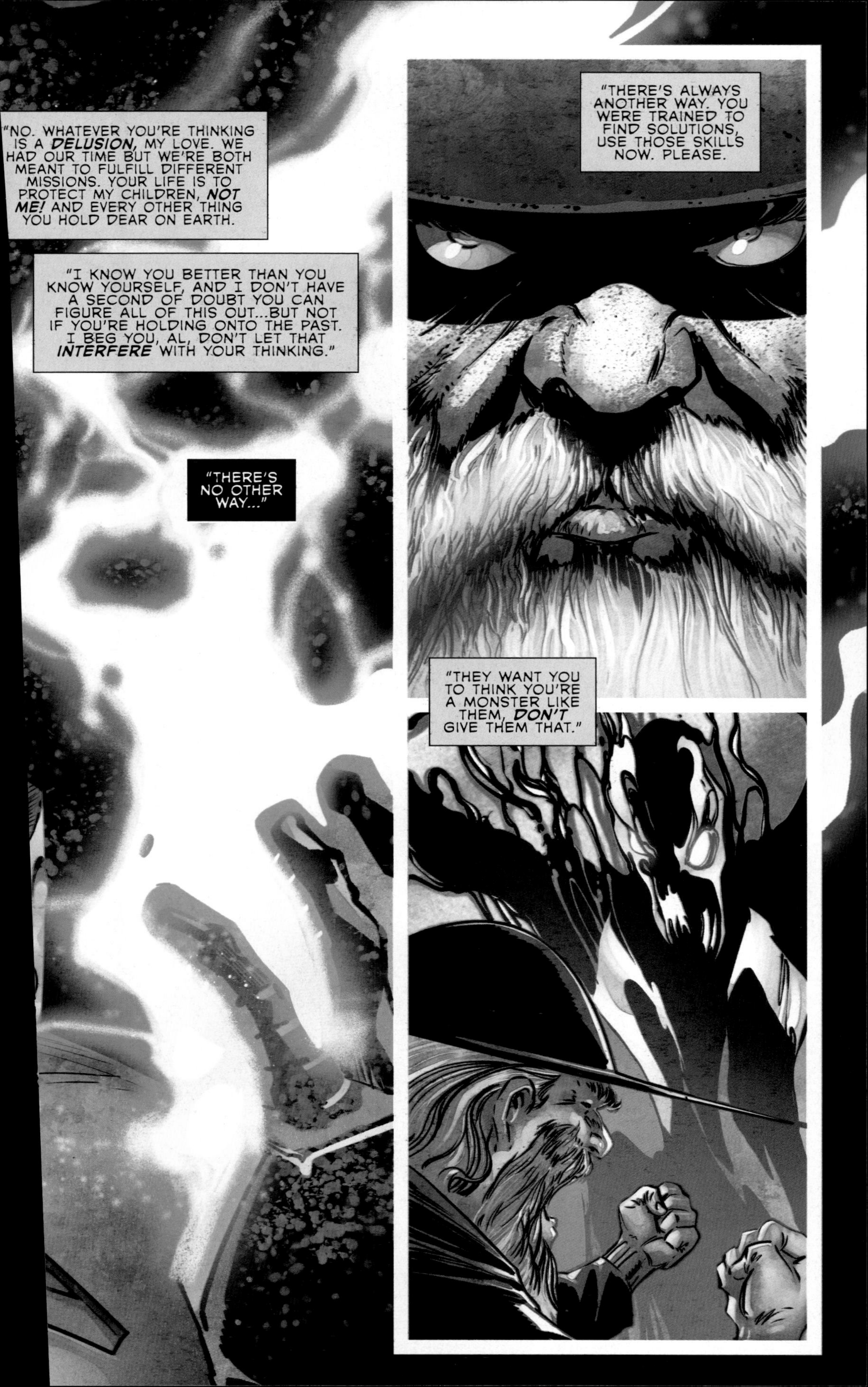
"NO. WHATEVER YOU'RE THINKING IS A DELUSION, MY LOVE. WE HAD OUR TIME BUT WE'RE BOTH MEANT TO FULFILL DIFFERENT MISSIONS. YOUR LIFE IS TO PROTECT MY CHILDREN, NOT ME! AND EVERY OTHER THING YOU HOLD DEAR ON EARTH.
"I KNOW YOU BETTER THAN YOU KNOW YOURSELF, AND I DON'T HAVE A SECOND OF DOUBT YOU CAN FIGURE ALL OF THIS OUT...BUT NOT IF YOU'RE HOLDING ONTO THE PAST. I BEG YOU, AL, DON'T LET THAT INTERFERE WITH YOUR THINKING."
"THERE'S NO OTHER WAY..."
"THERE'S ALWAYS ANOTHER WAY. YOU WERE TRAINED TO FIND SOLUTIONS, USE THOSE SKILLS NOW. PLEASE.
"THEY WANT YOU TO THINK YOU'RE A MONSTER LIKE THEM, DON'T GIVE THEM THAT."

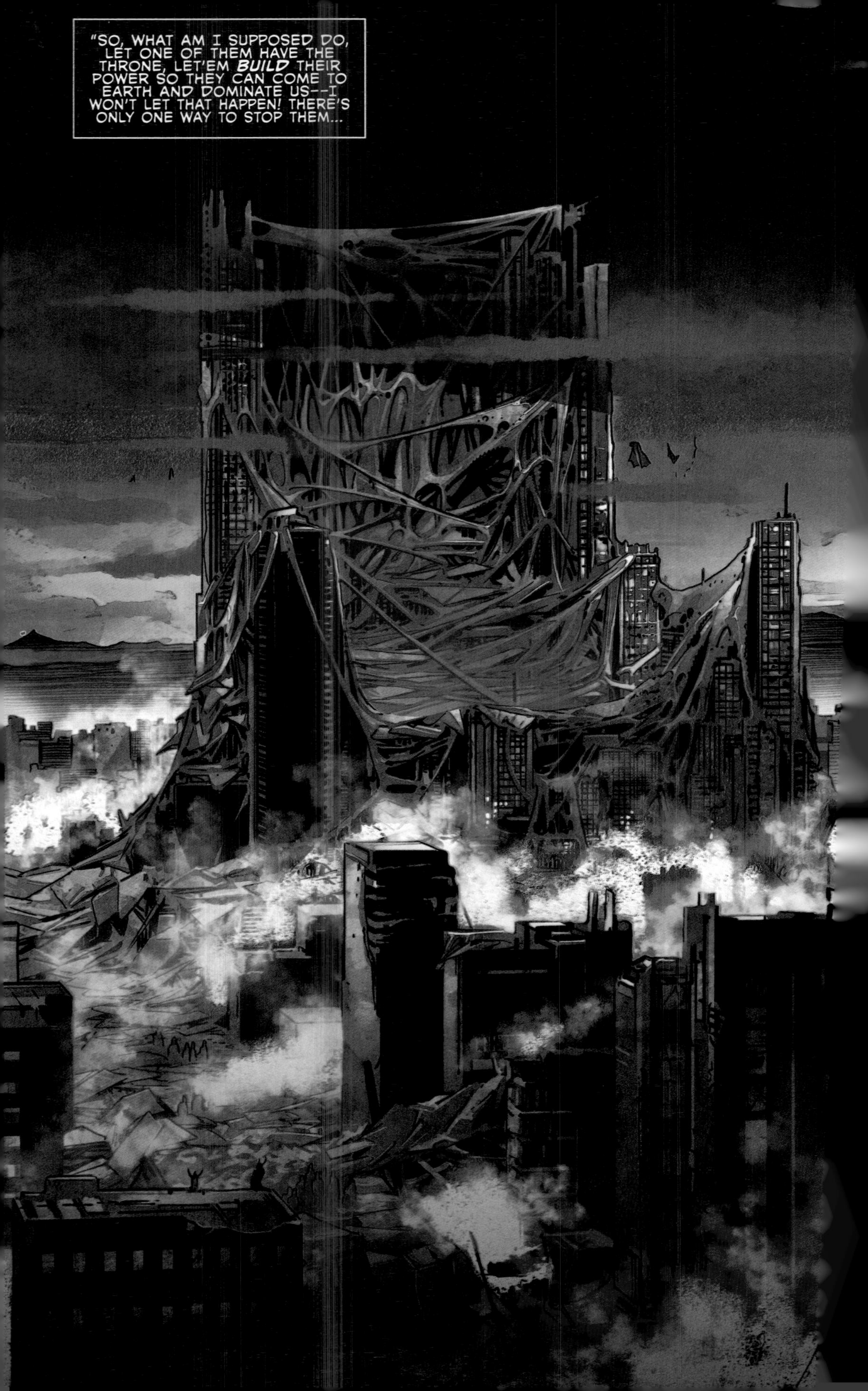
"SO, WHAT AM I SUPPOSED DO, LET ONE OF THEM HAVE THE THRONE, LET'EM BUILD THEIR POWER SO THEY CAN COME TO EARTH AND DOMINATE US--I WON'T LET THAT HAPPEN! THERE'S ONLY ONE WAY TO STOP THEM...

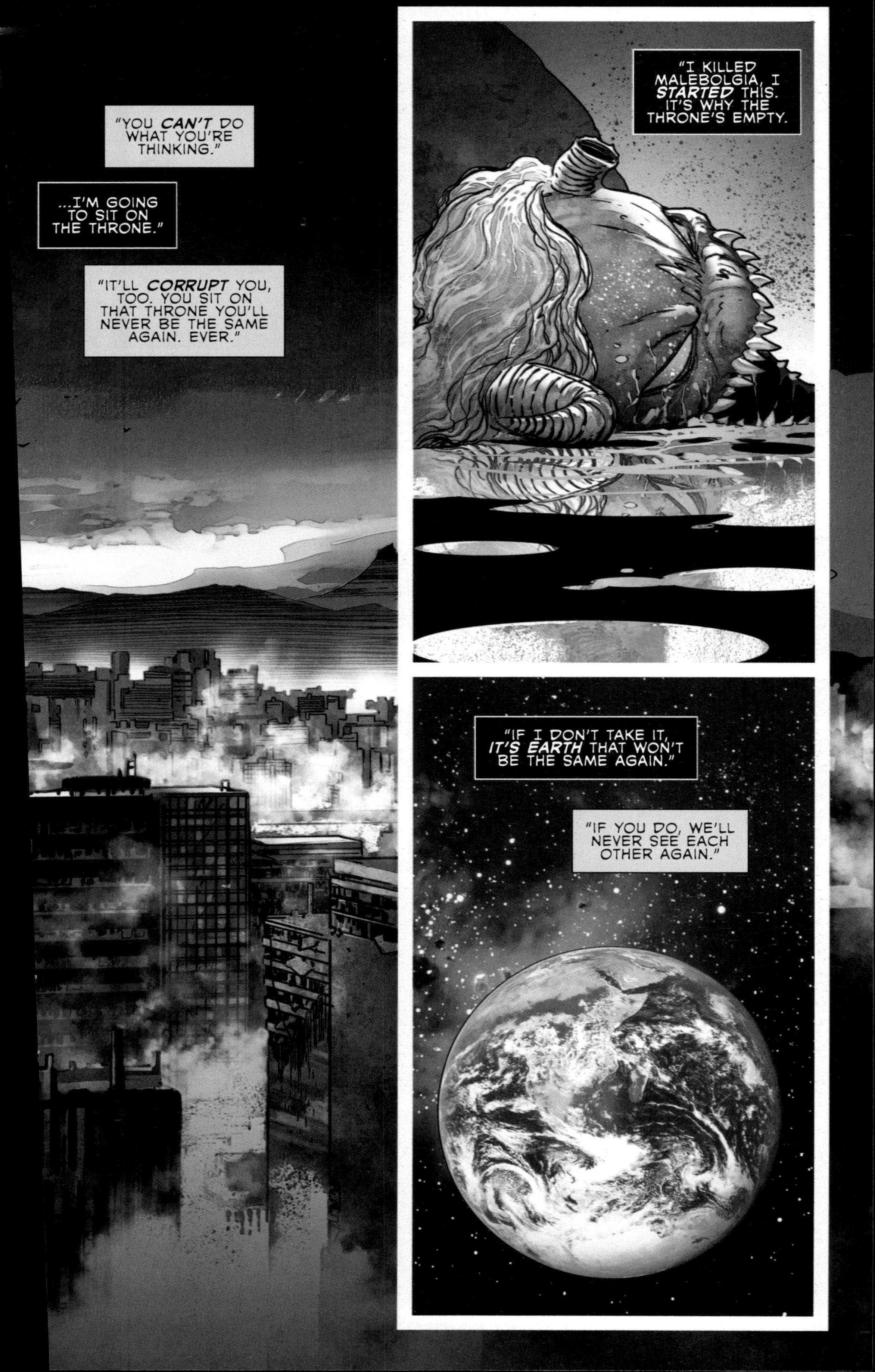
"YOU CAN'T DO WHAT YOU'RE THINKING."
...I'M GOING TO SIT ON THE THRONE."
"IT'LL CORRUPT YOU, TOO. YOU SIT ON THAT THRONE YOU'LL NEVER BE THE SAME AGAIN. EVER."
"I KILLED MALEBOLGIA, I STARTED THIS. IT'S WHY THE THRONE'S EMPTY.
"IF I DON'T TAKE IT, IT'S EARTH THAT WON'T BE THE SAME AGAIN."
"IF YOU DO, WE'LL NEVER SEE EACH OTHER AGAIN."

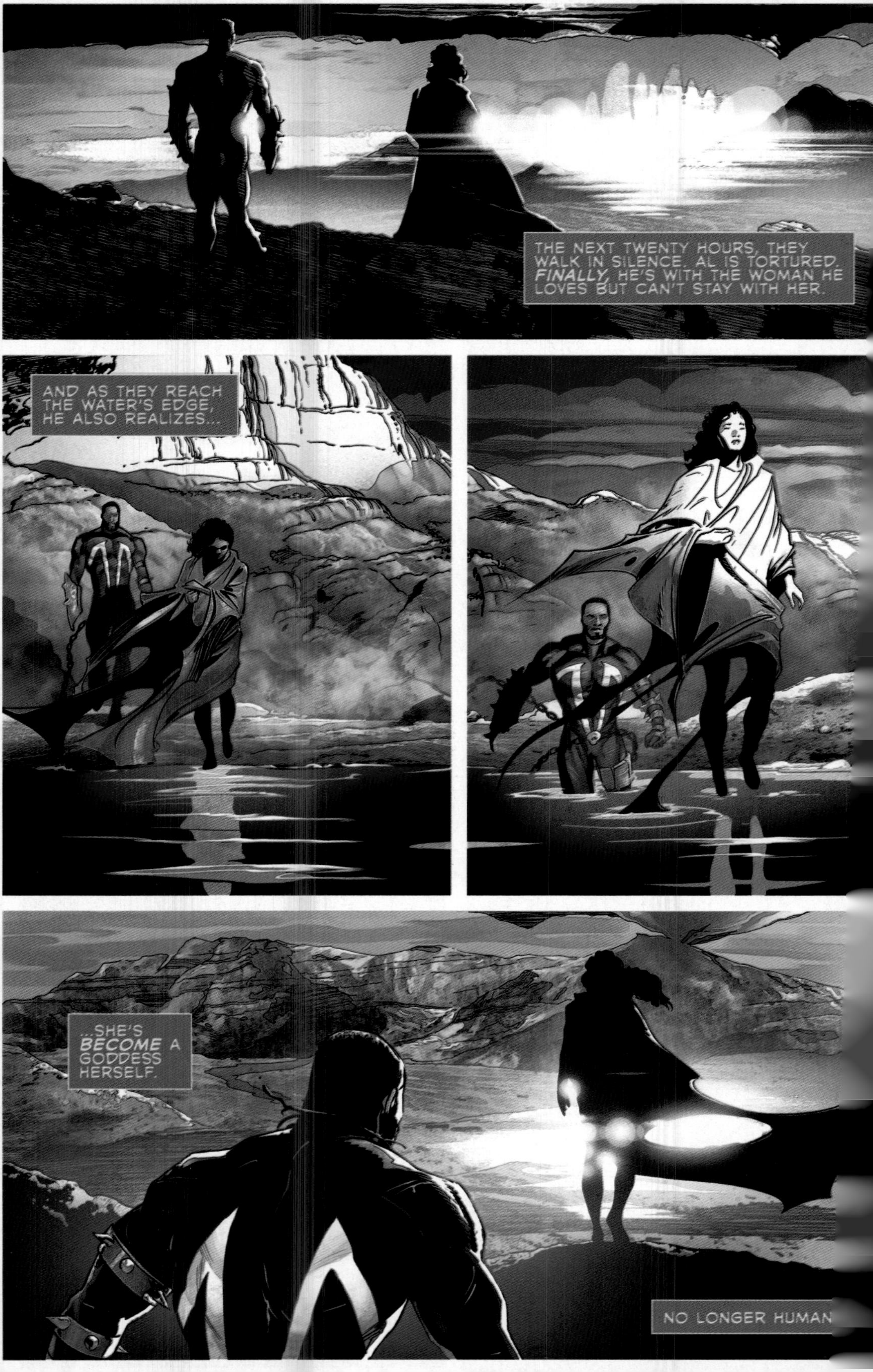
THE NEXT TWENTY HOURS, THEY WALK IN SILENCE. AL IS TORTURED. *FINALLY,* HE'S WITH THE WOMAN HE LOVES BUT CAN'T STAY WITH HER.
AND AS THEY REACH THE WATER'S EDGE, HE ALSO REALIZES...
...SHE'S *BECOME* A GODDESS HERSELF.
NO LONGER HUMAN

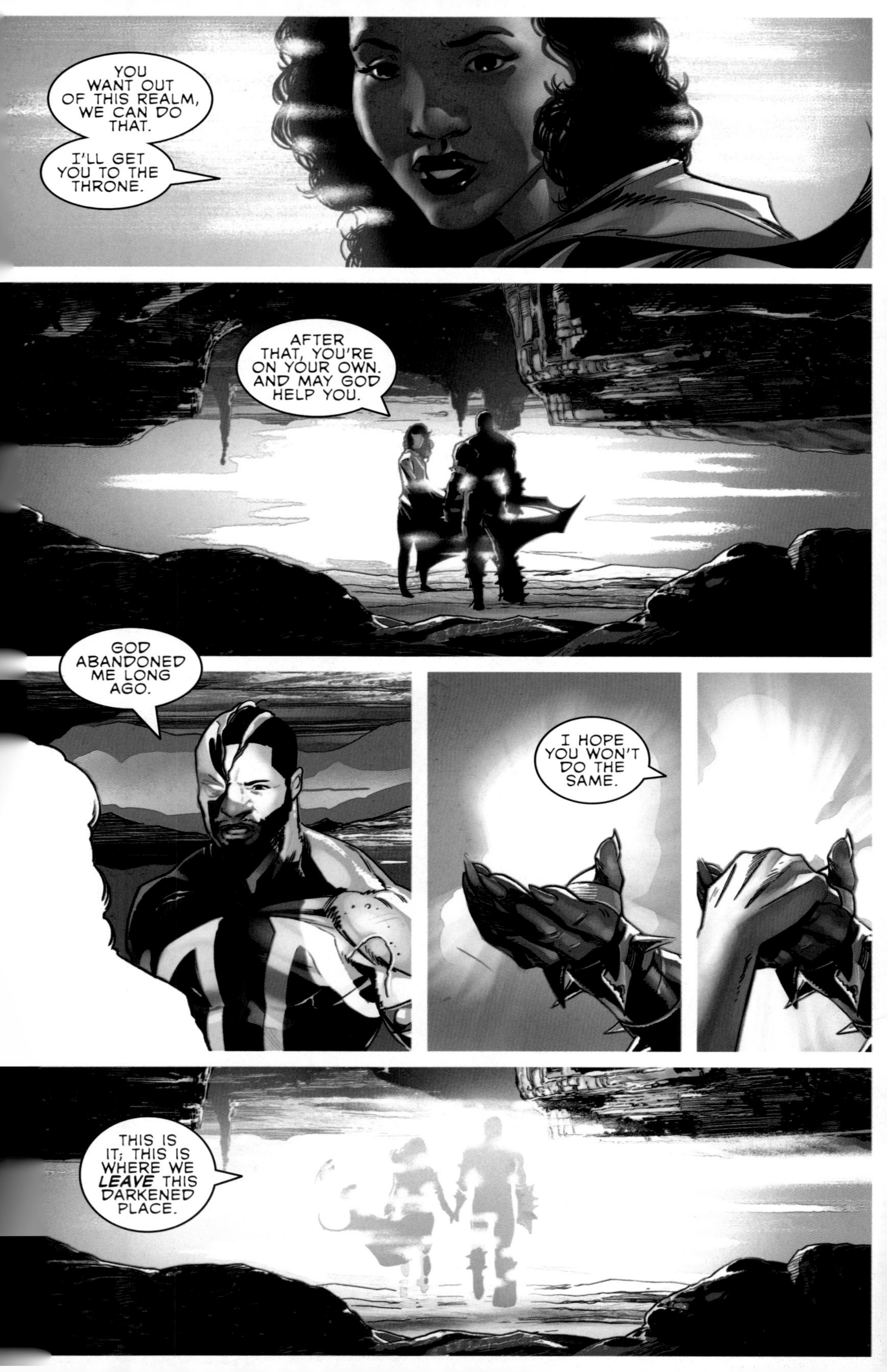
YOU WANT OUT OF THIS REALM, WE CAN DO THAT.
I'LL GET YOU TO THE THRONE.
AFTER THAT, YOU'RE ON YOUR OWN. AND MAY GOD HELP YOU.
GOD ABANDONED ME LONG AGO.
I HOPE YOU WON'T DO THE SAME.
THIS IS IT; THIS IS WHERE WE *LEAVE* THIS DARKENED PLACE.

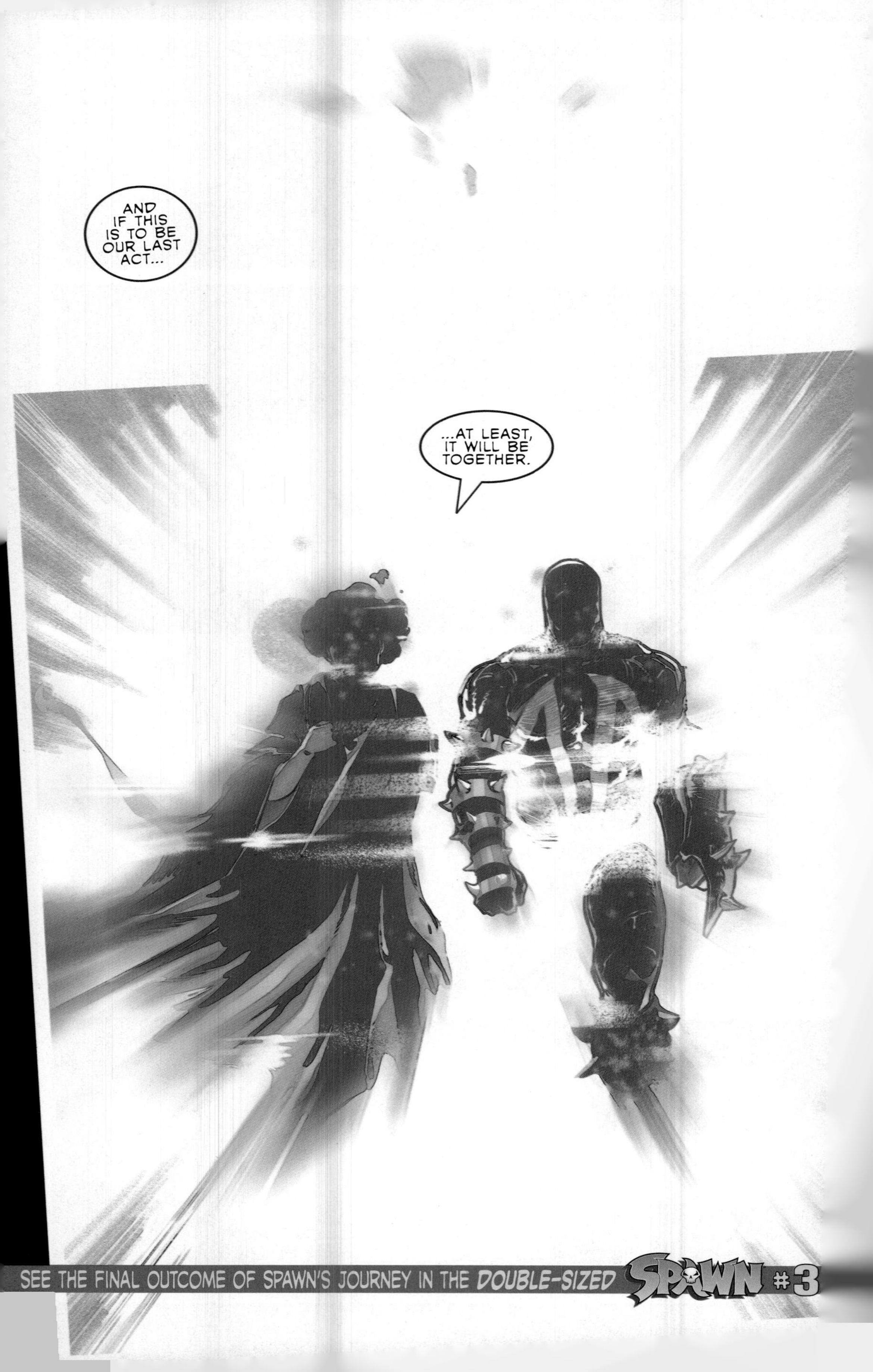
AND IF THIS IS TO BE OUR LAST ACT...
...AT LEAST, IT WILL BE TOGETHER.
SEE THE FINAL OUTCOME OF SPAWN'S JOURNEY IN THE DOUBLE-SIZED SPAWN #3

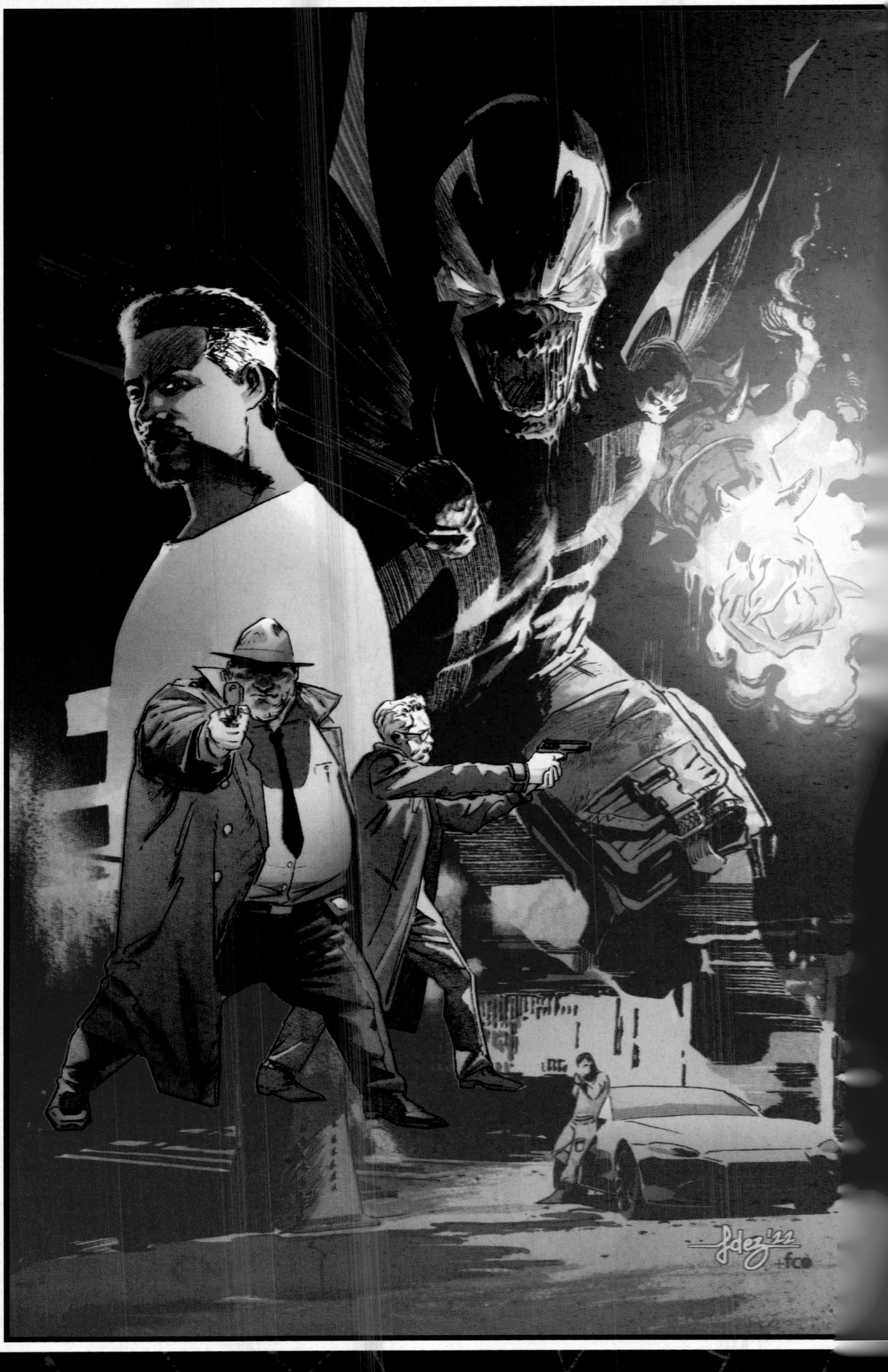
fdez'22
+fco

KING SPAWN 25 Cover 'B' by Javi Fernandez with FCO Plascencia

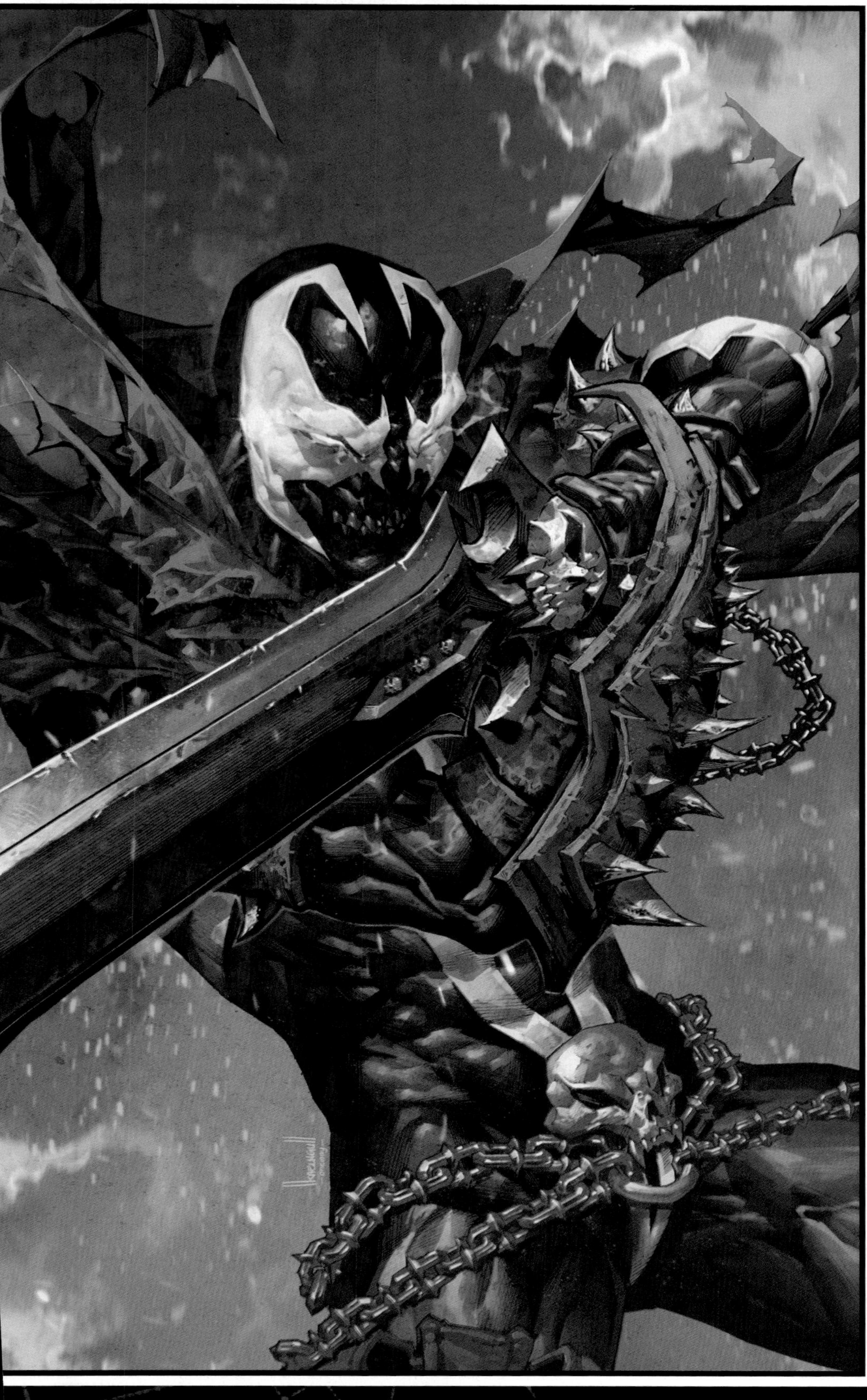

KING SPAWN 26 Cover 'B' by Kael Ngu

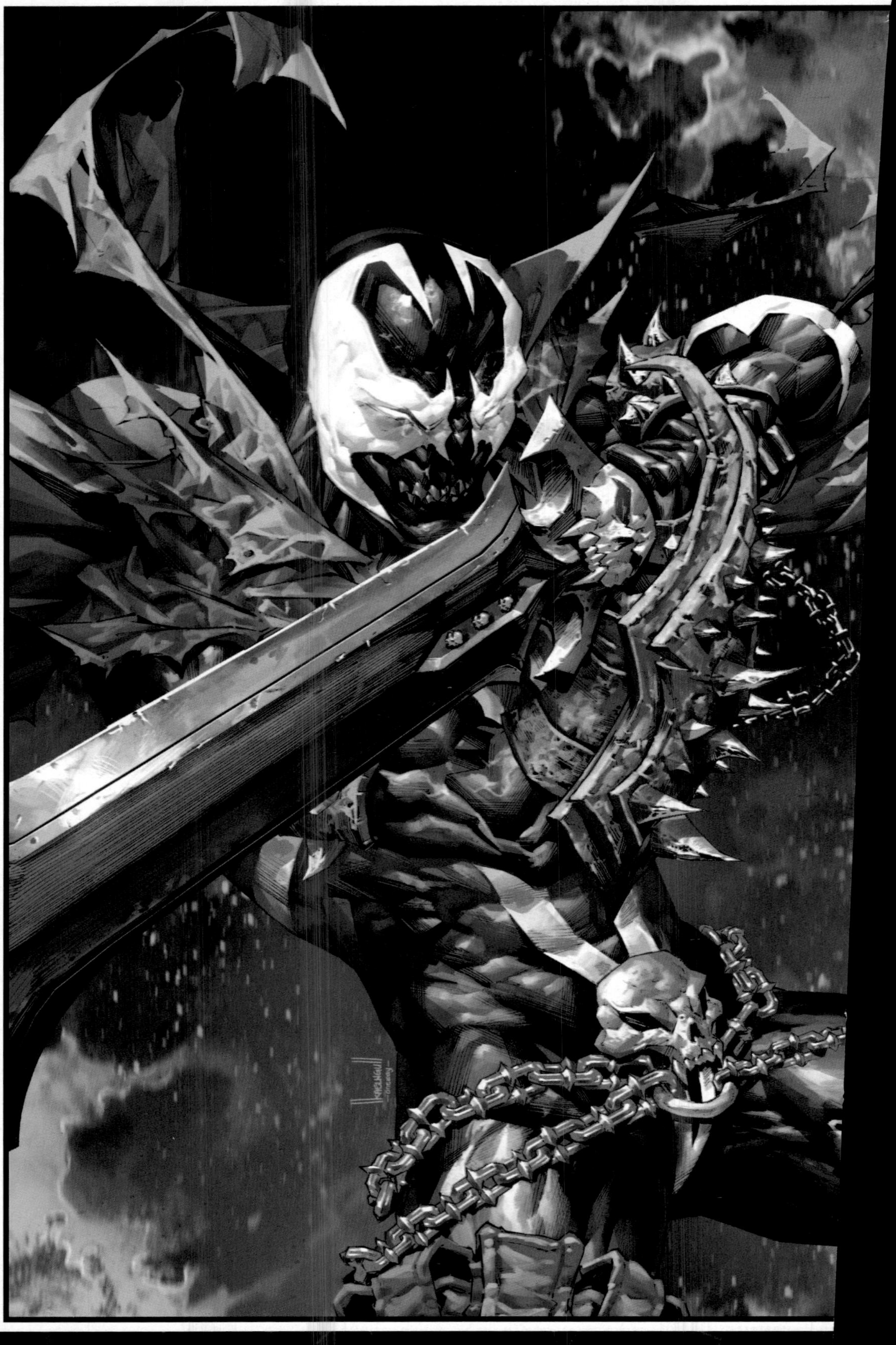

KING SPAWN 26 Cover 'C' by Kael Ngu

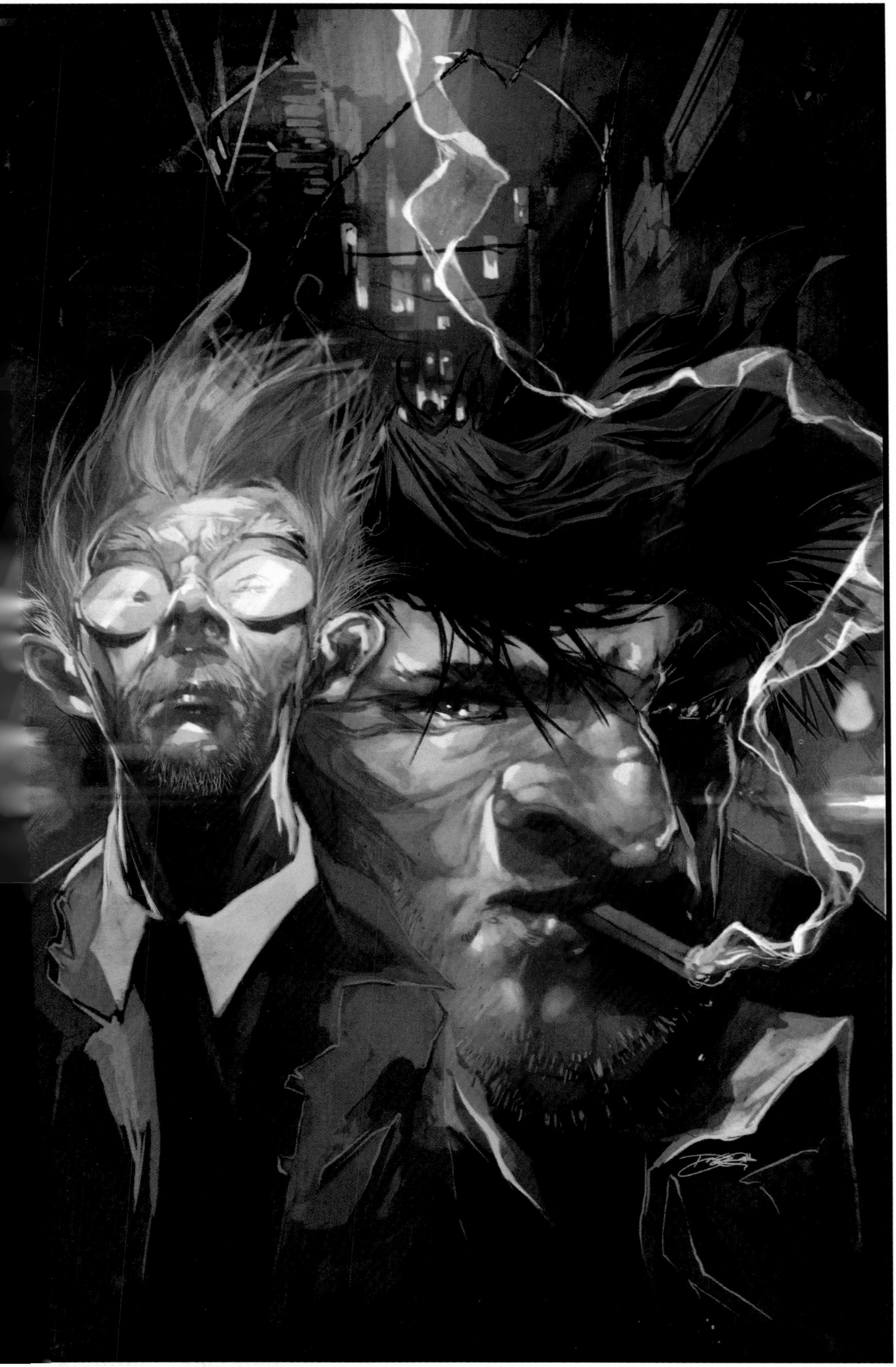

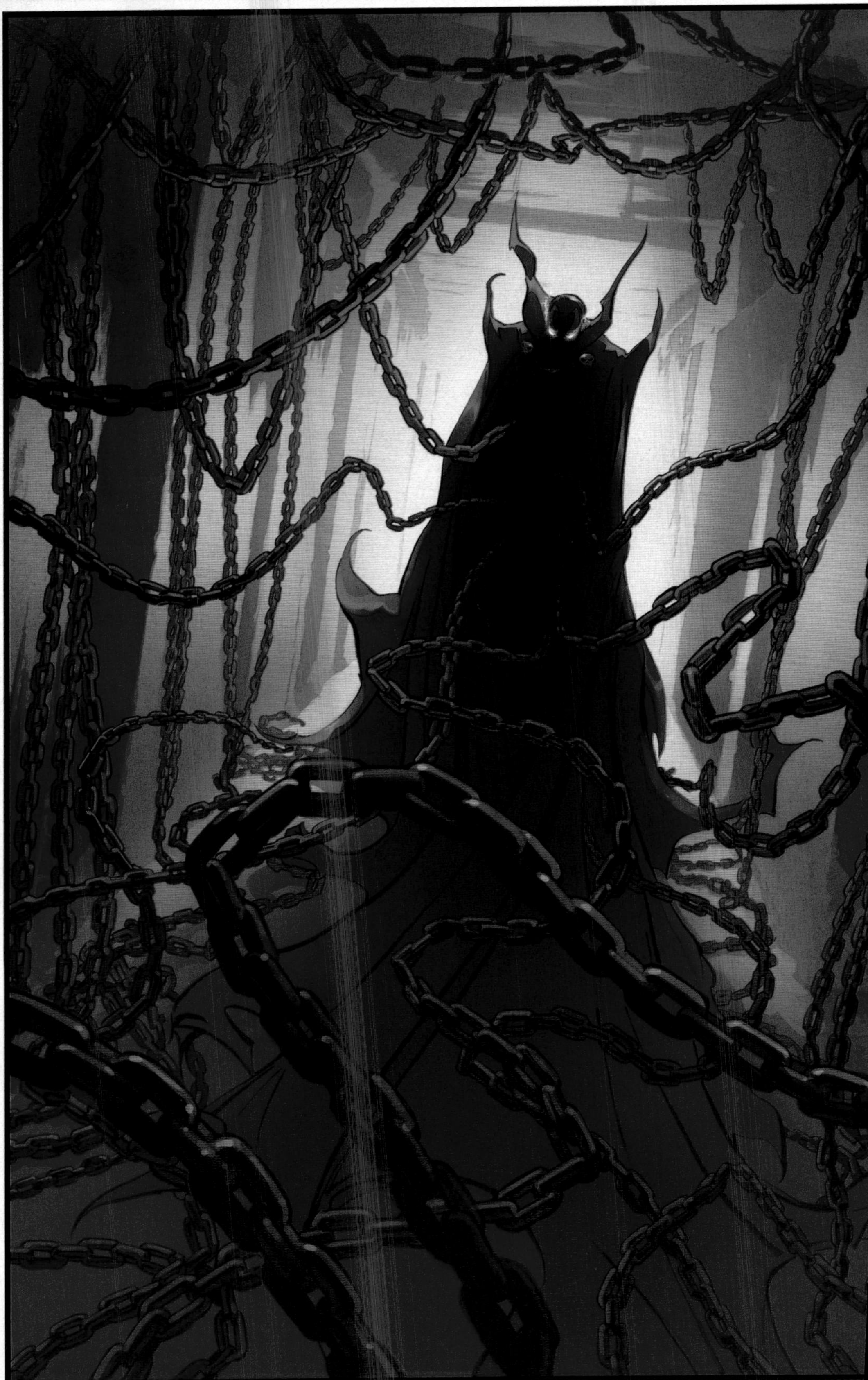

KING SPAWN 28 Cover 'B' by Marcial Toledano

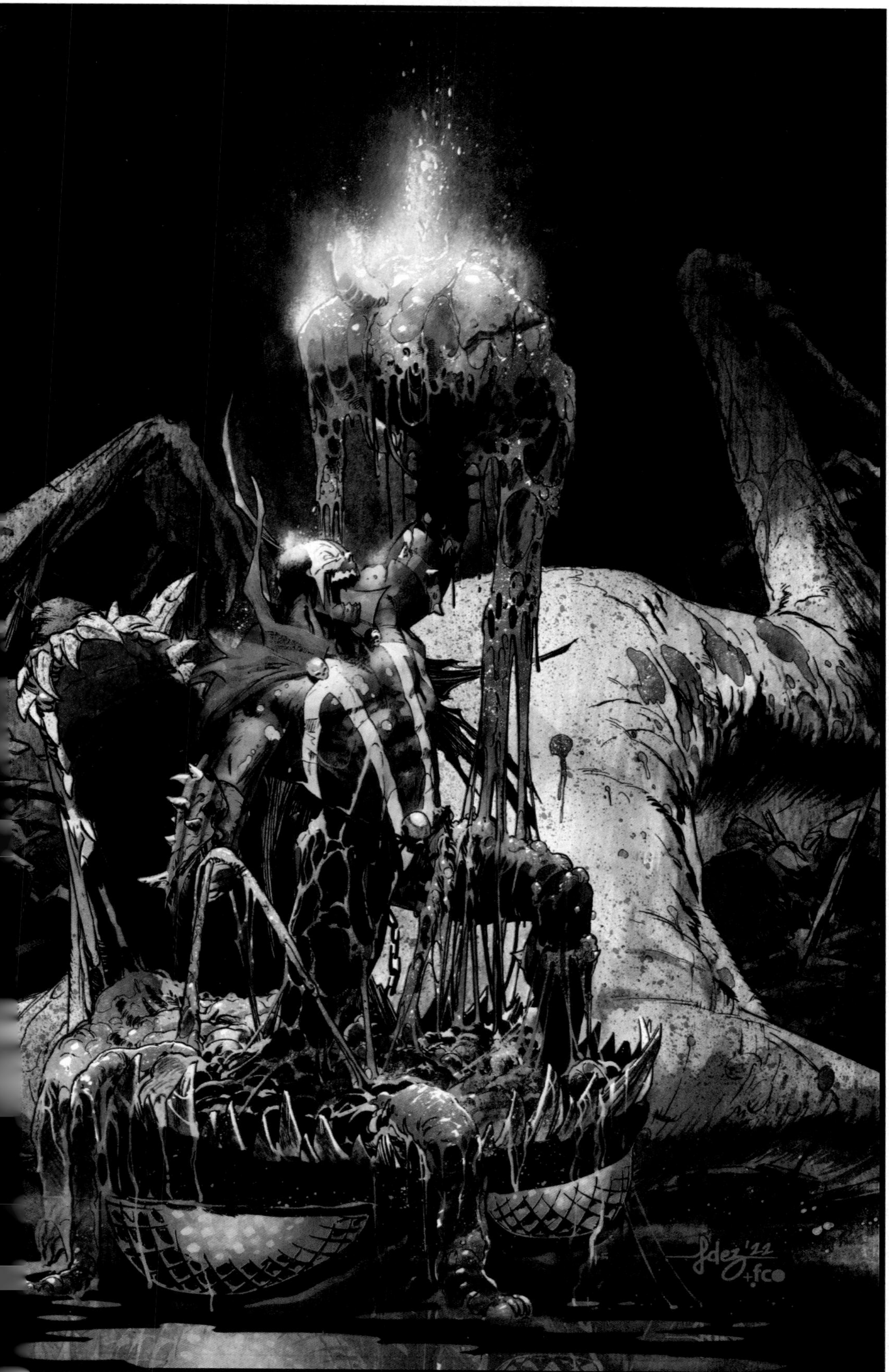
fdez'22
+fco

KING SPAWN 29 Cover 'B' by Javi Fernandez with FCO Plascencia

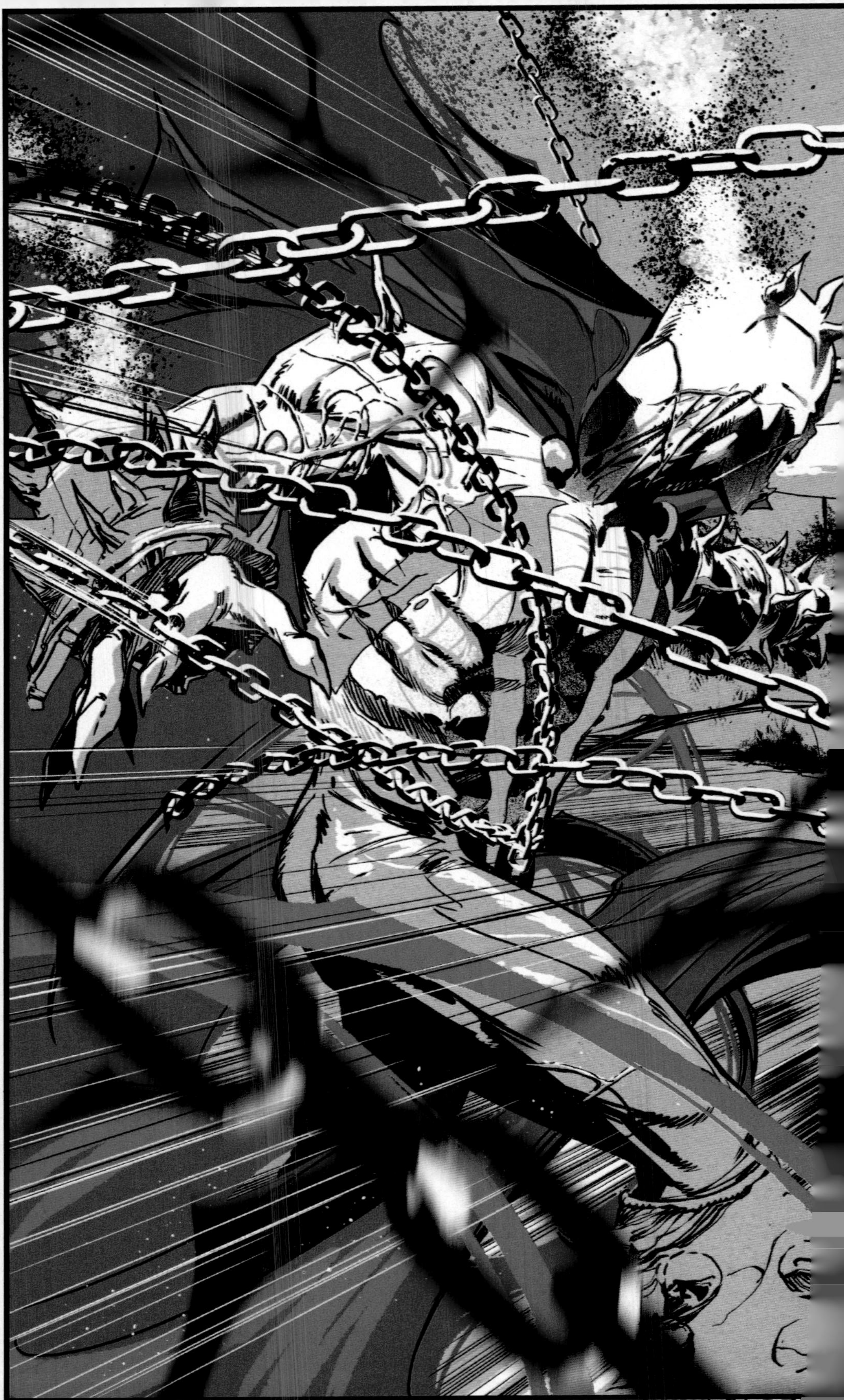

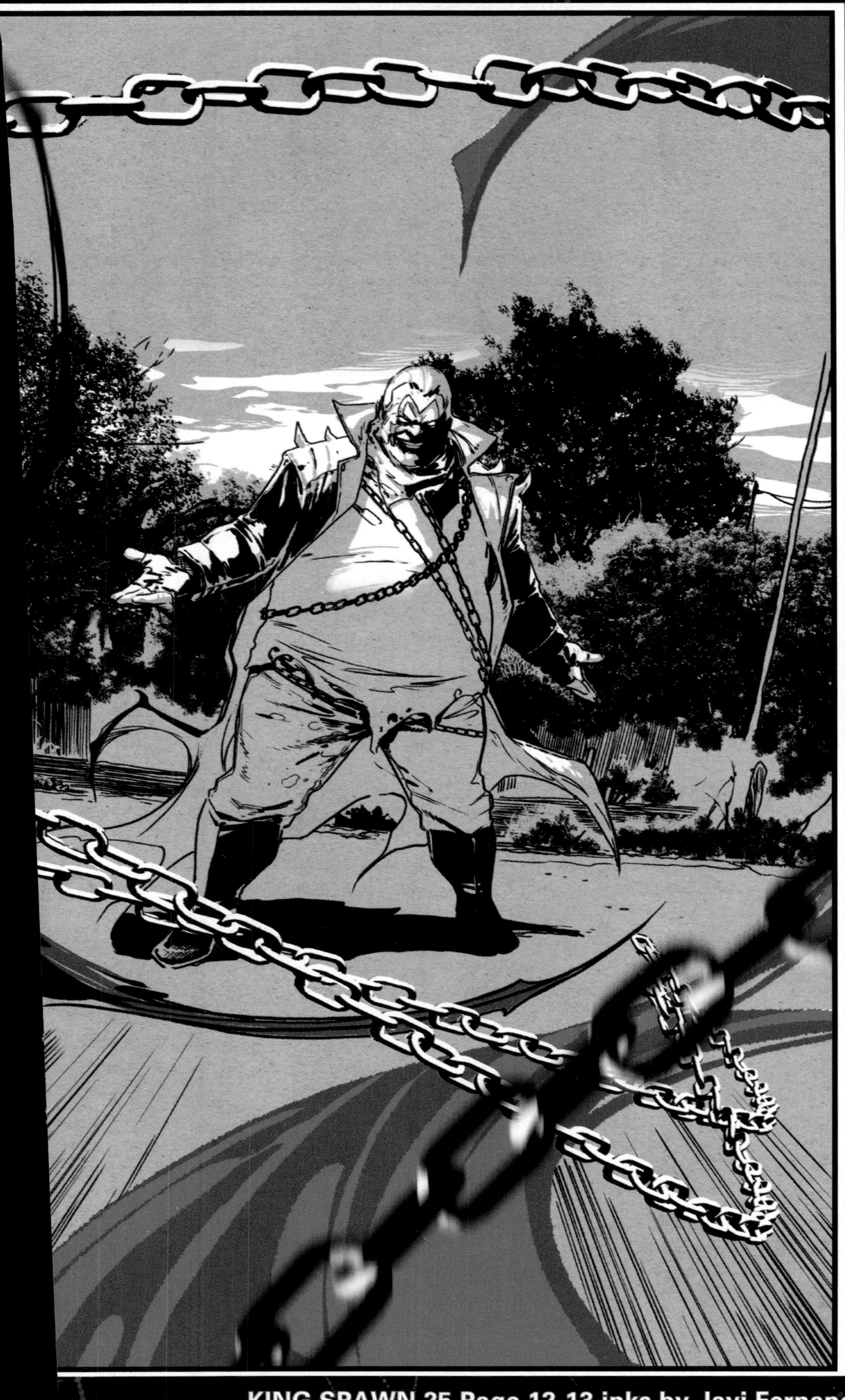

KING SPAWN 25 Page 12-13 inks by Javi Fernandez

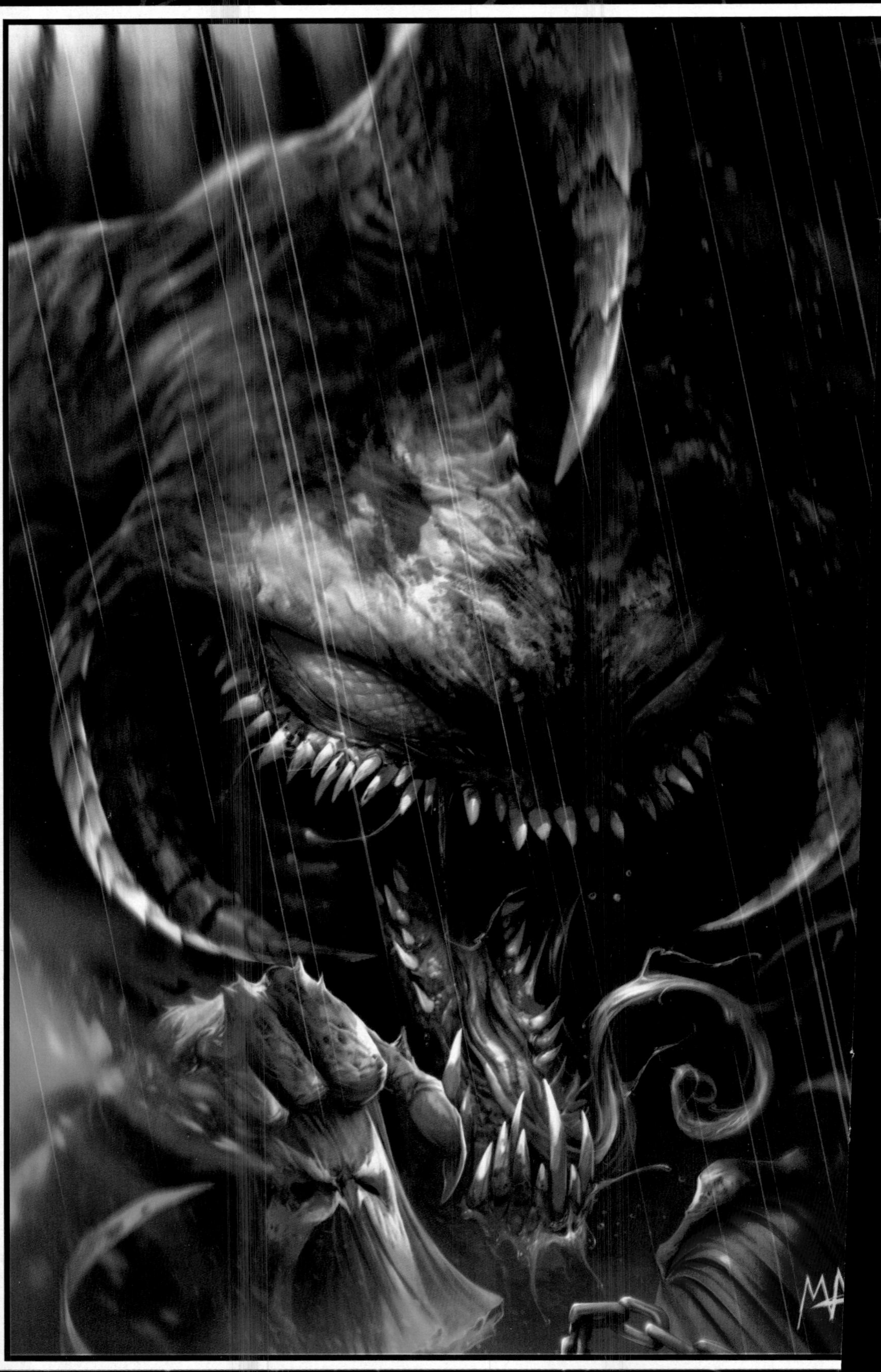

KING SPAWN 30 Cover 'B' by Francesco Mattina